HOUSE OF LORDS   SESS

22nd

SELECT COMMITTEE ON
THE EUROPEAN UNION

LABELLING AND TRACING OF GM
FOOD AND ANIMAL FEED:
INFORMING THE CONSUMER

WITH EVIDENCE

Ordered to be printed 30 April 2002

PUBLISHED BY AUTHORITY OF THE HOUSE OF LORDS
LONDON – THE STATIONERY OFFICE LIMITED

£18.50

HL Paper 117

EXECUTIVE SUMMARY

Under present EU rules all genetically modified (GM) products must be assessed for their likely health and environmental impacts before they can be approved for deliberate release into the environment (which includes being placed on the market as food). Any food or food ingredient produced from a GM crop which contains detectable levels of GM material has to be labelled as containing genetically modified organisms (GMOs).

Consumer concern about foods which are derived from GM crops or have been through processes involving use of modern biotechnology but do not have to be labelled have led a number of EU Member States to block further approvals of GM foods in the EU until new rules are agreed which would put consumers in a better position to decide whether or not to avoid food in which genetic modification has played any part in the production chain. The effect has been a moratorium on GM approvals in the EU since 1998. The European Commission and major commodity crop producers (particularly in the US) consider this to be illegal under WTO rules.

The Commission has responded with proposals to extend the labelling rules to all foods produced from GM crops, irrespective of whether GM material is detectable in the finished product, and to apply the regime to animal feed for the first time. Labelling would not be required for food (meat, milk and eggs) from animals fed on GM feed nor to products for which GMOs are used as processing agents (mainly wine and cheese). Since the need for labelling could no longer be determined by laboratory testing, the labelling proposals would be supported by a new traceability regime, which would create an "audit trail" from farm to supermarket shelf. The United States Government, the biotechnology industry and large-scale GM crop growers see the whole package as a possible technical barrier to trade under WTO rules.

The Committee's Report endorses consumers' right to choose between GM and non-GM products on the basis of the best information that it is practicable to make available, but concludes that it is not practicable to legislate for the degree of traceability envisaged by the Commission for bulk commodity imports from the United States and elsewhere.

Instead it recommends retaining the present labelling regime but to build on existing Identity Preserved (IP) and farm assurance schemes as a means of meeting consumers' demands for products which do not involve the use of GM technology. Although such products may command premium prices, the Committee considers it is better to leave these to market forces than to impose burdensome requirements on producers and consumers indiscriminately, which would be the effect of the Commission's proposals.

The Committee considers that use of the term "GM-free" should be restricted to products for which total absence of GM material, including food from animals fed on GM feed or produced with GM processing agents, can be guaranteed at all stages of production.

For practical reasons, the Committee accepts that the present rule which permits up to one per cent of a product to contain GM material without triggering the requirement to label should continue, provided that the material has been through the full EU authorisation procedure. Where this applies, it may be appropriate for the food to be labelled "non-GM", but the Committee feels this term is liable to confuse the consumer. It recommends further market research to establish more user-friendly terminology, backed by better information from the Food Standards Agency. It points out that there is a limit to what can sensibly be put on a label.

The Committee urges the Government to make every effort to persuade other Member States to lift their veto on approvals of new GMOs in return for a more pragmatic approach to traceability and labelling. It also expresses the view that the EU should not seek to influence developing countries' decisions on whether or not to adopt food and agricultural biotechnology practices without recognising the imperatives of developing economies. Finally it calls for closer and more transparent coordination within Government on all aspects of GM policy.

CONTENTS

ORAL EVIDENCE

NOTE: Pages of the Report and Appendices are numbered in bold type; pages of evidence are numbered in ordinary type. References in the text of the Report are as follows:

(Q) refers to a question in oral evidence;
(p) refers to a page of the Report or Appendices or to a page of evidence.

TWENTY-SECOND REPORT

30 APRIL 2002

By the Select Committee appointed to consider European Union documents and other matters relating to the European Union.

ORDERED TO REPORT

LABELLING AND TRACING OF GM FOOD AND ANIMAL FEED:

INFORMING THE CONSUMER

11576/01   COM (01) 425: Draft Regulation on genetically modified food and feed.

11496/01   COM (01) 182: Draft Regulation concerning traceability and labelling of genetically modified organisms and traceability of food and feed products produced from genetically modified organisms and amending Directive 2001/18/EC.

CHAPTER 1: THE CONTEXT

INTRODUCTION

The purpose of this Report

1. No new genetically modified (GM) foods have been approved in the EU since 1998, because of an effective refusal by certain Member States[1] to participate in the approvals process until rules on traceability and labelling are in place. The European Commission has responded with proposals to extend the GM labelling regime but these have provoked controversy which could unintentionally result in this *de facto* moratorium being further extended. The Commission considers the moratorium illegal, and is concerned that it might be challenged through the World Trade Organisation (WTO). The Commission's proposals are intended to extend consumer choice, but the UK Government and the food industry have expressed concerns that they might prove difficult to implement in practice.

2. This Report is concerned specifically with the proposals for labelling of GM food and feed and the associated proposals on traceability. It addresses them from the practical viewpoint of how best to meet the needs of the consumer. It is not concerned with the wider aspects of regulating the use of genetically modified organisms (GMOs) and their implications for health and the environment. These have been the subject of separate studies.

3. In view of the current controversy over the proposals, Sub-Committee D (Environment, Agriculture, Public Health and Consumer Protection, whose Members are listed in Appendix 1, decided to conduct a short inquiry between January and April 2002. An invitation for evidence was issued on 21 December 2001 (Appendix 2). The Specialist Adviser to the inquiry was Professor Alan Malcolm, Chief Executive of the Institute of Biology.

4. A list of those who provided evidence and other information is in Appendix 3. The Committee would like to express its thanks to Professor Malcolm and the witnesses for their valuable contributions, which were helpful in focusing the inquiry on the key issues in an area of policy which tends to be as confused as it is complex.[2]

---

[1] Initially Austria, Denmark, France, Greece, Italy and Luxembourg; later joined by Belgium.

[2] In summarising the essential features of the Commission's proposals we have drawn heavily on the Parliamentary Office of Science and Technology's *Postnote* No 172, February 2002, "Labelling GM Foods". We are grateful to the Director of POST for agreeing to the note being used in this way.

Box 1

GM and Biotechnology: basic terminology[3]

The term "GM" stands for the scientific or industrial process of "genetic modification" or the characteristics of material which has been "genetically modified". In simple language GM covers any of the following processes:

- the deletion, change or moving of genes within an organism;

- the transfer of genes from one organism to another (hence the term "transgenic");

- the modification of existing genes or the construction of new genes and their incorporation into any organism.

"Genetic modification" is for practical purposes equivalent to and interchangeable with "genetic engineering". It does not extend to the generation of organisms using standard breeding techniques, including cloning, hybridisation or controlled pollination (as these do not involve modification of existing genes). Nor does it cover mutagenesis not involving genetic engineering techniques.

"GM organisms" (GMOs) are organisms produced directly by genetic modification and therefore contain GM material in the form of protein or DNA. "GM products" (including foods) may themselves be GMOs but also cover products derived from GM processes (including the use of GMOs as processing aids).

In the United States the term "biotechnology" (or "biotech"), is preferred to "GM". It should be noted, however, that although "GM" is a key tool of modern biotechnology it is not the only tool.

Previous Parliamentary consideration of biotechnology and genetic modification

5. There have been a number of studies in recent years of different aspects of biotechnology and genetic modification by Parliamentary Select Committees. In the House of Lords, the European Communities Committee (as it then was) reported in 1998 on the implications for agriculture and the food industry of the Commission's proposals for amending the existing Directive 90/220/EEC on the deliberate release into the environment of genetically modified organisms.[4] These proposals were later to become Directive 2001/18/EC. The Report contains an extensive summary of the techniques of genetic modification, the place of GM in the wider context of biotechnology, the differences between GM and traditional breeding, the history and principles of regulation, differences between EC and US regulatory approaches, and international agreements relating to the movement of GMOs between countries. This summary holds good as a factual statement of the position as it stood at the time of the "moratorium" on EU approvals (paragraph 1) and we see no need to go over the same ground in the present Report.

6. The House of Lords Report came at a time of escalating media and public concern, particularly about the regulation of field trials of GM crops, which gave rise to inquiries and reports by separate House of Commons Committees, including a sequence of three by the then Agriculture Committee.[5] Its successor, the Environment, Food and Rural Affairs Committee, announced in February 2002 a brief inquiry into the current position in relation to GMOs, in particular developments since the Agriculture Committee's Report of March 2000 on segregation of GM Foods. The Committee began taking oral evidence in April.

The Committee's approach: focusing on the consumer

7. In the course of taking evidence Sub-Committee D found it necessary to inform itself—or witnesses thought it necessary to inform the Committee—on many of the wider aspects of

---

[3] Based on a simple definition in the Report of the New Zealand Royal Commission on Genetic Modification, 27 July 2001.

[4] ECC 2nd Report, Session 1998-99, *EC Regulation of Genetic Modification in Agriculture*, HL Paper 11, 15 December 1998.

[5] Science and Technology Committee (May 1999),*Scientific Advisory System: Genetically Modified Food*, First Report, 1998–99, HC 286–I/II.; Environmental Audit Committee (May 1999), *Genetically Modified Organisms and the Environment: Co-ordination of Government Policy*, Fifth Report, 1998–99, HC 384–I/II.; Agriculture Committee (June 1999), *Genetically Modified Organisms*, Sixth Report, 1998-99, HC 427; Agriculture Committee (March 2000),*The Segregation of Genetically Modified Foods*, Third Report, 1999–2000, HC 71–I/II; Agriculture Committee (July 2000), *Genetically Modified Organisms and Seed Segregation*, Eighth Report, 1999–2000, HC 812. For an account of reactions to the House of Lords Report, the various House of Commons Reports and subsequent developments in government policy, see Institute for European Environmental Policy,*Manual of Environmental Policy: the EU and Britain*, Elsevier Science Ltd, Oxford (updated every six months), at section 7.14.

biotechnology and genetic modification in order to place the Commission's proposals in context. In preparing this Report, however, the Committee has focused specifically on the practicality of the proposals in meeting the needs of consumers.

8. As always, the recitals to the Commission's documents and their opening Articles cite a multiplicity of aims. The draft Regulation on Food and Feed (COM (01) 425) states as its principal objective:

"to provide the basis for the assurance of a high level of protection of human life and health, animal health and welfare, environment *and consumers' interest* [emphasis added] in relation to genetically modified food and feed, whilst ensuring the effective functioning of the internal market".

9. The "consumers' interest" is backed by the recitals to the draft Regulation, which *inter alia* state that:

"... clear labelling, irrespective of the detectability of DNA or protein resulting from the genetic modification in the final product, meets the demands expressed in numerous surveys by a large majority of consumers, facilitates informed choice and precludes potential misleading of consumers as regards method of manufacture or production (20). Additionally, the labelling should inform about any characteristic or property which renders a food or feed not equivalent to its conventional counterpart ... as well as any ... which gives rise to ethical or religious concerns (21)."

10. There is further discussion of these principles in the Commission's explanatory memorandum that accompanies the proposal. The draft Regulation on Traceability and Labelling (COM (01) 182) simply states that its objective is to facilitate "accurate labelling, environmental monitoring and withdrawals of products". Promotion of consumer choice is implicit in the reference to accurate labelling.

11. This Report accordingly takes as its starting point our belief that consumers and producers have a legitimate interest in seeking to choose between foods and animal feeds which have been produced (whether directly or indirectly) with the aid of genetic modification. We have noted that the reasons why consumers wish to make these choices are varied, but we have not made it our business to question whether their motives are rational or well supported by science. Our concern is how far it is practical to meet consumers' expectations and whether this can be done in a proportionate way, having regard to the realities of the situation—particularly in relation to the international market for bulk agricultural produce such as soya and maize.

APPROVAL OF GM FOODS AND FEED IN THE EUROPEAN UNION

12. Under present EU rules all GM products must be assessed for their likely health and environmental impacts before they can be approved for deliberate release into the environment (i.e. planted as GM crops, marketed as GM foods, etc.). The "deliberate release" Directive that regulates this process was revised recently[6] to include new measures to refine safety assessment and enhance public confidence in the system. The Commission had also given an undertaking to introduce a more comprehensive labelling and traceability regime. The current proposals outlining such a regime were published in July 2001.

GM FOODS, FOOD INGREDIENTS AND ANIMAL FEED

13. There are several different types of GM food and feeds:

- Foods or ingredients produced directly from GM crops such as soybeans or maize. In certain countries, notably in the US but not in the EU, many widely available consumer products contain detectable GM material.

- Foods or ingredients produced directly from GM crops but which have been through refining and other processes which leave no detectable trace of GM material (e.g. highly refined soybean oil).

- Foods produced using GMOs purely as processing aids (e.g. enzymes), which similarly cannot be detected in the final product.

- Animal feeds produced from GM crops: GM material can be detected in the feed, but not in products from animals reared on it.

---

[6] i.e. Directive 2001/18/EC, adopted in March 2001.

CURRENT AND PROPOSED GM LABELLING REGULATIONS

14. Under current EU regulations, it is the presence in the final food of detectable GM material that triggers labelling requirements. Any food or food ingredient produced from a GM source which contains detectable GM material has to be labelled. Under the Commission's new proposals the labelling regime would be extended to include all foods and animal feed produced from GM crops, irrespective of whether they contain detectable GM material. The proposals would impose labelling requirements for two categories of GM products that currently do not have to be labelled: foods and ingredients produced from GM organisms but which contain no GM material (e.g. highly refined oil from GM soybeans), and GM animal feed. A more detailed description of the Commission's legislative proposals is in Box 2 and a summary of existing and proposed labelling requirements is in the table after paragraph 24.

Box 2

The Commission's legislative proposals

The way in which the Commission has presented its proposals is confusing to the general reader. This stems from the need to amend or enlarge the scope of separate legislative instruments. As a result, a package of essentially interdependent measures has come forward in two documents (the titles of which are themselves confusing). Despite the numbering of the proposals, they are intended to be read, and taken forward, in parallel. It is convenient, however, to consider them in the following order, since the second one depends on the first one in so far as it takes the objectives of the overall package as given.

- COM (01) 425: *Authorising and labelling of GM foods and animal feeds, including products derived from GMOs.* This proposal would replace existing EU authorisation procedures for GM foods, as contained in EC Regulation 258/97 (OJ L43, 14.2.97), and introduce for the first time rules for the authorisation of GM animal feed, within the general framework for the deliberate release into the environment of any GMO set by Directive 2001/18/EC (OJ L106, 17.4.01). The new authorisation procedures would assign a central role to the newly established European Food Safety Authority. Labelling would be required for all food and feed ingredients derived from GMOs, even when they are analytically identical to those derived from non-GM sources, instead of simply for food in which there is a detectable presence of DNA or protein resulting from genetic modification.

- COM (01) 182: Harmonised system for tracing, identifying and labelling GMOs and food and feed products derived from GMOs at all stages of the production and distribution chain. This would be a new Regulation and would require some amendment of the framework Directive 2001/18/EC. Without such a provision for traceability, which enables the control and verification of labelling claims, the parallel provisions for labelling of GM-derived products and ingredients cannot be put into effect.

---

15. Because the new labelling proposals would apply to some products that contain no detectable GM material, enforcement could no longer rely solely on sampling and testing for GM material in the laboratory. Instead, the Commission has proposed a new traceability regime, where operators at each point in the marketing chain—farm, storage, transport, processing, distribution and marketing—would have to record and pass on details of the genetic modifications present in each shipment and product. The idea is to establish an "audit trail" for GM organisms and the foods and feeds derived from them.

16. The operative provisions on traceability would not come into force until the EU had established a system of "unique codes" for GMOs for purposes of identification. Since imports of GMOs into the EU are largely from third countries, the EU system would have to be consistent with mechanisms being developed under wider international organisations, including work on unique identification codes currently in hand in OECD. It would also need to conform to the requirements of the Cartagena Protocol on Biosafety (see Box 3).

Box 3

The Cartagena Protocol on Biosafety

This is the First Protocol to the Convention on Biological Diversity, which was agreed at the Rio Earth Summit in 1992 by the majority of the world's governments and sets out commitments for maintaining the world's ecological resources whilst allowing for sustainable development. The Protocol's overall objective is to "contribute to ensuring an adequate level of protection in the field of the safe transfer, handling and use of GMOs resulting from modern biotechnology that may have adverse effects on conservation and sustainable use of biological diversity, taking also into account risks to human health, and specifically focusing on transboundary movements".

To achieve this objective, the Protocol introduces two main procedures to control the movement of GMOs from one country to another:

- A specific notification procedure which requires notification to, and the agreement of, the importing country before the export of a GMO (such as a seed) intended for deliberate introduction into the environment may proceed;

- A separate procedure for GMOs for food, feed or for processing which enables an importing country to declare, via an information exchange mechanism, that it wishes to take a decision based on risk assessment information before agreeing to accept an import.

The Protocol is of particular benefit to developing countries who lack existing legislation on GMOs since it gives them the necessary information and means to decide, before accepting GMO imports, whether there may be adverse effects on the conservation and sustainable use of their particular habitats and wildlife. To date, 107 countries have signed the Protocol and 13 countries have ratified it. The EU and the Member States, including the UK, signed the Protocol in May 2000. On 13 March 2002 the Commission adopted a proposal for a Council Decision on the conclusion of the Biosafety Protocol, with a view to ratification of the Protocol by the Community (COM(2002)127 final).

---

17. Existing GM food labelling rules contain a one per cent threshold for the accidental ("adventitious or technically unavoidable") presence of GM material in food from non-GM sources below which labelling is not required. Currently this applies only to material from EU-approved varieties. The Commission now proposes that the threshold should apply to non-approved varieties too, provided that the GMO concerned has passed a safety assessment by the relevant EU scientific committee(s). Current technology is not reliable enough to support a general threshold of less than one per cent, although lower levels of detection are possible in some circumstances[7] (see Box 4).

Box 4

Detection methodologies for presence of GM material

Detection methodologies vary according to the nature of the food. According to evidence from several sources (e.g. the Food Standards Agency and the Food and Drink Federation), one per cent GM-derived material in the case of foods such as purified oils, sugars and starches (where there is not expected to be either protein or DNA present) would be well beyond either current or anticipated technology. Where protein is present, antibody-based methodologies should be capable in principle of detecting one per cent provided that the genetic modification results in a new protein being produced. This is often not the case. On the (comparatively rare) occasions where it is anticipated that DNA from the GMO is present in the food as consumed, it would be possible to use methods based on the highly sensitive polymerase chain reaction. However, this might not be reproducible, depending on the extent to which the food had been subjected to acid or heat treatment.

LABELLING OPTIONS

18. The Commission considered four options for GM food labelling (a–d below). The Food Standards Agency (FSA) evaluated the costs, benefits, risks and uncertainties of these, along with a fifth option (c+):

- (a) maintain the current labelling regime;

- (b) maintain the current labelling regime and introduce a "GM-free scheme";

---

[7] Evidence to the inquiry from FSA (p 56 at paragraph 5.2), BBSRC (p 84 atparagraphs 9–10), Food and Drink Federation (Q 37) and Friends of the Earth (QQ 103–5).

- (c) introduce labelling of all foods derived from GM material (the option proposed by the Commission);

- (c+) introduce labelling of all foods derived from GM material and introduce a "GM-free" scheme;

- (d) introduce labelling of all foods derived with the help of GM material (including GM feed and GM enzymes).

EXTENDING THE LABELLING REQUIREMENTS

19. The current labelling regime allows consumers to choose whether or not to buy products containing GM material. Under the proposed new regime (option c above), this choice would be extended to allow consumers to identify food derived from GM material. In opting for this approach, the Commission recognised that some consumers may wish to avoid GM foods for reasons other than concern over avoiding exposure to GM material. However, the proposals have raised concerns. The FSA suggests they are inconsistent, in that they do not require labelling of all foods produced using GM technology (see table above). It also sees potential problems in enforcing the proposed new regulations.

20. Some of the products (e.g. oil from GM soybeans) that would need to be labelled under the new proposals do not contain GM material. The GM status of such products cannot be verified by testing for GM material in the laboratory. Rather, verification will rely solely on the Commission's proposed "audit trail". Audit-based systems have been established for other foods (e.g. organic foods, fair trade tea/coffee and animal welfare-friendly meat) and enjoy high levels of consumer trust.

21. There would be exemptions from the labelling requirements where GMOs have only been used as processing aids. This practice is widespread in the wine, cheese[8] and brewing industries. Permission has also been given for their use in the baking industries, although we understand they are not yet in use in the UK. Vitamins used to fortify food and sold as "supplements" may also be products from GM-derived processing aids. Because they are only used as processing aids, they are present at well below one per cent even during the manufacturing steps and will have effectively have been removed entirely by the time the finished product emerges. Such exemptions would therefore provide no comfort to those whose objection to GM technology is based on ethical grounds.

22. Since the proposals would apply only from the point of entry into the EU, some have questioned how the GM "audit trail" would work in practice, particularly for imported bulk commodities such as GM soybeans and maize from North America and elsewhere.[9] The American Soybean Association (ASA) suggests that it would not be possible to implement an "audit trail" that allowed GM material to be traced back to the farm.[10] This is because international trade in grains is based on a commodity flow system where no distinction is made between GM and non-GM crops. For instance, in the US distribution system, GM and non-GM varieties are assembled into successively bigger batches—a typical shipment arriving in the EU contains up to 50,000 tonnes of crops originating from thousands of farms. For an "audit trail" starting at the point of entry into the EU, the importer would have to sample and test each shipment for its GM content. This information would be passed on to each operator in the chain and form the basis for verifying labelling requirements. ASA are concerned that such a system would be open to fraud (a concern shared by the FSA), and would incur considerable extra costs.

INTRODUCING A "GM-FREE" SCHEME

23. The FSA sees option (b)—maintaining the current labelling regime and introducing a "GM-free" scheme—as representing the best balance between costs and benefits. Under this option, manufacturers could sell foods conforming to certain criteria as being "GM-free" (e.g. specifying measures to minimise contamination throughout the food chain and establishing a threshold for unavoidable with GM material). The Government sees this option as having advantages over the Commission's proposals as the current labelling rules are practicable and enforceable, and the introduction of a "GM-free" scheme would allow consumers to avoid GM technology if they so wish. US farmers also favour such an approach. They have been supplying "identity preserved" (IP) lines for years, including some IP "non-GM" lines. These are generally in smaller quantities and are kept

---

[8]   An example is chymosin ("vegetarian rennet").

[9]   According to the FSA, the US grows 68% of the world's GM crops, Argentina 22%, Canada 6% and China 3%. In the US alone 70% of its soya bean crop is GM, 75% of its cotton crop, 50% of oilseed rape and 25% of maize (evidence to the inquiry, p 55 at paragraph3.1, footnote).

[10] Evidence pp 77–78.

entirely separate from the usual bulk distribution system through all stages of harvesting, transport, processing, etc. IP lines command a premium in the market to cover the additional costs incurred in maintaining integrity.

24. In general, consumer groups support option (c+)—the Commission's proposal to extend labelling requirements to include all foods produced from GM sources backed up with a "GM-free" scheme. There is strong support for the separation of GM and non-GM foods throughout the marketing chain and for measures to allow GM foods to be traced.

Summary of current and proposed GM labelling requirements

Food/feed	Labelling currently required?	Labelling required by Commission's proposals?	Labelling required by FSA's proposals?
Food produced from GM crops and containing GM material	Yes	Yes	Yes
Food produced from GM crops but not containing GM material	No	Yes	No
Food produced using GM organisms but not containing GM material (e.g. wine and cheese)	No	No	No
GM animal feed sold to livestock producers	No	Yes	Yes
Food from animals fed GM animal feeds	No	No	No
Non-GM foods with less than 1% presence of GM material	No	No	No (unless claimed to be "GM-free")

THE WIDER PICTURE

25. There has been a *de facto* moratorium on approvals of new GM products within the EU since 1998, pending revision of the deliberate release Directive.[11] This Directive is due to be implemented in national laws by October 2002; the Commission had hoped this would signal the end of the blockage in approvals, which it considers to be illegal. Several Member States have suggested that the approvals process should not be restarted until the new traceability and labelling regime is implemented; this could extend the blockage until mid 2003 and possibly into 2004. Any such extension could increase the likelihood of the EU facing action through the WTO. It is also possible that the Commission's labelling and traceability proposals might themselves be the subject of action through the WTO.

26. The EU's proposals on traceability and GMOs were notified to the WTO Committees on Sanitary and Phytosanitary Measures (SPS) and on Technical Barriers to Trade (TBT) in 2001. At meetings of those Committees, most recently in March 2002, the US has complained about the lack of scientific justification for the *de facto* moratorium, and Canada has suggested that the proposals discriminate against products produced by GM technology, thus raising the question whether they might be perceived as a barrier to trade.

27. The assessment of rules for the regulation of GMOs fall within the remit of the WTO Committee on Trade and Environment (CTE), set up in 1994 at the end of the Uruguay Round. The Committee also aims to clarify the relationship between WTO rules and the specific trade obligations of certain multilateral environmental agreements (MEAs), such as the Convention on Biological Diversity and the Cartagena Biosafety Protocol (see paragraph 16 and Box 3). Another issue, to be examined in the CTE as well as the TBT Committee, is that of policies on eco-labelling (i.e. labelling which provides information on the environmental characteristics of a product) and whether existing WTO rules stand in the way of such policies.[12]

---

[11] Directive 2001/18/EC.

[12] Information about the Committee is on the WTO's website at http://www.wto.org.

CHAPTER 2: POINTS FROM THE EVIDENCE

28. In this chapter we record briefly the views of the main stakeholders on the question with which this Report is primarily concerned—whether the Commission's proposals represent a practical and proportionate response to consumers' legitimate wish to exercise choice in relation to GM and non-GM food and feed (*cf* paragraphs 7–11 above). Not all of the evidence we received, though interesting and important in a wider context (e.g. safety testing, the approvals regime and the role of the European Food Safety Authority), was directly relevant to this question.

THE SCIENTIFIC COMMUNITY

29. The Royal Society of Edinburgh pointed out that the EU imports each year 37 million tonnes of maize, soya, rapeseed or derived food products. The likelihood of adventitious presence of GM material was inevitable. As some consumers object to the application of GM technology as well as having concerns about the risk to environment and health, the Society favoured a system of labelling which identified products as made either "with genetic engineering" or "without genetic engineering".[13]

30. The Biotechnology and Biological Sciences Research Council (BBSRC) said that zero level contamination of GM food and feed was not practical. It suggested that GM feed could have a higher threshold without the animal products themselves approaching the one per cent threshold that is permitted for a food ingredient. Alternatively, it suggested that the application of the one per cent threshold to feed as well as food might simply reflect the practical consideration that one per cent was about the current minimum limit of reliable quantification of transgenic sequences in complex samples.[14]

31. The Royal Society[15] drew attention to its 1998 report *Genetically modified plants for food use*[16], in which it concluded that the use of GM plants potentially offered benefits in agricultural practice, food quality, nutrition and health, but recognised that there was public concern about potential environmental effects of GM technology and the safety of GM food for human consumption. In relation to labelling and traceability the report's conclusions were:

- Strong support—in the interests of consumer choice—for the labelling of foods containing GM material where the foodstuff was substantially changed from that of its conventional counterpart.

- Recognition that segregation of commodity crops and derivatives through long supply chains on a global scale would cause difficulties of traceability for those manufacturers and retailers who wished to source products which did not contain GMOs or their derivatives.

- There were problems in relation to the complexity of international trade, detection limits, complexity of product formulations or processing techniques.

- For enforcement purposes it would be essential to recognise a minimum level, based on scientifically validated testing methods, for adventitious presence of GM material, below which a product could be considered to be free of GM derivatives.

32. The Royal Society had since produced an update[17] to the 1998 report. This did not deal specifically with the issues of labelling and traceability but *inter alia* stressed the need for criteria for safety assessments to be made explicit. It noted that changes in the nutritional status of GM foods could occur both in GM and in conventional, non-GM food; eating GM DNA was no different from eating DNA from a wide range of sources. There was no evidence that GM foods caused allergic reactions, but it was suggested that vulnerable groups such as infants needed special guidelines. The Institute of Food Research echoed these findings.[18] The Royal Society planned to review developments on the environmental aspects of GM crops separately.

---

[13] p 117 at paragraph 15; p 116 at paragraph 7.

[14] p 84 at paragraphs 6–7.

[15] p 115.

[16] *Genetically modified plants for food use*, Statement 2/98, The Royal Society, London, September 1998.

[17] *Genetically modified plants for food use and human health—an update*, Policy document 4/02, The Royal Society, London, February 2002.

[18] p 99.

CENTRAL AND LOCAL GOVERNMENT

33. The view of the UK Government, in a memorandum submitted by the Food Standards Agency,[19] was that the proposal to label ingredients where no GM material was present was neither enforceable, practical nor proportional. Full traceability of food and feed was unlikely to be achievable. The current situation was unsatisfactory; there was an urgent need to clear the approvals backlog and end the *de facto* moratorium.

34. On the other hand, FSA considered that the Commission's proposals did not go far enough for those who wanted to avoid food produced by using GM technology, such as cheese, meat, milk and eggs from animals fed GM animal feed. The Agency therefore wished to see the Commission's proposals supplemented with a "GM-free" labelling option. However, supply chains in developing countries in particular lacked formal contractual arrangements as produce was sourced from hundreds of producers. There were therefore limitations to the extent that unique identifier codes[20] could be an effective tool for the traceability of commodity crops which were traded on the open market world wide and which passed through a complex supply chain. The Agency agreed with the Commission that non-EU-approved GMOs would also need a one per cent threshold.

35. The Minister for Environment, the Rt Hon Michael Meacher MP, told the Committee that the traceability proposals were "probably not practicable, and . . . certainly disproportionate" (Q 193). On the one per cent threshold for adventitious presence of GM material, he confirmed the FSA's view that this was the best that current technology could reliably offer, but he felt that consumers had the right to expect the threshold to be lowered as technology improved (Q 201).

36. The FSA Chairman, Sir John Krebs, described the proposals as a "cheat's charter". He said: "If the Commission's proposals were implemented, then in a couple of years' time people would turn round to us and say 'Well, how are you checking that actually these products that claim to contain no GM-derived products are in fact doing that?' I would have to say 'Well, I am sorry, there is no way of guaranteeing it other than a paper trail which refers to a batch of soya grown perhaps in South America, shipped in a bulk transporter, processed in a bulk mill, then shipped in a large container arriving at the door of Europe when, under the European Commission proposals, the traceability starts.'. . ." (Q 218).

37. He went on to illustrate the point: "Last month we published a research study in which we had looked at the GM soya content of 200-odd examples of baked goods from the shelves of the shops of Britain. We found that about 15 per cent of those baked goods contained small traces of GM soya. Sometimes the soya was actually in wheat flour, so it was an adventitious presence in a wheat product. In three out of the 200 or so cases the presence of GM soya exceeded the one per cent threshold. Now all of those products were products which were produced through a traceability and IP system. . . . This is to me a practical demonstration that traceability and IP does not give a guarantee." (Q 219) He added: "Even for the major retailers, whilst certainly they have more capability to deploy resources right back through the chain and demand proper systems from their suppliers, even there the evidence I have heard from the retailers themselves is that they cannot provide guarantees in many cases." (Q 222)

38. The Local Authorities Coordinating Body on Food and Trading Standards (LACOTS) felt that "non-GM" and "GM-free" were likely to convey the same message to the consumer. An international standard was required. It was desirable to specify standard criteria for determining levels of GM contamination. Traceability was feasible so long as there were effective systems in countries of origin; imported commodities would therefore need certificates of compliance. Local authorities would need significant additional resources to meet the requirements of sampling and analysis, which could range from £600 to £1000 per sample.[21]

CONSUMERS AND ENVIRONMENTAL ORGANISATIONS

39. The Consumers' Association (CA) argued that public concern could not be resolved by science alone. There was a need for an open, transparent, inclusive procedure reflecting social attitudes and beliefs. A clearer idea of consumers' attitudes to GM developments was needed. Labelling was only one aspect of consumer choice. Identity Preservation systems should be encouraged and supply chains developed. However, confidence and acceptance of GM foods would depend on the extent to which GM products were perceived to offer benefits to consumers when balanced against perceived risks. CA considered that GM-derived food should definitely be labelled, and that the one per cent threshold

---

[19] p 55ff.

[20] See paragraph 16.

[21] LACOTS response (4 September 2001) to the Food Standards Agency's consultation on the Commission's proposal (*not printed*).

for unapproved GMOs—provided that the unapproved varieties had undergone a risk assessment—would provide some reassurance.[22]

40. In oral evidence CA's representatives cited evidence from opinion surveys which strongly supported the case for labelling (QQ 1–4, 10). They criticised the FSA's proposal for a "GM-free" label, which they felt would mislead the consumer and create a niche market (as with organic food) for which consumers would have to pay a higher price. Ms Sue Davies said this would be unfair, "because most people want to buy the standard products which were on the market before GM came into food products. ... If something did say 'GM-free', for it not to be misleading it would be essential that there has been no GM near the product" (Q 21).

41. The National Consumer Council (NCC)[23] did not support the one per cent threshold. There was clear consumer support for the right to know whether food was from GM crops or was the produce of animals fed on GM feed. NCC urged the Commission to bring forward consistent proposals on enzymes at an early date. Like CA, it did not consider the FSA's proposal for "GM-free" to be helpful. Low income customers would be disadvantaged. Once a traceability system was established and ongoing, the costs should be minimal for small businesses.

42. NCC did not accept the proposal to set a threshold for non-approved GM material until full authorisation was in place. A zero tolerance threshold for non-approved varieties should remain in force. There was a need to clarify more fully the roles and responsibilities of, and liaison between, the European Food Standards Agency (EFSA), risk management bodies and Member States' competent authorities in order to facilitate greater consumer and scientific confidence in the whole risk analysis process. NCC advocated consumer representation on any risk assessment bodies and scientific panels responsible for conducting assessment under the approval process. Assessments should be conducted in an open, transparent and inclusive way.

43. Friends of the Earth (FOE) welcomed the extension of the present regime to GM derivatives. They objected to the one per cent threshold for unapproved GMs, which they argued would water down unacceptably the deliberate release Directive. They did not regard it as reasonable to put the burden of avoiding GMOs on to the consumer.[24]

44. FOE's GM campaigner Adrian Bebb disagreed with the FSA's criticisms of "paper trails", pointing to the fact that such systems existed and worked for products such as organic, fair trade and kosher food. On the question of bulk commodity crops, his colleague Peter Riley commented: "Increasingly companies will be looking to go to particular farmers to supply them with what they want because of the uncertainty that the commodity market provides. This is exactly what companies like Tesco are doing—they have gone down to the farm level in Brazil to get their soya at the moment. If farmers see there is a business to be made by providing European consumers with what they want ... they will provide the companies with the assurances that (they) are looking for." (QQ 100, 106)

45. Greenpeace argued that Article 153 of the EC Treaty required that consumers should have the right to know what was in their food. They felt the Commission's proposals did not go far enough. Eggs, meat, milk etc from animals consuming GM feed should be labelled, and the one per cent threshold was considered too high. IP traceability systems need not add significantly to the cost of products as they only added paperwork, the cost of which could be incorporated into the invoicing process. They wanted to see national authorities playing a bigger role in the initial evaluation of new GMOs.[25]

46. Neither GeneWatch[26] nor the Genetic Engineering Alliance[27] supported the FSA. They considered that labels should be introduced for cheese and all other products from GM technology. It was unacceptable that the majority of consumers should pay more for a "GM-free" option. It was more appropriate that GM foods became the niche market. The "GM free" option denied the low-income consumer the right to purchase such products as they would be priced too high. They would like meat, milk and eggs from animals fed on GM feed to be so labelled and wanted the moratorium to continue.

---

[22] Points from CA's response (September 2001) to FSA consultation *(not printed)*.

[23] p 102ff.

[24] pp 29–31.

[25] pp 94–98.

[26] pp 89–91.

[27] pp 91–92.

THE FOOD CHAIN

Farmers

47. The National Farmers' Union[28] described how farmers and growers had developed farm assurance schemes. It welcomed other food industry initiatives for Identity Preservation as a means of ensuring meaningful labelling. Transmission of information on GMOs could possibly be integrated with other on-farm traceability systems, such as the UK's assured combinable crops scheme. The cost of testing for the presence of all GM varieties would be extremely high and appropriate reference material would need to be lodged with the Commission. The NFU was disappointed that clear guidelines on the use of the term "GM-free" had not been addressed in the Commission's proposals. This term should mean total freedom from any linkage with any GMO whether directly incorporated into the final product or used in its production.

48. The National Farmers' Union of Scotland[29] welcomed the Commission's proposals and believed that the labelling requirements should meet the needs of most consumers. It also welcomed the proposal to provide the same level of assurance for both food and feed. Zero tolerance was, however, impossible to achieve without 100 per cent testing. The moratorium on EU approvals was illogical, given that some GM-containing food and feed products were already on the market.

49. The Ulster Farmers' Union drew attention to the serious cost implications for UK farmers. The EU needed to import protein as it was only one-third self-sufficient. The UK farming industry would be pricing itself out of the market if the Commission's proposals were implemented.[30]

The food supply industry

50. The Supply Chain Initiative on Modified Agricultural Crops[31] (SCIMAC)—a grouping of industry organisations (including the National Farmers' Union) along the UK farm supply chain—has drawn up guidelines for the identity preservation of GM crops from initial seed stock through to delivery of the harvested crop ex-farm, thus establishing a framework for continued identity preservation and traceability beyond that point. The measures specified build on existing, proven systems within UK agriculture and combine provisions for record-keeping and transfer of information with specific requirements for on-farm management practice. SCIMAC stressed that "labelling exists to promote choice, not to provide a route for denial of access and choice." It considered that a meaningful and enforceable framework of consumer information could be delivered only by regulations which focused on the product rather than the production process. It therefore opposed a traceability system which could not be verified through end-product testing, since that could lay the way open to fraud and confuse rather than inform consumers. Instead it favoured an enforcement regime based on auditing of records and stock inspections during spot checks.

51. The British Society of Plant Breeders and the British Sugar Beet Seed Producers' Association[32] suggested it was not the responsibility of regulators to attempt to gauge or reflect prevailing public attitudes or consumer preferences. They noted that certain details of the traceability regime were left flexible in the Commission's proposals and would to some extent depend on how individual Member States decided to implement them. Implementation should not seek to re-invent the wheel but should build upon proven systems of traceability. Identity preservation (IP) was already established within the food chain.

52. The United Kingdom Agricultural Supply Trade Association[33] (UKASTA) argued that there were distinctions between food and feed which the proposals did not adequately recognise. There were many opportunities for feed to be commingled. The proposals could involve great cost and delay, with no apparent benefit. The UKASTA Feed Assurance scheme and the Feed Materials Assurance scheme were the key to the non-GM sourcing and traceability of feed materials. Clumsy legislation could harm their development and expansion. The Grain and Feed Trade Association (GAFTA), however, considered that a single food and feed approval system was sensible.[34]

53. GAFTA raised a number of points on the traceability proposals. They felt that their application to imports into the EU could only be viewed as a technical barrier to trade since the scientific basis

[28] pp 109–11.

[29] pp 112–13.

[30] UFU response (31 August 2001) to FSA consultation *(not printed)*.

[31] pp 120–23.

[32] pp 86–89.

[33] pp 130–32.

[34] p 93.

was invalid—they were not able to address environmental damage or human health. They offered consumer choice with no scientific validity and therefore potentially violated WTO rules, laying the EU open to challenge under the WTO dispute procedures.[35]

Food processors and retailers

54. The Food and Drink Federation (FDF) approved of the Food Standards Agency's preference for retaining existing labelling arrangements with the addition of a "GM-free" labelling scheme. It considered the Commission's proposals disproportionate, unworkable and unenforceable, and saw no need to label derived products.[36] The Provision Trade Federation said that importers could not guarantee the GM status of a derived product. The Federation welcomed the fact that the Commission's proposals did not extend to food produced "with a GMO" (as opposed to "from a GMO"). A label which identified cheese, meat, etc as derived from animals fed on GM feed would be detrimental to sales.[37]

55. The British Retail Consortium (BRC)[38] welcomed the inclusion of feed in the proposed new arrangements. BRC believed that the best way of ensuring that products did not contain GM ingredients was to have a robust identity preserved system. BRC and FDF had published a technical standard based on best practice to assist in the supply and traceability of non-GM material. BRC expected that this would be widely adopted throughout the EU on a voluntary basis but would prefer to see it officially recognised. It considered the "GM-free" status favoured by the FSA was unattainable for commodity crops.

56. Mr John Longworth, group trading law and technical director for Tesco and representing BRC, was more optimistic about the practicality of ensuring traceability as the supply chain expanded and became more complex. He said that there were a number of Asian countries that were keen not to have GM crops because of the importance of their export trade in edible oils. He added that there was a potential for parts of Brazil to maintain production of non-GM crops for a long time (Q 76).

57. The British Beer and Pub Association, speaking for several trade associations from the retail trade and restaurant catering sector, believed it was vital for Member States to have sufficient flexibility to introduce their own legal requirements, appropriate to national culture and traditions, on labelling of food served in restaurant and other catering outlets, whether pre-packaged or not.[39] The Scotch Whisky Association felt that the requirement to label food not containing detectable GM material could set a dangerous precedent; the proposal was not based on science or justified on health and safety grounds. There were practical difficulties in crowding too much information on labels. Association members might be forced into IP schemes which would be unworkable, given the long time that whisky took to produce and mature, and would argue that the proposed regulations should apply only to spirits distilled after the date of implementation.[40]

THE BIOTECHNOLOGY INDUSTRY

58. Monsanto[41] suggested that a specific (non-GM) class of feedstuffs would reduce confusion. The one per cent threshold had been established to allow consumer choice, not safety. It was inevitable that there would be differences around the world in interpreting and implementing the Cartagena Biosafety Protocol[42]. Similarly Syngenta[43] said that labelling of GM products was not a food safety issue but a consumer choice issue. The one per cent threshold would require further revision because of future changes in cost and consumer expectations. The purpose of the EFSA should be to harmonise the risk assessment process and to ensure scientific scrutiny of information. Risk assessment conducted by OECD countries, not just EU, should be acceptable for unauthorised GM material.

---

[35] p 94.

[36] Unprinted material summarised at p 13.

[37] pp 113–14.

[38] pp 27–28.

[39] p 85.

[40] pp 118–19.

[41] pp 99–102.

[42] See paragraph 16 and Box 3.

[43] pp 126–130.

THE UNITED STATES GOVERNMENT AND MAJOR US STAKEHOLDERS

59. The American Soybean Association[44] was concerned about excessive documentation, which they estimated could involve several thousand different farms in one shipment alone[45]. Identity Preserved systems were in their view the only possible approach. The current EU moratorium was preventing US and EU farmers from gaining access to benefits from up to twelve products which had been cleared by the EU scientific experts.

60. The United States Embassy, in a memorandum submitted on behalf of the US Government,[46] commented that the proposed regulations were more restrictive than necessary. The burden to be placed on suppliers did not reflect considerations of health, safety and environment on the one hand and those of perceived consumer desires on the other. Traceability and labelling would be very expensive to implement and there was room for significant fraud. It was not possible to achieve "no risk": the one per cent threshold could not reliably be tested or consistently met. "Genetically modified" applied to all breeding methods and "biotech" was considered a more relevant term. The US asked why foods produced through biotechnology required to have additional labelling requirements, and who determined when a biotech food could "give rise to ethical or religious concerns".[47] The US did not believe that expanding mandatory traceability and labelling requirements to animal feed was justified or that it would enhance public health.

61. In oral evidence, Mr Peter Kurz, Minister-Counsellor for Agricultural Affairs, said: "Frankly, it is not clear to us what risks the proposed labelling requirements are attempting to address. . . . If consumer choice is truly the objective of the proposal, how will this regulation increase consumer choice given that even under less stringent EU labelling regulations processors and retailers are re-formulating rather than labelling, due to perceived concerns about the customer reaction and market share?[48] The United States would argue that it is equally important to give guidance as to what would constitute a food that has *not* been produced through biotechnology." (Q 131)

62. He suggested that identity preserved (IP) schemes were "the only way to assure that the consumer really gets biotech-free foods" (Q 144). Asked to comment on the argument that the onus should be on producers of GM crops to provide the information which is required by the consumer rather than expecting the consumer to pay a premium for IP lines, he drew a parallel with organic food: "Hopefully with organics we will move to a point where, if the demand is sufficient, the premium that has to be paid will be relatively modest and then hopefully that would serve as a model for biotech foods as well. We are also dealing with the market place here and the realities of production of grain and foodstuffs, and to ask producers to take the onus on themselves in view of the fact that this is only a relatively small percentage of the world market asking for biotech-free foods frankly is not going to happen." (QQ 145–6)

63. Asked if the US would accept the Commission's proposals if it meant that the moratorium on GMO approvals could be lifted, Mr Kurz said the US administration was concerned that they would "set a precedent that could also be applied to non-agricultural industries. . . . Frankly, we do not see any ground for compromise in these proposals." He added that they agreed with Sir John Krebs's view that the proposals were unworkable. (Q 141)

OTHER VIEWS

64. The Rev Professor Michael Reiss[49] commented that most of the objections to the Commission's proposals had been based on practicality, fairness and cost. One argument for labelling was that it was ethical and because people wanted it. Surveys of the public did not provide the relevant information any more than the answer to the question "do you want lower taxes?" Choice did not always require mandatory labelling. It was better to permit retailers and restaurants to decide whether to label. Those who wanted to know would seek those who did so label. The duty of regulatory process was to prevent harm and to provide special protection for those unable to take legal actions against those responsible

---

[44] p 77ff.

[45] A single boatload of commodity soybeans can contain 50,000 tonnes of soybeans, of which each tonne would contain over 7 million beans. In a shipment from the US the beans will have been collected and mixed together at every point of a ten-stage handling system from several thousand different farms. Each farm will typically have grown between six and ten different varieties—which could be either biotech or non-biotech, according to practice on the individual farm—from the several thousand soybean varieties available to growers. (ASA evidence, p 80.)

[46] pp 39–43.

[47] COM(2001)425 final, Article 14(2)(b).

[48] This comment confirmed what Mr Longworth told the Committee about Tesco's decision to remove GM ingredients from its own-brand lines, after which others followed suit (Q 69).

[49] pp 114–15.

for harm. There was therefore (as the Royal Society had suggested[50]) a role for mandatory labelling to prevent harm such as allergenic effects and to provide extra safeguards for vulnerable groups, particularly infants.

CHAPTER 3: THE COMMITTEE'S CONCLUSIONS

WHY IS LABELLING NEEDED?

65. The proposed Regulations seek to extend existing EU legislation on labelling (and hence traceability) of GM crops, food and animal feed, including products containing or derived from GM material. Although we have consciously restricted the scope of this Report to the practical aspects of meeting consumer demands for labelling, taking those demands as given,[51] we will start by briefly running through the case for labelling under several headings. These take into account the considerable variation in consumers' motives in wanting to know which foods are "GM" in one sense or another (see Box 1, after paragraph 4 above).

Safety

66. None of our witnesses, either in writing or orally, provided any specific evidence that there was any increased risk to public health in general, or to susceptible individuals in particular, from the consumption of GM products currently available or under development. There has been increasing consumption of products derived from GM maize and soya in the US during the past five years. Our attention has not been drawn to any deleterious effects to the health of individual consumers. It may of course be too early to make any assumption about the safety of these two crops. It would also be inappropriate to attempt any wider generalisation from these two examples.

67. Testing of GM products is considerably more exhaustive than traditional crops and food. This has enabled problems such as the unintended transfer of brazil nut allergenic material in protein-enriched soybeans to be dealt with before the product actually reached the market place. On the other hand the "StarLink" incident[52] illustrates the difficulties of restricting a GM food crop to animal or industrial uses when its non-GM counterpart, used for human consumption, is virtually indistinguishable, as well as the practical difficulties of segregating GM and non-GM crops to prevent contamination or cross-pollination.

Nutritional benefits

68. Since many GM products are chemically identical to traditional products, no effect (positive or negative) on nutrition can be asserted. While various claims have been made, those products available so far (e.g. yellow rice) are relevant more to countries with large undernourished populations. This is not generally the case in the EU. It seems unlikely that nutritional benefits for developed countries will appear in the near future. Current UK and EU legislation in this area is already very tight, and certainly more restrictive than in the US.

Environmental implications

69. The inquiry did not specifically address the adequacy of existing legislation to prevent inappropriate releases of GMOs into the environment. No extra benefits in this respect are likely to flow from the present proposals. Some of the earlier experiments in plant biotechnology have, however, led to public concern (coupled with distrust of the industry) about effects on biodiversity and ecosystems. Much greater transparency of information and independence of scientific research is needed to allay this concern.

70. Food is an unusual consumer product. There are many examples where the consumer is concerned not only with the product itself but also with the means of production and the implications for the environment and animal husbandry. These concerns are well demonstrated by the demand for organic vegetables, free range eggs, etc.

71. The fact that a food is determined to be safe to eat does not necessarily mean that it cannot harm the environment. Many crops which are grown for food may themselves be, or contain, seeds (e.g. apples, potatoes, sweet corn etc), which could lead to the spread—whether by accident or design, and irrespective of the scale of production—of novel, including GM, varieties into non-native

---

[51] See paragraphs 7–11.

[52] StarLink™ was a proprietary variety of maize, modified to contain insecticidal properties. During the period 1998–2000 the US Environmental Protection Agency approved its use as animal feed but not as human food, because of suspected allergenic effects. Fragments of the modified DNA were subsequently found in a popular brand of taco shells sold in the US. It was thought that this had arisen from physical contamination of seed corn but cross-pollination from GM crops could not be ruled out. Voluntary action was taken to withdraw manufactured products at risk from similar contamination. (See Friends of the Earth at Q 96.)

environments. Good environmental monitoring is needed in order to protect against undesirable gene leakage of this kind, which may compromise identity preserved (IP) schemes.

72. On the other hand there are frequent claims that GM crops can offer substantial benefits to the environment, such as reduced need for pesticides which harm flora and fauna and disrupt ecosystems. The validity of such claims is outside the scope of this Report.

Ethical considerations

73. In 1985, the United Nations adopted a series of consumer rights in their "Charter for Consumer Protection". Among these were (i) the right to be informed and (ii) the right to choose. It seems to us that the second follows logically from the first; certainly without information, choice must become more limited.

74. We were interested in the views expressed by the Rev Professor Michael Reiss, who suggested that the market place, rather than legislation, may be an effective way of providing this. Those who wish to have such information will choose those products and suppliers who make it available. This does not of course remove the onus on the authorities to protect the vulnerable, such as babies or those with allergies.

Consumer preference

75. The principle that consumers are entitled to know whether they are eating GM food or not is already part of existing EC legislation on GMOs. That is why the conclusions of this Report are mainly concerned with the practicalities of extending that knowledge to all types food and feed in which genetic engineering has played a part.

FEASIBILITY OF TESTING AND TRACING OF GM CONTENT

76. A variety of products produced with GM technology are not merely substantially equivalent to existing products but are actually identical (oils, sugars etc). Not only is there now, but there never can be, any scientific means of identifying their source. This is why the Commission's proposals on labelling would need to rely on an "audit trail". We are not convinced that either for bulk commodities (soya, maize, wheat etc) or for products from countries with less sophisticated supply chains could such a trail be relied upon. We are also concerned that the cost of such surveillance would fall upon producers and consumers with no obvious benefits in nutrition or food safety. We feel that unenforceable legislation could devalue the system, and a higher price would unavoidably have to be paid for enhanced consumer choice.

DERIVED PRODUCTS

77. We consider that all derived products should be treated in the same way. This would not be the case with the Commission's proposals. Most of the world trade in soya and maize is now in the form of GM or GM-derived and this situation must, realistically, be accepted as unchangeable. Whilst therefore it is realistic to label food and feed which are themselves genetically modified, products derived from GMOs can be identified only by audit trails.

WHAT SHOULD BE LABELLED?

78. We were convinced by the arguments of the FSA and the farming and food industries[53] that the Commission's traceability proposals would be largely unworkable, because of high costs, practical difficulties of ensuring universal traceability and the opportunities for fraud or misleading claims. We have therefore concluded (with the FSA) that it would be more practical to go for something like option (b) in paragraph 18 above—i.e. to continue with the existing labelling regime, which meets consumers' wish to know whether they are eating something which contains detectable amounts of genetically engineered DNA or protein, and to couple this with a scheme of identity preserved (IP) products for people who wish to go further and avoid food from any source or process in which genetic engineering has played a part. For reasons which we discuss below, we do not think it would be appropriate to label these products as "GM-free", but they would be presented as having been produced without the use of GM techniques and with every reasonable step having been taken to avoid the accidental presence of GM material.

79. In coming to this conclusion we recognise that a possible consequence might be the creation of a two-tier price structure (as is already the case with organic and non-organic food); but it is

---

[53] See paragraphs 33, 47, 50, 48 and 52.

unrealistic to expect increased costs to be borne by all consumers, including those who have no wish to pay for audit trails and who have no concern about GM-derived food. We think every effort should be made, working alongside normal market forces, to keep the additional costs of IP and assurance schemes as low as possible.

80. We appreciate that this may be an imperfect response to the aspirations of consumer and environmental organisations. Nevertheless we see encouraging and positive scope for building on existing IP and farm assurance schemes. Evidence from the farming and food industries suggested that such schemes (e.g. the British Farm Standard scheme) could deliver a standard of traceability which should command consumer confidence.

TERMINOLOGY

81. We were unhappy with the UK Food Standards Agency's proposed use of the term "GM-free". Sir John Krebs envisaged that it would represent, at least initially, a niche market, for which people would be willing to pay a premium, as with organic food, and would be "based on local production systems with short supply chains where traceability could be guaranteed and where the sources could be identified as definitely not having a GM basis" (Q 227). The Commission does not attempt a definition of "GM-free" or similar terms, since its proposals work the other way round—i.e. by requiring all food and feed within the defined categories[54] to be labelled as containing or produced from GMOs.

82. Zero level of GM food and feed is not usually practicable. Therefore in our view the term "GM-free" should not be used unless the seller can guarantee a true zero level. We feel that as long as the adventitious presence of GM matter is tolerated up to a limit of one per cent, the term "GM-free" is unhelpful and, in a strictly literal sense, positively untruthful.

83. Alternative wording such as "non-GM", "contains no intentionally present GM material", or "produced without the use of genetic engineering" were suggested in the evidence. We consider that the term "non-GM" might be acceptable, provided that:

(a) it is used only for products in which the presence of *authorised* (our emphasis) GM material[55] is below the threshold of one per cent;

(b) its meaning is rigorously defined; and

(c) it is supported by a strenuous campaign of public information, led by the FSA.

Otherwise we fear—as Sir John Krebs conceded (Q 226)—that many consumers would not recognise a difference between "GM-free" and "non-GM". There is a parallel with "lead-free" and "unleaded" petrol. "Unleaded" is the term favoured by the oil industry because during the period when leaded petrol was being phased out there was a possibility that petrol which was entirely lead-free when it left the refinery could become contaminated in the distribution chain. In practice most motorists would regard the terms as interchangeable.

84. We therefore think that the FSA should consider following up the recent report of the former Food Advisory Committee on Food Labelling[56] by arranging consumer research into the form of words that might be most useful and least ambiguous in this area. In this context words like "impurity" and "contamination" have implicit negative connotations, which we think should be avoided.

85. We have already commented that in our view all GM-derived products should be treated in the same way. We consider that meat etc from animals fed on GM feed and any products (wine, cheese, etc) made with GM processing aids should be no more eligible to be labelled "non-GM" than the highly refined oils and sugars referred to in paragraph 76 above. We recognise the particular problems that industries with lengthy production processes—notably the wine and spirits trade (paragraph 57)—would face if the Commission's proposals were to be adopted.

CLARITY OF INFORMATION

86. We were concerned about the impact on the size and legibility of labels if the requirements for what should appear on them compulsorily were too detailed or prescriptive. A label is only one way of conveying information to consumers. Much information is already provided that in practice is not readily accessible to the average consumer. We think that the FSA and producers throughout the food chain should explore alternative and more user-friendly means of getting information to those

---

[54] See paragraph 14.

[55] See paragraph 17.

[56] Food Advisory Committee, *Review of Food Labelling 2001*, Food Standards Agency, FSA/0354/0102, January 2002.

customers who want it. This information needs to provide as many details of the methods of production (including husbandry) as possible. Only rarely is commercial sensitivity a valid excuse for non-disclosure.

87. For instance, it would be open to cheese producers to include labels or other forms of information voluntarily which explained to customers why chymosin was preferred to natural rennet as a processing agent.

THE MORATORIUM ON APPROVALS OF GM IMPORTS TO THE EU

88. We support the ending of the present *ad hoc* moratorium, which we consider to be an unfortunate abuse of Community procedures and could expose the EU to international litigation. Quite apart from averting major potential difficulties in the WTO forum, it would help to resolve the growing problem of unapproved products finding their way on to the EU market. The Commission's current proposals envisage an expert committee conducting safety assessments of GM material which has not yet been approved by the EU but is contained in food at a level below the one per cent threshold. The FSA describes this as "unsatisfactory".[57] We think it is unacceptable and adds weight to the case for unblocking the moratorium.

DEVELOPING COUNTRIES

89. The Sub-Committee's call for evidence (Appendix 2) included a specific question on the implications of the Commission's proposals for developing countries. There are two aspects. The first is whether the proposals would inhibit trade with countries who have already embraced, or might wish to embrace, agricultural biotechnology on an extensive scale. The second aspect is the possibility that exploitation of a technology that appears to benefit their agronomy may be retarded. Deaths from organophosphate poisoning in China have dropped dramatically since the advent of Bt cotton[58]. We believe that EU legislation on tracing and labelling would probably have only a neutral effect on developing countries' economies, but it is likely to be perceived by them as restrictive.[59]

90. We are concerned that traceability and labelling requirements for exports to the EU should not inhibit developing countries from developing GM technology, if they consider this would be appropriate for meeting their needs for food security and improved nutrition and can satisfy themselves that it there are no potentially harmful implications for their environments.[60] We welcome the Department for International Development's initiative for capacity building in these countries,[61] but are convinced that far more resources will be needed to provide adequate levels not simply of technological know-how but also the capacity to take decisions on social and environmental grounds. However it would appear that little progress is possible until the Cartagena Protocol on Biosafety is ratified.[62]

91. We recognise that difficult issues are involved here. In the final analysis developing countries will have to make up their own minds on whether to embrace food and agriculture biotechnology. We do not think that the EU should seek to influence decisions without recognising the imperatives of developing economies.

---

[57] p 56 at paragraph 5.3.

[58] Cotton seeds genetically modified to contain a common bacterium (bacillus thuringiensis) which protects against bollworm, the main pest that attacks cotton crops.

[59] In the hope of getting first-hand evidence on these issues, follow-up letters were written to the Brazilian, Chinese and Mexican Ambassadors and to the Indian High Commissioner asking for statements of their governments' views. In response to the first of these the Committee was told that the Brazilian Government had not yet decided on its policy in this area and therefore would not be making a submission. The High Commission replied that it was seeking information from the relevant authorities in India, but at the time of reporting this had not arrived. It is apparent from the Indian Government's recent decision to approve the introduction of Bt cotton that policy on biotechnology has been undergoing review in India, and no doubt in other countries too. No replies were received from the other embassies.

[60] We note that the UN Development Programme's Human Development Report 2001 *Making new technologies work for human development* (http://www.undp.org/hdr2001/), concludes that many developing countries might reap benefits in reducing malnourishment through the unique potential of GM techniques to produce new biotech foods and crops, although these have be balanced against challenging issues of risk management. We have also noted recent statements by the President of the Rockefeller Foundation, Professor Gordon Conway, about the potential of benign uses of biotechnology for tackling world food shortages. He believes that biotechnology's potential is currently seriously threatened by "a polarized debate that grows increasingly acrimonious". (See, for example, G Conway and G Toenniessen, "Feeding the world in the twenty-first century", *Nature*, Vol 402 Supp, 2 December 1999, p C55.)

[61] Q 186.

[62] See paragraph 16 and Box 3.

HANDLING OF GM ISSUES WITHIN THE UK GOVERNMENT

92. We find the allocation of responsibilities for GM policy issues within Government confusing, even after cross-questioning the Minister and Sir John Krebs on the matter (QQ 178–82, 208–15). We recognise the pivotal role played by the FSA but are puzzled that it should describe itself as a "Government Department" and we remain unclear as to its relationship with the Department for Environment, Food and Rural Affairs when formally its accountability is to Health Ministers. We note that there is a Cabinet committee, currently chaired by the Leader of the House of Commons, whose remit is to pull together the various interests within Government. Its proceedings, however, fall short of full transparency and we would like to see the lead responsibility being held by a senior departmental Minister.

RECOMMENDATIONS

93. We now make the following recommendations (references in brackets are to supporting paragraphs in the Report):

(a) Consumers have a right to choose between GM and non-GM products on the basis of the best information that it is practicable to make available (11);

(b) It is not practicable to legislate for the degree of traceability envisaged by the Commission for bulk commodity imports from the United States and elsewhere (76);

(c) Identity preserved (IP) and farm assurance schemes already exist and should be encouraged as a means of meeting consumers' demands for products which do not involve the use of GM technology (78);

(d) Rather than imposing indiscriminate burdens on producers and consumers at large (as the Commission's proposals would imply), we believe that it should be for the market to determine the prices of non-GM products from IP schemes, although we would urge that these should be kept as low as possible (79);

(e) Use of the term "GM-free" should be restricted by law to those products for which 100 per cent absence of GM material (including use of processing agents) can be guaranteed at all stages of production (82);

(f) We accept that, for practical reasons, the present threshold of one per cent is necessary to allow for the unintended presence of GM material in the generality of products which might otherwise be described as "GM-free" (83);

(g) This threshold should however apply only to GM ingredients which have been through the full EU authorisation procedure (83);

(h) For products to which the threshold applies, the term "non-GM" may be appropriate, but it is liable to confuse the consumer: we recommend that the FSA, following the advice of the former Food Advisory Committee, should conduct consumer research to establish more user-friendly terminology (84);

(i) In any event, we consider that all GM-derived products should be treated in the same way: we endorse the proposal to extend the labelling regime to animal feed; it follows that meat etc from animals fed on GM feed should not be classified as non-GM (77, 85);

(j) Although products obtained through use of GMOs as processing aids fall into a different category, we feel the same principle applies: it would, however, be open to producers to use voluntary labelling to explain the advantages of the processes and the trace quantities involved (85);

(k) Whatever terms are chosen, they need to be backed by better information for the consumer, on which the FSA should take the lead, supported by all other parts of the food production chain (86–87);

(l) A sensible balance should be set between what can be put on a label and what needs to be communicated by other means, such as in-store notices or company websites (86–87);

(m) Every effort should be taken at Ministerial level to persuade other Member States to lift their veto on GM approvals in return for a more pragmatic approach to traceability and labelling which should nevertheless go a long way in meeting their current concerns (88);

(n) The EU should not seek to influence developing countries' decisions on whether or not to adopt food and agricultural biotechnology practices without recognising the imperatives of developing economies (91);

(o)   There should be closer and more transparent co-ordination between the FSA, the Cabinet Office and other Government Departments, with one departmental Minister having overall responsibility for all aspects of policy on GMOs and related biotechnology issues (92).

RECOMMENDATION TO THE HOUSE

94. The Committee considers that the European Commission's proposals on labelling and traceability of genetically modified food and animal feed raise important issues of policy to which the attention of the House should be drawn. It makes this Report for information.

APPENDIX 1

Sub-Committee D
(Environment, Agriculture, Public Health and Consumer Protection)

Members of the Sub-Committee

Baroness Billingham
Lord Crickhowell
Lord Christopher
Lord Dubs
Lord Fyfe of Fairfield
Baroness Maddock
Baroness Miller of Chilthorne Domer
The Countess of Mar
Lord Palmer
Earl of Selborne (Chairman of the Sub-Committee)
Lord Walpole

The Specialist Adviser was Professor Alan Malcolm

Members of the Sub-Committee declared the following interests in relation to this inquiry:

Lord Fyfe of Fairfield
Former Chairman, Co-operative Wholesale Society 1989-2000

The Countess of Mar
Farmer
Cheese Maker

Baroness Miller of Chilthorne Domer
Somerset County Councillor
Chairman Somerset Food Links

Lord Palmer
Arable Farmer
Member of NFU for Scotland

The Earl of Selborne
Director, Blackmoor Estate Ltd (a farming company)
Fellow, The Institute of Biology
Fellow, The Royal Society
President, The Institute of Agricultural Management
Trustee, The John Innes Foundation
Trustee, The Lawes Trust (Rothamsted Experimental Station)

APPENDIX 2

Sub-Committee D's Call for evidence

Sub-Committee D, under the chairmanship of the Earl of Selborne, is conducting an inquiry into the European Commission's proposals for assessment, authorisation, traceability and labelling of genetically modified (GM) food and animal feed, including products derived from genetically modified organisms (GMOs) (COM (2001) 182 and 425).

The inquiry will focus on the issues of traceability and labelling and the implications of the proposals for consumers and third countries. In particular answers will be sought to the following questions:

1. Do these proposals adequately address the requirements of European consumers for regulation, traceability and labelling of GM food and feed and of food and feed products derived from GMOs?

2. Do they make sensible distinctions between the requirements of animal feed and those of food for human consumption?

3. How effective are the proposals likely to be in ensuring full traceability of GM material at all stages of the chain from producer to consumer?

4. Are the proposals likely to be enforceable in practice, particularly where no novel genetic material is contained in the food or feed?

5. A threshold level of 1 per cent or lower for the accidental presence of GM material in food and feed has been proposed, below which there would be an exemption. Is a threshold of this level, common to both food and feed, appropriate?

6. Is the role proposed for (a) the European Food Authority and its scientific committees and (b) Member States in the authorisation process for GM food and feed appropriate?

7. Are the proposals likely to be compatible with the requirements of the Cartagena Protocol on Biosafety and with other international commitments, including OECD programmes?

8. Are the proposals compatible with obligations towards non-Member States seeking to export food and feed to the EU?

9. Should the present EU-wide moratorium on approving GM food and crop product applications be maintained until the issues concerning traceability and labelling of GMOs have been resolved?

10. What other aspects of the proposals require further consideration before the UK Government can sign up to them?

21 December 2001

APPENDIX 3

List of Witnesses

The following witnesses gave evidence. Those marked * gave oral evidence.

American Soybean Association
Biotechnology and Biological Sciences Research Council (BBSRC)
British Beer & Pub Association
* British Retail Consortium
British Society of Plant Breeders and British Sugar Beet Seed Producers Association
* Consumers' Association
* Food and Drink Federation
* Food Standards Agency
* Friends of the Earth
GeneWatch UK
Genetic Engineering Alliance
The Grain and Feed Trade Association
Greenpeace
Institute of Food Research
Monsanto S.A.
National Consumer Council
National Farmers' Union of England and Wales (NFU)
National Farmers' Union Scotland (NFUS)
Provision Trade Federation
The Reverend Professor Michael Reiss
The Royal Society
Royal Society of Edinburgh
The Scotch Whisky Association
Supply Chain Initiative on Modified Agricultural Crops (SCIMAC)
Sygenta Seeds
United Kingdom Agricultural Supply Trade Association (UKASTA)
* UK Government
* United States Embassy, London
University of the West of England, Faculty of Applied Sciences

Information (not printed as evidence) was also received from:

Consumers' Association
Food and Drink Federation
Local Authorities Coordinating Board on Food and Trading Standards (LACOTS)
Ulster Farmers' Union

MINUTES OF EVIDENCE

TAKEN BEFORE THE EUROPEAN UNION COMMITTEE (SUB-COMMITTEE D)

WEDNESDAY 6 FEBRUARY 2002

Present:

Billingham, B
Christopher, L
Crickhowell, L
Dubs, L
Fyfe of Fairfield, L
Maddock, B

Mar, C
Miller of Chilthorne Domer, B
Palmer, L
Selborne, E (Chairman)
Walpole, L

Examination of Witnesses

Ms Sue Davies, Principal Policy Adviser and Ms Mona Patel, Senior Public Affairs Officer, Consumers' Association, examined.

Chairman

1. Could I welcome Sue Davies and Mona Patel from the Consumers' Association? We are grateful to you for helping us in our inquiry today. You will find on the table a list of interests which some of us have declared. Could I thank the Consumers' Association also for the copies you have given us of your responses to the Commission's Green Paper on consumer protection? In fact I suppose the inquiry we are doing here is a subset of that—a very specific corner of consumer protection but an important one. When we asked if you could manage today we did indicate that we would have to share the time with others from the American Embassy. In fact they are not now coming this morning so in fact we shall not be under such time pressure as we indicated. I am going to ask Lord Fyfe if he would like to ask the first question, but before I do that I wonder if there is anything you would like to say by way of introduction about the Consumers' Association?
(Ms Patel) We are very grateful for the opportunity to give evidence today and particularly for the Committee's decision to hear evidence from consumer organisations first. We feel that especially because we feel that the way that GM has been approached in the past has been in such a way that consumer concerns have not been given sufficient weight. But consumer concerns are obviously very important and science alone in relation to GM does not have all the answers. We believe that all other factors should be taken into account and obviously one of these factors is consumers' views. At international level the Codex Committee has recognised the importance of other factors besides science, as has the European Commission in its current proposals on food and feed. As you know, CA has been working on GM issues for many years and we have had a two-pronged approach; in the first place to ensure that GM foods are safe, and by that we mean that we are presented with the level of risk that consumers find acceptable, and the second facet of our approach is to ensure that consumers have a choice about whether or not to eat GM foods. We feel that the European Commission's proposals do go a long way towards ensuring those two objectives. They will strengthen many aspects of the approvals process and will give consumers meaningful choice about whether or not to buy GM foods. We also feel that there will be traceability throughout the food chain as a result of these proposals and this will be important in providing consumers with comprehensive information. The proposals will also ensure effective withdrawal of products in the event of safety problems arising in the future. They will also be useful for monitoring the long-term implications and claimed benefits of GM foods. So, in conclusion, overall we very much welcome the thrust of the European Commission's proposals.

Chairman: Thank you very much. Thank you too for the written material you have submitted, which makes the same points. Now, Lord Fyfe, you would like to ask a question.

Lord Fyfe

2. I am very interested in consumer opinion and how it is defined. Has there been a shift in consumer opinion, do you believe, since your Association was started, and how would you categorise the motives of consumers who want to avoid consuming food which is possibly derived from GM material? Also it would seem that citizens of the United States are not nearly as conscious of GM as people in this country and in Europe as a whole. Is there any particular reason for this, do you think?
(Ms Davies) Consumers' Association, as you say, has been working on GM foods for many years. We first reported on GM foods back in 1989 in one of our magazines and it is quite interesting, looking back, to see exactly what stance we took on the issue and, to quote, we said "Consumers will want reassurances on a range of issues, from product safety to environmental or ethical concerns. A drawing up of controls and codes of practice in this field should reflect those demands. More than ever before, consumers will want to know exactly what they are eating and why." We also acknowledged there could be benefits from GM. We have tended to do consumer research to track any key developments, so when vegetarian cheese first came on the market we carried out a survey, when tomato purée came on the market we carried out qualitative and quantitative research, and the same when soya and maize came on the market. It is clear that individual reservations will obviously vary from person to person but it has always been shown that there is a general concern

Lord Fyfe contd.]

about what the long-term implications of GM are going to be—the idea that this is something new and we do not know what the implications are going to be—and therefore we have to take a precautionary approach. Some people may feel that it is unnatural in some way and it is tampering with nature and therefore they feel they want to know more about it. Some people are concerned with environmental effects. So there are a whole range of different reasons why people may be concerned, but it is quite clear that people feel that this has shown just how complex the food supply chain has become. Particularly when soya and maize came on to the market, a lot of people did not realise they ate that much soya and suddenly they became aware that it was in a whole range of products where they did not expect to find it. So with some people it is just the idea that this is the food that I am eating and therefore I should know what is being put in that food—they want to have that information. In terms of whether or not public opinion has changed that significantly, when we started doing the research back at the beginning of the 1990s there was clearly a lack of awareness about GM by most people because it was not being reported in the media and people did not know about it, but the same concerns were raised in the research that we did. When soya and maize came on to the market, there was then obviously much greater awareness. In terms of US opinion, it is very interesting. We work very closely with our sister organisation, Consumers Union, in the United States. We are both members of Consumers International and we are also members of the Transatlantic Consumer Dialogue, which is a more recent body, which brings together US and EU consumer organisations—there are 25 US groups and 40 EU groups—and we have developed a joint position on GM foods. The US groups feel just as strongly about the need for full labelling of all derivatives, the importance of traceability and the importance of a mandatory approval process, for example. But also looking at consumer opinion in the US, it seems that the main difference is that because products are not labelled people do not really know that it is an issue. There is some interesting research that the Food and Drug Administration did on their website which sets out the results of some focus groups that were carried out in 2000, trying to find out what US consumers thought about GM. They had about 12 focus groups in four cities across the US that were representative of the population as a whole—one focus group was screened so it was composed of people who had a particular concern about GM—and it was clear that the findings were very similar to what you would get if you asked UK consumers. It was clear that people did not really know that much about it. To quote a few of the comments that the FDA have on their website, "Virtually all participants said that bioengineered foods should be labelled as such so that they could tell whether a given food was a product of the new technology." The researchers presented them with a list of the GM products that were on the market in the US and they said "Most participants expressed great surprise that food biotechnology has become so pervasive in the US food supply. Even among participants who considered themselves well-informed about biotechnology, many registered amazement. The typical reaction of participants was not one of great concern about the immediate health and safety effects of unknowingly eating bioengineered foods, but rather outrage that such a change in the food supply could happen without them knowing about it." They therefore felt that there must be something that the industry was trying to hide from them. I could give you the reference for that, if you would like to see it in more detail, but I think it is very interesting, particularly as it is research that the US Government have done themselves. Other surveys have been carried out; there was, for example, one last year by ABC News ëwhich again shows similar results to the surveys we have done, where 92 per cent of US consumers said that they wanted to have information about which foods were genetically modified.

Chairman

3. Would you mind sending that reference to our clerk; it might be of help to us.
(*Ms Davies*) Certainly.

Lord Fyfe

4. Could I suggest that the subject of genetic modification is hardly a regular topic at dinner tables or in pubs, clubs and so forth, and that the majority of the population of this country might not be just as aware as we are in this room of the pros and cons or indeed the dangers of genetically modified food? Is it not something which is promoted by various organisations such as your own in order, perhaps, to add to the interest in the subject – and there is no harm in that—but it is a very convenient subject for groups such as your organisation to latch on to as a suitable topic for research, to publicise it generally and perhaps to publish a document? Are people as conscious of genetically modified food as we think they need to be?
(*Ms Patel*) I will come back to the surveys which Sue mentioned to give you some statistics. In 1994 we carried out some research among a nationally representative sample of the population and we did so at a time when cheese had come on to the market containing GM chymosin. At that time only 21 per cent had heard of GM technology and there was a general reluctance to buy it, and about 70 per cent said that it was because they were not aware of what it was, they were not interested in it and did not know enough about it. There was quite a high percentage of unawareness or lack of interest. 40 per cent of the people in that survey also wanted to be cautious in relation to GM foods, partly because they probably did not know what it was about. In 1996 tomato purée went on sale and we did another survey then, where we did face-to-face interviews around the country, and at that time 41 per cent of the people claimed to have some understanding of GM; that is almost doubling the statistic in 1994. 44 per cent of those people said they did have concerns about GM. 32 per cent were concerned it was interfering with nature somehow and that it was unnatural, and a

Lord Fyfe contd.]

similar percentage felt that they did not know enough about the long-term consequences of GM to make a decision about it. Roughly 13 per cent said that they did have enough information about it but thought the technology was somehow wrong. Recently there was a Eurobarometer survey, published in December 2001, which was a survey of consumers across the EU, and 70 per cent said they did not want GM foods and about 95 per cent wanted to have the right to choose whether or not they actually ate GM foods. I think the issue of choice is very important and underlines a lot of what consumers believe about this issue, and that is very much the perspective from which Consumers' Association comes. It is one of choice. We are not opposed to GM technology. We believe in the right of the consumer to choose, based on comprehensive and accurate labelling.

Baroness Billingham

5. I happen to think that on this issue your Association bears a huge responsibility; you really do bear the responsibility of evaluating and being knowledgeable in a way the general public is not. As Lord Fyfe said, this is not something that is generally understood by most of us. The consequence of all that is that the information the general public has varies widely, from a tabloid headline "Frankenstein Foods" to issues coming out of more learned areas like recent reports from the Royal Society. It is all very well to advise us on which car to buy and which is the safest, but this goes completely beyond that. Your job is so fundamental because you have the confidence of the public and to a certain extent we are going to be relying on you to give us the information that will say, "Look, these are safe products, they are not life-threatening, long-term we believe etc etc." That is a huge responsibility and I am just wondering if you have the resources in your organisation actually to confront those issues and to deal with them?

(Ms Davies) The way we have been trying to deal with it is that we very much see our role as one of trying to distil all the complicated information out there in a way people can understand and this is a very complex area. We have done over the years reports in Which? on GM foods where we have tried to condense this information down to a four page magazine article, and what we have prided ourselves on is taking a balanced and independent view on these issues. We have never been opposed to GM foods in any way but have always considered it could have benefits but then there could be risks as well. We have tried to focus on what kind of control measures you need to ensure that people can use these products safely and can have an effective choice as well. We do have a lot of in-house resources within the Communications Division, where we both work. We have Which? magazine and Health Which? magazine, and Gardening Which? has also taken an interest in this issue. But in addition we rely on external expertise so we get a range of different perspectives when we are writing our articles. We are obviously trying to represent the views of the majority of consumers. We have 700,000 members but they tend to be better informed people. We always do our research on a representative sample of the population and try to make sure that the issues we are trying to address are the ones people want to know about.

Baroness Miller of Chilthorne Domer

6. Going back to the point you made that people in the US and the European Union were in your opinion not as vociferous until they became aware that such alterations had been made in the food chain, do you think that people, both here and perhaps in the US, understand why this technology is being developed? In our country we have not only enough food but in many cases too much food; the developing countries can comment for themselves and we hope to be hearing from them. Why do you think this is being developed in the UK?

(Ms Davies) When we have asked people what they see the potential benefits of GM could be, people do say, for example, better quality food, better tasting food, longer lasting food. The problem has been that the first products to come on the market have not shown any consumer benefits and at the same time you have a lot of consumer concerns about GM, so people seem to feel that they are the ones having to take the risks, for example, but they are not actually getting any benefit from it. The introduction of soya and maize was handled so badly. When tomato purée came on the market, retailers put it in its own tin, it was clearly labelled, and the idea was, "We will clearly label it, let consumers have a choice, let the market decide whether there are benefits from this technology." When soya and maize came along and it was, if you like, hidden in products and people did not know they were eating it. That intensified people's concerns about it and they felt they were not being given any decision in whether or not it was a worth-while product.

Lord Crickhowell

7. You have been talking about there being benefits as well as risks and I welcome that. We have had a great rush of statistics and changing reactions recorded by those statistics, but one of the things I have learned over the years about statistics is that they very much depend on the questions you ask. There is widespread evidence there is a great deal of public concern about the effect of fertilisers; indeed one of the reasons I suspect for the growth of interest in organic products is because people do not want to feel that their apples are covered with some nasty chemical. There is also a great deal of concern, and the Prime Minister is off to Africa today, about the starving people of the world. If you asked the question in terms of, "One of the reasons for the introduction of GM products is to reduce the amount of chemicals going into the environment or to increase yields for the benefit of under-developed countries", you might get rather different answers from answers you would get if you asked simply, "Are you in favour of GM foods or not?" Would you be able, perhaps later, in written form, to give us some guidance as to the kind of questions that are being asked of people? Are they questions that actually enable them to make judgments of that kind

Lord Crickhowell *contd.*]

or are they being just asked the question about GM foods, where they may be more influenced by a picture of some cow that is being misguidedly produced by manipulation, rather than that the major products they are talking about are being developed to reduce the amount of fertiliser, the amount of chemicals and to increase the yields of the under-developed world? I would like to know more about the background to your statistical information.

(*Ms Davies*) We can certainly send you a lot more information about how we approach our own research. We have a market research department so we always talk to them about how to do surveys and what are the most appropriate methods to use and they are always very careful to make sure that, as you say, they are not asking questions so that you can make sure you get a certain answer. Also in the case of GM it is often very difficult to do a straightforward survey because there are so many different aspects to it, particularly when you are dealing with the complexity of the supply chain and the possible risks and the possible benefits. We have often opted to do qualitative research through focus groups, for example, where you can try to get into much more detailed description about what the possible risks and possible benefits are, and it is certainly the case there that we have been able to get into much more detail about what people would see as benefits and we have not been giving them some kind of nightmare scenario; we have really been trying to talk through what the possibilities could be. But we could give much more detail about that.

Lord Dubs

8. I was interested to hear what you said about choice and the importance of choice, because if you ask any consumer whether they want more choice over whatever it is in food they are almost bound to say yes, are they not? I cannot think of any question about giving consumers more choice to which the answer would not be yes. I cannot think of any reason why I would not want to know about something in my food even if I had never heard of it before. So I am slightly sceptical about your view that consumers want choice. My real question is this: choice is important if one knows what the significance of the choice is. I fear beyond some not very well articulated anxiety about GM foods most people do not actually have a view about them – they do not have very much knowledge. So they are bound to say yes, they want to know—and how do they obtain it? If there are fears expressed by yourselves or by some organisation about GM foods, that will encourage people to say, "We don't want GM foods", regardless of whether or not that is an informed choice. Is there anything in that argument or are you going to shoot me down?

(*Ms Patel*) The issue with GM is that it is a new technology and it is an evolving technology and we do not necessarily have all the answers to it. Going back to what we said at the beginning, science will not provide us with all the answers, it is very much an evolving technology and because we do not know all the answers about the safety and about the long-term

implications we feel it is important that this is an area where choice should prevail. There are lots of things that happen in the food supply chain which perhaps consumers do not know very much about; the way that animals are reared, the way food is actually produced, there is a general lack of knowledge about how food is produced but it is produced in a way that has been prevalent for many, many years. Now with GM there have been many changes in the way it is produced—quite significant changes—so it is important to be clear about that. These are very significant changes and people should be told about them.

9. One could put forward the counter-argument that, after all, since the beginning of time the world has tried to modify the way in which its food is produced—it has tried to breed better strains of wheat and so on; years ago there was the green revolution which made a big difference to output in countries like India. So it is not all that new, is it, or are you saying it is new as a concept?

(*Ms Davies*) I think that is true. If you look at traditional breeding practices over time, people often say, "Why are you talking about this kind of biotechnology when biotechnology has been around for a long time?" but the difference here and the reason why there is more concern about it is that it is much more specific and much more targeted, where you can transfer genes potentially between different types of species, and it is the timescale in which it is happening as well. It is happening much more quickly to crops like soya and maize. If you look at the amount that has already been grown in the US, for example, it is a very rapid change over a short period of time. In terms of your question about people always wanting to have more choice, we do a great deal of work on labelling. For example we have been calling for ingredients; labelling and nutrition labelling but we have always made the distinction between information people may want to know about—for example how animals are being reared and whether pesticides are used—and we have always seen that as being something that maybe retailers could voluntarily provide for those consumers who want to have that level of information where there are perhaps specific concerns but it is not something which generally we would see as being put on the label—and here where probably the only kind of equivalent may be food irradiation on a scale that the public are concerned about, and the public perception is that there is a fundamental change in the food supply. So this is why we think it definitely needs to be on the label. People want to have this information on the label and know about the derivatives. So we have tended to make a distinction between the sort of information which it would be useful for people to have and that which definitely needs to go on the label.

Baroness Maddock

10. We know from your introduction and the papers we have that you welcome the European Commission's proposals but I think we would be very interested to know whether you think they actually meet the demands of European consumers.

Baroness Maddock *contd.*]

I am also interested to know whether their concerns are similar to the ones you have outlined in the research you have done with British consumers.

(*Ms Davies*) From the research we have done and for example the Eurobarometer surveys the European Commission have done, it is clear that people want to have choice and people want to have as much information as possible about the use of GM in their foods. We have supported these proposals because we have tried to bear in mind what we think is practical, given the situation that we are in at the moment and the complexity of the supply chain. So, for example, ideally some people may want to have information about whether GM processing aids are used, whether or not the meat they are using or the eggs they are using came from an animal that was fed feed that contained GM ingredients, and we felt that these are a significant move forward, bearing in mind what is practical at the moment. We have been calling for traceability as a general concept across the food chain anyway. If you look at BSE, for example, it just really highlighted how you need to know what is going into the food so that industry has proper systems in place, so that if something should go wrong they can withdraw products from the market. So I think this combines the benefits of actually having a system based on traceability which can deal with safety aspects but at the same time can make sure that people actually for the first time have clear information about things like soya oil and soya lecithin which, because they are derivatives, are not detectable in the final product using the test methods that are available because they are not that sensitive. You probably saw the Food Standards Agency survey that came out last week which suggests they are becoming more sensitive, although there is still a lot of variation between different laboratories. We think this is really a good way forward. I think it is going to require a different form of enforcement because the traditional approach has been that we are very reliant on trading standards officers to go along and take products off the shelves, for example, and then analyse them. But GM has shown just how complex the supply chain is now and how we need to develop more effective systems of enforcement based on auditing throughout the food chain, which obviously is not straightforward but we think is something which we need to shift towards. If you look at other claims as well as GM, if you look at claims about quality characteristics of food, certain quality assurance schemes, organic foods, country of origin, there are lots of different claims that are made on products which cannot be tested in the final product. We think that these are a significant step forward in giving consumers information. In terms of the perspective of other European consumers, the Eurobarometer survey published at the end of last year showed that 85.9 per cent of people wanted to have a choice over whether or not to eat GM foods and 70.9 per cent said they did not want to eat GM foods at the moment. That was a survey of about 16,000 people which worked out at about 1,000 people per Member State. We also worked very closely with BEUC the European consumer organisation, and their position has been very similar to ours, based on research that our sister organisations in other European countries have been

doing on representative samples there. So it seems to be a fairly consistent picture. Probably the one difference would be that maybe in certain of the Scandinavian countries they feel they want the proposals to go even further because they want more information about meat, eggs and milk, for example, and also about processing aids.

11. You talked about the different concerns of people here, whether they are environmental or whether they are about safety. Do you have any idea of the balance within European countries? You have touched a little on Scandinavia.

(*Ms Davies*) Not in that level of detail. We can try to find that out and give you more information if that would be helpful.

Lord Crickhowell

12. I am in difficulty over this question of giving people choice and how you do it. There are certain known hazards where you do labelling—nuts, for example—where it is known certain people are instantly affected, even lethally, but when it comes to GM foods I am very critical about statistics. If I can give a specific example, I have just been visiting Llanos in Venezuela, a very flat and wet central area of the country, full of an amazing mixture of birds and wildlife, largely untouched. In parts of the Llanos they are now trying to grow rice and they are crop spraying from the air with a lot of pretty nasty chemicals, having a fairly lethal effect on the neighbouring parts of the country where they do not use the chemicals. If you just put on the label "GM produced" you do not know really why it is being GM produced, but if you put on the label "This is GM rice which does not involve crop spraying that destroys wildlife" you get a totally different consumer reaction. My difficulty is this simple "GM" label tells you very little about the kind of GM technology that is being used, so I am lost as to whether the general public are really being given any real choice at all. How do you get round it?

(*Ms Davies*) We have always supported giving people as much information about why the modifications take place and what the possible benefits are. To go back to the tomato purée example, they gave you the information on the can, but it has obviously been more difficult with soya and maize. I cannot see how it would be so much of a problem if we do start to see these products giving benefits, because the people who will be producing these products will clearly want to promote what the possible benefits are of GM food so it will be put on the label if that is the case. I think there is a balance to be struck on how much information you can get on the label and we have discussions with the industry over what is practical. Ideally we would like to see information, but I think the European Commission's proposals are probably quite practical under the circumstances and just require information about whether or not ingredients are genetically modified. Certainly we would support wider dissemination of information about why modifications have taken place so people can make informed decisions. We want to emphasise that we do not see choice as something for the sake of it, it has

Lord Crickhowell *contd.*]

to be informed choice, so people can make up their minds about what the risks and benefits are. Some people may think, "I want to buy GM" but at the moment it seems the majority of people do not want to eat it.

Lord Christopher

13. I think in part your response to Lady Maddock's question leads into this. You criticise the proposed 1 per cent threshold for the GM content of food: can you expand your case for this and how practical you see it?

(*Ms Patel*) Fundamentally we think the approvals process is important. With new technology there is obviously a lot to learn and technology by its nature is an evolving issue, so we think it is important that the approval processes are robust. At this stage we do not think we can know the full implications of GM technology so there is a need to make sure the approvals are carried out in a satisfactory way. The idea of allowing unapproved varieties on to the market does give us some concern. For example, you could be allowing GM products on to the market where countries have very different approval processes from the EU. For example, in the US there is no mandatory approvals process, there is just a notification process. GM is developing in a very advanced way in China and we do not know enough about how approvals are made in that country. If you allow unapproved varieties from other countries around the world, you may actually make a mockery of the EU approvals process. Sue has mentioned that we do appreciate the difficulties of keeping GM ingredients out of the supply chain, and this is especially because of the failure to segregate in North America, but we do not feel this should be a reason for potentially putting consumers at risk. We believe the EU proposals on risk assessing these unapproved varieties may give us some reassurance, but we feel we need more clarity as to the scope of the risk assessment that the EU is proposing for these unapproved varieties. We would like to know who is going to carry out these risk assessments and what they are going to involve. We are particularly concerned at the EU level about the lack of openness and transparency of decision-making and also the lack of consumer representation on EU committees. We are very keen to see this risk assessment process opened up, transparent, public and involving consumer representation. Moving on from that, we are concerned about how these unapproved varieties will be picked up in the EU because they will need reference material from the countries where these GM foods are freely circulating, so we have concerns about how this material will be made available to the EU so they can see what they are looking for and use the reference material as a check. In any case, we think surveillance will be hugely important in this area and that will be surveillance by both the Food Standards Agency and the new European Food Safety Authority, so we can see the scale of contamination with these unapproved varieties if it is allowed to happen.

14. In your paper you say the 1 per cent threshold could be reduced—you do not say instantaneously—

but you have not, even now, applied yourself to the practicalities of this. If you set a standard which is in practical terms not possible for suppliers to meet, it is inviting them to cheat. How practical is it with the great grain silos in Canada and the States? How practical is it?

(*Ms Davies*) The retailers and manufacturers have told us that the 1 per cent is realistic at the moment. Our concern is for consumers who are concerned about GM who do not see the point of any threshold, so we hope as the supply chain is developed that will be able to be minimised. It is important to look at it on a case-by-case basis as well, because you are talking about different types of crops here. In the future, you could be talking about things like GM fish, for example, so it is important to bear in mind what is practical given the different types of products as well but with the aim of minimising it as far as possible, bearing in mind what the limits of detectability are. The Food Standards Agency survey which was published last week showed that 1 per cent did seem to be feasible at the moment, but then, as Mona has pointed out, there is a slightly different issue between adventitious contamination when you are talking about non-GM supplies, when they are contaminated with food crops which have been approved in Europe, and the 1 per cent threshold where you are talking about crops which have not been given any approval at all where, because of the supply chain, it is very difficult to pick them up but you could be dealing with a potential safety issue as well.

Lord Crickhowell

15. I wanted to pursue this practicality question and the 1 per cent, which is a point very much made by the US Under-Secretary, who gave a press conference in Europe just before Christmas. He pointed to the difference in demand from people to have organic products where you are dealing with a relative minority market, very often products which are separable, easily identified and for which people may be prepared to pay more. He mentioned that in America it is perhaps ten or eleven per cent of the market. I do not know what it is over here but when I go into my supermarket it is a relatively small stall which offers me organic products. Clearly there the supermarket is offering you a product where it can set up a system of traceability which can be audited because it is a specific, clearly identified market. When you come to something like maize or soyabean, in which the major world producers are now using GM, and for which the whole arrangements for storage and shipment tend to be in bulk and it is very difficult to separate individual packages, you do not know exactly what happens as they go down the trading market. How do you propose to introduce a system that is credible, is verifiable, which can be audited? Do you actually believe that such a system is capable of being enforced, and how?

(*Ms Davies*) We do think it can be enforced and implemented. As we have explained, we have been following the GM debate for many years and what has been interesting is that things you were once told

Lord Crickhowell *contd.*]

were completely impossible become possible. We were told it was impossible not to have GM soya or maize, for example, but the retailers and manufacturers through their buying power have been able to secure non-GM supplies and have been able to set up identity preservation systems throughout the food chain. It is important not to assume that because there may be some difficulties now, the supply chain cannot adapt to providing that kind of information. What we are pleased that the EU proposals will require, and it is following on from a previous Directive 2001/18 which deals with environmental releases of GMOs, is that there is going to be a general requirement throughout the food chain so that all operators will have to pass on information about GMOs and then subsequently about products produced from GMOs. The requirement will be that each operator will have to have information and pass it on to the next person in the supply chain. As you say, that does present opportunities for fraud but in most areas of food legislation there are opportunities for fraud. The Food Standards Agency has just been dealing with all the contaminated chicken, for example, which was supposed to be destroyed but ended getting back into a thousand different products. There are always going to be problems. The challenge that GM presents is not unique, it is a challenge more generally about how you legislate and enforce within the global food market we are dealing with now. Through Consumers International we have been closely following the discussion within the Codex Alimentarius Commission and there is a committee meeting in the spring which will look at GM labelling. One crucial aspect will be to have an international standard on GM labelling so then you will have some kind of consistent standard across the world. In terms of the practicality of enforcement, we would see it as a combination of using test methods where you can to verify what ingredients you are using, and then passing that information on, but a lot of it is going to be auditing throughout the food chain as well. One of the things lacking in the regulations at the moment is that there is not any clear guidance from the Commission about how they see that working, so we hope they will give clear guidance to industry but also to enforcement officers as well. One of the crucial things is that the enforcement officers have enough resources to actually do this. We think that although the Food Standards Agency has been very critical of the proposals rather than dismissing them outright their role should be to work with the Commission and with the retailers. When we talk to the retailers and the main manufacturers about whether or not this is practical, they say it is practical; when we talk to the enforcement officers, they say it is going to be difficult but that is mainly because of concerns about their resources and the fact that trading standards officers, who would have responsibility for this, are dealing with so many other aspects of food legislation as well as other more general trading standards issues. So it is making sure they have sufficient guidance but also sufficient resources to actually ensure it is enforced.

Lord Crickhowell: You say the retailers say it is practical, and I do not know whether that is right, but

Mr Larson said in answer to a question that he had been told by the European food processing industry that what was likely to happen was that you would simply have labels which said, "May contain GMOs", or they would take the product off the market, and then you would have no consumer choice at all. The further you go down the processing chain, the more difficult it is to trace, because many of the GMOs cannot be scientifically identified whilst they are in the process. So unless you have an audit trail so that you can actually know who bought from whom, you have not got an identification process that works—you may simply exclude whole markets and then you may get world trade conflicts as well. Do you disagree with the argument that you may simply get some general labelling—"It may contain"—or things will be taken off the market, and what is your response to the argument that that actually involves less consumer choice and not more?

Chairman

16. Before you answer that I wonder if I could add a rider to what Lord Crickhowell has pointed out? We have been given evidence that some people in the food chain may ultimately decide that these labelling and traceability regulations might make it desirable to remove products from the market, which presumably reduces choice. Given that the reason why producers produce GM crops is presumably to lower their costs of production, and given that presumably lower costs of production should ultimately feed through—although I accept they do not always—to the consumer, does that not imply that there is a danger ultimately that these regulations we are deliberating on could lead to less choice and higher prices?

(*Ms Davies*) It is possible that some suppliers, retailers or manufacturers may decide that it is easier to use other ingredients rather than to use the ones concerned because they decide that is more effective. Certainly that is what happened when there was concern and some of the retailers shifted towards non-GM supplies, and in some cases they shifted to using different ingredients. In terms of the question of choice, there is a difference in using GM crops or GM products where there is an obvious benefit for the consumer so they would want to choose that product. At the moment with soya and maize we do not see any benefits from those products at all for consumers and it is clear that most consumers do not want to buy those products at the moment. So it is not necessarily an issue at the moment but obviously quality is a factor and if that means moving to a different ingredient then that would be an issue. I think probably the difference here is that the system we have at the moment puts the onus on the end supplier to give information about whether or not there are detectable levels of GM DNA or protein in the final product, and what this is shifting towards is an approach where responsibility is spread throughout the supply chain, where each operator has responsibility for passing information on to the next supplier. So rather than it all falling on the last stage in the chain, we would see this as being

Chairman *contd.*]

something where the costs are spread across the food supply chain. It may be an issue for some manufacturers who think, "It may be more costly to do this, so we will just take out the ingredients", but I do not think that necessarily will be the case. As we have already tried to emphasise, we think that having traceability is something which will become a requirement in any case, because under the EU proposals for general principles of food law, the ones which they are introducing in the European Food Safety Authority, they are also going to make traceability a general requirement throughout the food chain, so it is something that we need to be shifting towards in any case and it is going to become a more general requirement for everybody, not just people who use GM ingredients.

Lord Dubs

17. I very much agree with your point about traceability and I think as regards Western Europe and North America it probably could be made to work. May I put it to you that for the developing countries there are, I understand, some significant advantages as regards introducing some GM products in terms of high yields, fewer pesticides and so on? Is it not possible that developing countries will be faced with a real dilemma? Do they go down the path of improving output, helping their people not to starve, but risk not being able to sell their products to Western Europe, or do they do the opposite? Given that traceability of derivatives of GM products is, I understand, often not possible, are we not going to be in a position where the argument will fall down insofar as we open up or keep open our markets to developing countries? If we then say, "We are not prepared to take a risk", and we are not then actually slapping the developing countries in the face? Is there not a real dilemma for us between our responsibilities to buy from developing countries and ease their dreadful poverty and say that "No, we are going to stay clean of these things and not buy your products"? Is that not going to be a dilemma?
(*Ms Davies*) I think it is a dilemma but the argument as to what the benefits are for developing countries from GM are very complex. On the one hand, probably some of the benefits have been over-estimated but there is certainly a potential for GM to have a role, but I do not think it is the answer to everything. There are a lot of issues around distribution of food, for example, not merely the fact there is not enough food at the moment. We are part of Consumers International, which involves consumer organisations from around 120 countries around the world and some of their members, particularly in India and Brazil, are very concerned about what the implications of GM will be for consumers in those countries and about the influence of multinational companies who are developing these products over their own systems of agriculture. So there are pros and cons and it is very unclear at the moment what the benefits will be, and that is why it is important that developing countries have a real say in how and whether GM can contribute to their systems of agriculture. Consumers International have tried to make sure that they take a consistent

view so if you are talking about safety controls in developing countries you do not assume, "This is okay for the developed world but this is what we need in the developing world", so the issues around safety and traceability should be just as important for the developing countries as well. A lot of the problems we are talking about around traceability come from North America where these crops are being grown; there was a reluctance to segregate products and therefore we now have the problem where the products are already in the food chain and how do we distinguish where they are. If other countries are starting to develop GM products, including if they are grown in Europe, it is important to look at things like separation distances, looking at clear criteria for how they should be grown as well. I am not saying it is simple in any way whatsoever but a lot of the difficulty is that we are doing it back to front, that the crops are grown in a certain way, they are put in certain products and we are now trying to sort that out, rather than looking at starting from meeting all these different needs in the way they are produced.

Chairman: We had better press on. You are giving us some very interesting information. I am sorry we are taking longer than you expected but we are on to a good thing here.

Countess of Mar

18. What role do you see for the European Food Safety Authority?
(*Ms Patel*) We think its role will be important but we do have concerns about the limited powers which it has been given, particularly because it has been focused very much on safety, and we have concerns about what role it might have in the whole risk management process. We agree with the centralised approvals process which is proposed in the Commission's proposals on food and feed, but we feel it must be open and transparent, again going back to the point that consumers' views must be taken into account in the approvals process. A wider concern is that there should be consumer representation on the board of the European Food Safety Authority and also on-going dialogue between consumers and their representatives and representative organisations. The scientific committees of the European Food Safety Authority will also be important and we think it is very important that they are opened up. At UK level we have seen an increasing opening up of scientific committees. We lobbied long and hard for there to be a consumer representative on the Spongiform Encephalopathy Advisory Committee (SEAC) for example, and now there is one. We are seeing increasing requests from the Food Standards Agency and other government departments for consumer representatives on a wide range of committees, from ACNFP (Advisory Committee on Novel Foods and Processes) to ACRE (Advisory Committee on Releases to the Environment) and other non-GM committees, but the EU has not followed that pattern and we think it is important that the consumer voice does prevail at European level as well. We would also like to see access to papers. We would like to see the European Food Safety Authority following some of

Countess of Mar *contd.*]

the practices of the Food Standards Agency and opening up committees and making papers available, agendas of meetings available and, specifically in relation to GM, opening up the dossiers which are put forward for approval at European level. We think the Authority should also have a role in considering the risks and benefits of GM but we are concerned that the legislation in setting up the Authority actually gives this role to the European Commission and also allows Member States to have a say. We think the European Food Safety Authority has to have a role in the risk management process as well. It will also have a role in giving guidance to industry and enforcement bodies on a wide variety of issues; it will have a monitoring role so it can look at long-term developments in the food chain, monitoring the long-term implications, horizon-scanning as well to see what is coming up in the future, so we are not caught out by new technology or products being introduced on to the market and us not having done enough to make sure they are safe and the processes for introducing them are robust. The Authority will also have a role in developing effective test methods in relation to GM and other new technologies which might come along and it will obviously have a role in research so that we get better methods for assessing risks and we can look more at the unintended effects. So it really does have a very wide range of roles in relation to ensuring the safety of food throughout Europe.

19. Are all these benefits of the European Food Safety Authority already written into its articles, or are these things you visualise them having? I was thinking particularly about monitoring because if you are monitoring over a lot of countries—and I am very interested in post-monitoring surveillance and the failure of chemical monitoring—this is going to be monitoring at a minute level, so how do you visualise them doing that? There is going to have to be very high scientific integrity to find out whether things are going wrong.

(*Ms Davies*) Many of those things are things which we think the European Food Safety Authority should be concerned with. It is very difficult because obviously it has not been set up yet and it is difficult to see how its role will develop but our concern was, looking at the regulation, that its role does seem to be limited too much towards giving scientific and technical advice. There is often a blurring between what is risk assessment and what is risk management but we always hoped it would be able to come up with recommendations to the European Commission for legislation that it should be taking forward. It is also difficult because it is important that it has close links with the enforcement role of the Food and Veterinary Office which is based in Dublin and we hope that eventually the Food and Veterinary Office might move within the European Food Safety Authority because the European Food Safety Authority may have responsibility for surveillance but not for enforcement. We certainly would like to see its role boosted. It will have a strong role in research and it is going to be crucial that it has really good people on its board, a really strong chief executive. It is also going to have a forum where Member States will be feeding into the work it is

doing, but it is also important that it has close links with organisations around the world like the US Food and Drug Administration, the Australian New Zealand Food Authority as well, so there is a sharing of expertise around the world and an understanding of what the different research institutes are doing so, as in the UK now, even if we do not have the right expertise in the UK we make sure we are consulting experts in other countries where they might have that knowledge.

Lord Walpole

20. You have criticised the Food Standards Agency for advocating "GM free" labelling (analogous to "organic" labelling) as an alternative to the Commission's proposals. Could you enlarge on that?

(*Ms Davies*) We have been very disappointed with the stance that the Food Standards Agency has taken because, as you know, we campaigned very vigorously for the Food Standards Agency and for it to put consumers' interests first, and although the Food Standards Agency has said it is in favour of consumer choice we think this idea of the GM free label could work against consumer choice. If you ask people, "Do you want to have GM free food, do you want to have a GM free label?" I am sure most consumers would say they do because that is why they have been going to the supermarkets and saying, "Which products have GMOs and which have not?" The difficulty we have is that by developing a GM free label you are almost developing, as with organic products, a niche market that consumers would have to pay more for if they wanted to avoid GM free ingredients. We do not think that is right at the moment because most people want to buy the standard products which were on the market before GM came into food products and therefore do not see a reason why they should have to pay more to have that choice. That is going to be a particular issue for low income consumers. I mentioned before the Eurobarometer Survey which showed that 70.9 per cent of people said they did not want to eat GMOs, so it is certainly not a niche market at the moment in terms of people wanting to avoid GMOs. We also have concerns about the actual practicalities of having a GM free label. If something did say "GM free", for it not to be misleading it would be essential that there has been no GM near the product.

21. In other words, 0 per cent?

(*Ms Davies*) Yes. So there was no possibility of contamination. The only way you could work to that is by developing identity preservation systems which the retailers and manufacturers have developed already. We have been supportive of what they have been doing and saying they should extend that as far as possible. Some of them have already extended it, for example, to include GM animal feed and we would hope that ultimately they may start to look at processing aids as well. That seems to be the way you would have to go if you wanted to have a GM free label. The difference is that at the moment those Identity Preserved (IP) supplies are available to consumers at no extra cost with no label on them at all, whereas under the Food Standards Agency

Lord Walpole *contd.*]

proposal you would have the same system with a label saying "GM free" which consumers would have to pay more for because it would be making some claims which went beyond what was already on the market. The other issue we have is, as I have said before, if it happened that GM had been near the product it could not be so labelled and in terms of the feasibility of that the Agriculture and Environment Biotechnology Commission has just come out with a report saying it would be difficult to achieve GM free at the moment. We are also concerned that the Food Standards Agency has criticised the EU proposals because they could be potentially misleading and confusing to consumers but we think the GM free label would be much more confusing. If you introduce a GM free label, what would be the potential labelling options? We worked it out that there would be five alternatives and it does get very confusing. There would be products which would not have a label on because they would not have any ingredients which had been genetically modified. At the moment, for example, no soya or maize so you could be talking about a tomato sauce or something like that, and you would not expect there to be GM in there at the moment. You would then have products with no label on that complied with EU legislation as it stands at the moment, so there would be no detectable levels of GM DNA or protein in them but there could be GM derivatives. You would then have products which did not have a label because they have been produced using IP systems and therefore the 1 per cent threshold would apply. You would then have the GM free label which, as we understand it, would be the same as the one I have just mentioned, because that would also have been produced using the IP system. Then you would have those products which were labelled because there were detectable levels of GM DNA and protein in them. So you could have this whole proliferation of labelling options which would be very confusing and basically consumers would be paying more than they are at the moment for what would be produced through an IP route but they would also be misled by looking at the GM free label rather than the claims of the retailers and manufacturers that they are using non-GM ingredients; it would actually be telling consumers it was completely GM free. The Food Standards Agency has also said it prefers this approach because it thinks there are difficulties about enforcing the EU proposals but the same issue would obviously arise because here you have a system which is based on an audit trail as well. So we think it would be much more helpful for consumers if, instead, you had labelling based on whether or not derivatives were present based on a system of traceability. Rather than just dismissing the EU proposals the Food Standards Agency should actually try to work with retailers and manufacturers and enforcers as well as with the European Commission to come up with a system which works. For example, some of the manufacturers have been trying to develop ways they can see how this could be implemented in a practical way. Generally, we think that GM free labelling would be very confusing and misleading, and also very expensive for consumers, and would not provide them with any more level of choice than they have at the moment, and a lot less choice than the EU proposals would allow.

(*Ms Patel*) The Agriculture and Environment Biotechnology Commission published a report called *Crops on Trial* in January of this year. Secretary of State, Margaret Beckett, responded to that report on 17 January this year and in that report she says that because of the practicalities around seeds it would be "virtually impossible to guarantee a GM-free seed". So we have one government department saying it would be virtually impossible to guarantee a GM-free seed and the Food Standards Agency saying they want to see a GM-free label, and there is a question about how practical the Food Standards Agency proposal is given what the Department for the Environment, Food and Rural Affairs has said.

Countess of Mar

22. You mentioned earlier that you acknowledged the audit trail would raise the costs of food products and manufactured products, and yet you are talking now about GM-free and GM labelling. As I can visualise it, it seems to me that any food producer or manufacturer is going to have to have an audit trail which is going to increase the costs. It does not matter whether it is GM or GM-free, they have to prove their product is what it says it is right the way through. I wonder whether with all this regulation of food production you have considered what it will do in the end to both the producers and to consumers as far as price is concerned, because there is no such thing as cheap food. I notice in a lot of your publications you stress the necessity to have cheap food.

(*Ms Davies*) We have not done any detailed analysis on what the costs would be throughout the food chain, but we have talked to some of the retailers and manufacturers about it. Where they have developed preservation systems already there has not been any extra cost to consumers. When we asked them about that they said that the costs generally get absorbed at various stages throughout the food chain in any case because it is spread throughout the food chain, through the different suppliers. In many cases this is something that suppliers and manufacturers would be required to do as part of their due diligence defence in any case. They would be required to have a clear track of who was supplying their ingredients and where it was coming from, if they are responsible and if they have got proper quality assurance systems in place. We appreciate that there may be some cost but we think it is not going to be hugely significant and it should not have a significant impact on the product price at the end of the day.

23. With the increase in the use of this technology spreading to all sorts of other ingredients apart from soya and maize, and I ought to declare an interest, I am a cheese maker. I do not use chymosin because my customers do not like it. I also do not use calf rennet, I use a microbial one. As I see it, allocating costs at each stage would make it difficult for some of the early stage producers to be able to make a living because of having to keep up the trail all the time. It

Countess of Mar *contd.*]

needs to be simplified—that is what I am trying to say.

(*Ms Davies*) Who do you mean by the "early stage" producers?

24. For example, the dairy farmer. He has got to go back to the manufacturer of his cattle feed. Manufacturers of cattle feed have been notorious over the years for their lack of transparency, shall we put it that way, and yet he carries responsibility for the quality if he says that his milk is GM free. He has not got the scientific ability to test the cattle feed himself in order to say that he can say it is guaranteed GM free, so what is he going to say? He is going to say you cannot have that guarantee.

(*Ms Davies*) That shows you have to be careful about GM free claims and how meaningful they are going to be for consumers. We are generally supportive of the fact that the EU Commission is extending the regulations to include animal feed. As you mentioned with BSE and a lot of food safety problems we have had recently, it is clear people should have more information about feed. Although that information does not have to be passed on to the final consumer at the moment, those having non-GM or GM free claims would need to know about it. There is a real need in the case of GM (but also more generally) for producers to know exactly what they are feeding their animals. That has been a big gap in terms of choice and also for safety reasons as well.

Baroness Miller of Chilthorne Domer

25. For the US and other major exporter countries that are growing GM crops, how would you imagine that the EU should respond to their concerns about this proposed regime?

(*Ms Davies*) The concerns seem to be that it would be discriminating against their producers because they are losing a market in Europe for GM products. Our concern is that basically GM should be left up to the market to decide and if people want to buy it then it should be available. The problem has been that by putting it on the market without it being clearly labelled, as we have already discussed, people have felt quite outraged that they have not had a choice over what they are eating. I would hope that the US suppliers (although it does not seem to be the case at the moment) would appreciate that by giving people more information they may help build consumer confidence in products rather than them feeling that there is some reason why they are not giving them the information in the first place. So we would hope they would support that and the evidence from US consumers appears to be that they would like the same level of information as well, although the US regulatory authorities have taken a completely different approach to GM in both the approval process and labelling requirements more generally.

26. Are Consumers Union in the United States and the Trans-Atlantic Consumers' Dialogue going to raise the profile of this issue in the States? Obviously there is quite a fear in the EU about it getting to the World Trade Organisation level of retaliatory action, as there was in the case, for instance, of bananas and Scottish cashmere and so on.

(*Ms Davies*) Consumers Union is a very similar organisation to CA. It has a magazine *Consumer Reports* and it has published articles on GM fairly regularly and it certainly lobbies the US Government. In terms of the Trans-Atlantic Consumers' Dialogue, GM is a priority and so we have been talking regularly. We have annual meetings with US officials and European Commission officials and have raised the concerns we have about the need for clear labelling and traceability and a proper approval process. There does seem to be a reluctance within the US at the moment to take these on board within the approach they take. It is certainly something that we have been pushing for.

Baroness Billingham

27. Clearly there are going to be economic impacts, some positive and some negative, and so the question I want to raise is whether there are there grounds for concern over the potential impact of the EC proposals on small and medium-sized enterprises? Is there a risk of even greater concentration of the food manufacturing sector, which in fact will be detrimental to the consumer?

(*Ms Davies*) We hope that will not be the case. As we have seen the proposals it seems that the current system could be more onerous on SMEs because at the moment it is based on detectability in the final product, so it is up to the person who is marketing the product to check that information. Whereas under this approach it seems that the cost would be spread more evenly throughout the food chain because it would be the different suppliers' responsibility to pass on that information about whether or not they are using GM (although you may need testing at some stages to help to verify that). We see it being spread more evenly across the food chain rather than the emphasis on whether there is GM material in the end product.

28. But surely there are going to be burdensome implications from this which will fall more heavily on smaller companies than larger companies? I think the implication of my question is that some small companies are going to be driven out of business by this and therefore the concentration of food production will be going to the multinationals that we have already been talking about earlier this morning.

(*Ms Davies*) We have not done enough detailed analysis, to be honest, to give you a really clear answer about that. We would hope there might also be opportunities for some of the small suppliers to offer non-GM products and non-GM alternatives that people would want rather than it being just the case that the main retailers and manufacturers are doing that.

Baroness Miller of Chilthorne Domer: Have you got any comments about the conclusions of the OECD conference that was held in Bangkok entitled "New Biotechnology Food and Crops: science, safety and society?". In particular, I am interested in the recommendation that governments and industry should prepare dossiers which would satisfy both the

Baroness Billingham *contd.*]

regulatory process but also as part of their accountability to society at large?

Chairman

29. When you are answering that I hope you will not be inhibited by the fact that I chaired that conference. If you thought that recommendation was rubbish you must say so!

(*Ms Davies*) We very much welcomed the conference. One of the things we thought very useful was the fact that the conference tried to be very inclusive and Consumers International, for example, was represented on the steering committee that set up the conference. Although it was set up at quite short notice an effort was made to try and ensure that a range of NGOs and people from around the world were represented at the conference. It also brought together a lot of the different regulators and international bodies that are dealing with GMOs. Part of the problem has tended to be that, for example, environmental issues may be dealt with by one organisation and food standards by another. It tends to be dealt with very separately rather than taking a broader overview of what is happening with GM. We definitely supported the recommendation regarding greater openness and transparency, including the idea that dossiers should be prepared so that they are accessible to the public as well so as to make things more accountable in general. One of the things that we thought was a very useful idea was the idea of making more use of stakeholder fora at national and international level. As an example of that, we were involved with the EU/US Consultative Forum on Biotechnology, which you might have heard about, which was set up by Bill Clinton and Romano Prodi. The idea of that was to try and alleviate some of the tensions between the US and the EU over GM by bringing together a range of stakeholders from the US and from the EU to come up with a consensus position. It did do that and it came up with a recommendation regarding the need for a mandatory approval process, regarding the need for greater transparency and regarding the need for mandatory labelling. There were about 20 recommendations. That was a useful process but it shows if you are setting up stakeholder fora the important thing is that you have the buying policy makers as well. The group was set up at a bad time because it came at the end of the Clinton administration and, although the Bush

administration has acknowledged it, it does not appear to have any intentions at the moment to act on the recommendations. Part of the problem with the whole issue of GM is that there has not been a proper dialogue between the different interests particularly early enough in the process. We mentioned the European Food Safety Authority having a role in horizon scanning but that is not unique to the EFSA. We see that through our Food Standards Agency, for example, and other international bodies as well, trying to gain an indication of what is happening with GM as well as with other technologies and what the implications are and what issues they raise for stakeholders, to try and address them earlier on in the process rather than trying to deal with them once products are on the market when consumers may reject them. The other recommendation from the conference that seemed very useful was the idea that you need to have a better balance between publicly-funded research and industry-funded research and the importance of having effective peer review as well, in particular the need to develop better ways of having long-term monitoring of GM products. We obviously hope that the recommendations will be followed through.

Lord Palmer

30. The whole subject really is a nutritional mine field. I am extremely glad I am no longer a food producer because it is extremely complicated. Are there any other issues in the Committee's call for evidence on which you would like to comment, either now or indeed at a later stage?

(*Ms Davies*) I do not think there is anything specific. We have already said that there are some things we will send you more information on—for example, about the way we approach or surveys.

Chairman: That would be helpful in answer to Lord Crickhowell's question and we would all find it helpful to have that. If there is any other evidence that you feel on reflection you would like to add, do please send it in. I am aware that we have kept you for rather longer than we originally suggested we might. By happy chance we had a little bit more time than we expected. We certainly found it very helpful to us. Once more, I apologise for the length of the session but it has been very helpful to us. Thank you both for your help.

WEDNESDAY 13 FEBRUARY 2002

Present:

Billingham, B
Christopher, L
Crickhowell, L
Dubs, L
Fyfe of Fairfield, L
Maddock, B

Mar, C
Miller of Chilthorne Domer, B
Palmer, L
Selborne, E (Chairman)
Walpole, L

Letter from the Food and Drink Federation

This is in response to your call for evidence of 21 December 2001 in respect of the above enquiry.

Regrettably, due to the unforeseen length of absence from FDF, due to illness, of the Executive directly responsible for GM issues, we have not had opportunity to prepare responses to the questions which you have identified.

In accordance with the fourth paragraph of the Instructions to Witnesses, however, we are able to send to you the attached commentaries (*not printed*) on the Commission's proposals, which were sent to the Food Standards Agency on 4 September 2001. These remain entirely relevant to the continuing discussion of the proposals and will, we hope, make a valuable contribution to the Sub-Committee's deliberations. Whilst the comments on the GM food and feed proposal run to ten pages, some key points are made in the general comments on the first page and there is an overall conclusion at the end.

FDF subsequently welcomed the FSA Board's affirmation (at its September 2001 meeting) that GM labelling should be practical, proportionate and enforceable, and its decision to maintain its previous position of supporting existing labelling provisions (based upon detectability of genetically modified material) supplemented by the introduction of rules on "GM-free" labelling and the provision of additional information for consumers on the use of GM technology in food production.

Michael Hunt
Manager, Food Law and Labelling
Scientific & Regulatory Affairs Division
Food & Drink Federation
1 February 2001

Examination of Witnesses

DR GERALDINE SCHOFIELD, Chairman of the GM Issues Group, MR JOHN WOOD, Head of Scientific and Regulatory Affairs, MR NEVILLE CRADDOCK (Nestlé), Chairman of the Scientific and Regulatory Affairs Committee, the Food and Drink Federation, examined.

Chairman

31. Dr Schofield, Mr Wood and Mr Craddock, thank you for joining us today. We are doing, as you know, a short inquiry on labelling and tracing of genetically modified food and animal feed. I should just report that on the table there is a list of the Members of this Committee's declared interests in this subject. Dr Schofield, would you like to start by introducing your colleagues, and would you like to say anything about the Food and Drink Federation by way of introduction?

(*Dr Schofield*) Thank you, my Lord Chairman. I am Geraldine Schofield, I am Head of Regulatory Affairs for foods in Unilever for research and development. I chair the Food and Drink Federation's (FDF) genetic modification issues group. I am a past member of the Advisory Committee on Release into the Environment (ACRE) and a past member of the advisory committee on genetic modification. I would like to call on my colleague, Mr Craddock, to introduce himself.

(*Mr Craddock*) Good morning. I am Neville Craddock. My role is chairman of the FDF Scientific and Regulatory Affairs Committee. I am employed by Nestlé UK, where I am Head of Regulatory and Environmental Affairs. I am a former member of the very recently dissolved Food Advisory Committee, and I have just been appointed to the Advisory Committee on Novel Foods and Processes (ACNFP).

(*Mr Wood*) Thank you, my Lord Chairman. I am John Wood, from the Secretariat of the Food and Drink Federation, where I look after scientific and regulatory affairs, which encompasses all things GM. The Food and Drink Federation is the principal trade association for the UK food and drink manufacturing industry.

32. You have very kindly sent us your response to the Food Standards Agency's consultation paper on the same proposals. Is there anything, at the moment, before we start with some of the questions we would like to ask you, you would like to add to that?

Chairman contd.]

(Dr Schofield) Not at this time. I think our position is clear. The main points are that while the food industry supports the overall objectives of the Commission's proposals, particularly in terms of the one-tier system, "one door, one key", there are reservations about the practicalities of the way those objectives are being met in practice with the Commission's proposals. I think the main objections are about the enforceability. A recent communication on biosciences from the Commission stressed the enforceability of regulation and stressed appropriateness. We would question these proposals on both of those grounds and on the fact that there is really no sound scientific basis. I hope that the FDF position puts those points quite clearly.

33. I am sure that is what we will wish to explore with you, as to what in your view would be the proportionate response, what is a legitimate requirement of consumers and how this can realistically, within the realities of international trade, be appropriate. Those are the issues we would like to address. Could I just ask you, if we did ask you from the perspective of production elsewhere than the UK—for example in a developing country—would any of your companies have experience? I rather guess Unilever might?
(Dr Schofield) With what particular aspect—genetic modification, or . . .

34. The traceability of genetically modified food or feed imported into the European Union from a country where, perhaps, there is not the same amount of infrastructure in relation to traceability.
(Dr Schofield) Not, as far as I am aware, from the developing world. The imports into Europe of the major commodity crops which are genetically modified would be mostly soya. At the moment all our supplies of maize, for all our needs in Europe, are actually supplied from the European market which is not genetically modified. The only other one would be, as I said, the soya feed and, potentially, some soya oil. Most of the other systems in Europe are now Identity Preserved systems either sourced from the United States or from South America. We also do not import any rapeseed kernel oil from Canada where a large proportion is genetically modified. From the developing world as yet, in terms of commercialisation, we do not import anything into Europe. There are some grains in GM crops in China, a very small quantity in South Africa, but we do not import any of those into Europe.

Chairman: We may have to ask you to anticipate what would happen in the event of their being put on to the international market and how you would expect to respond.

Lord Dubs

35. Good morning. I am interested in the claim that may be made about food products being GM free. Do any of your members make such claims?
(Dr Schofield) We are not aware of any members of the FDF claiming GM free on their products. In fact, at the FDF we had discussions on labelling going back as far as 1995 when, as a group, we realised there would be plantings of GM soya in the

United States. Anticipating that we looked at labelling as a Federation. We also did this through the Institute of Grocery Distribution. We voluntarily, as an industry, decided to label products where there was novel protein derived from soya and other ingredients. This came into place between 1996 and 1998. The manufacturing industry had quite a lot of branded products on the market which were labelled. We considered "GM free" and we also considered "may contain" labelling which we felt was unsuitable as not providing the correct information to consumers. Unfortunately, most of that ceased with the very negative, intense media campaigns in 1998/1999 which resulted in most manufacturers withdrawing those ingredients which were mainly GM soya, from their products. That resulted in no labelling at all. We have seen a plethora of GM free labelling over the past year or so and it is of great concern because it seems to be leading the public into the misconception that anything that is not labelled "GM free" actually is GM. That is causing some problems. In fact, there are many instances where people are now slightly confused and think that there are a lot of GM foods, particularly fruit and vegetables, on the market. We have seen quite a lot of illegal labelling "GM free" where, for example, packets of fruit and nuts are labelled "GM free" which of course have not been anywhere near anything genetically modified. So, no, our members do not make such claims. I think it is an area where the Commission should act to stop this illegal practice.

Countess of Mar

36. A minimum amount of contamination of 1 per cent has been proposed. Do you think this proposal is workable and how can it be controlled?
(Mr Craddock) Before I come straight on to that I would like to add a couple of words on GM free and Identity Preservation, because there is a little bit of confusion amongst the general population about the distinction between them. Our view on GM free is that it should mean precisely what it says: that the materials have not been touched at any point in their supply by genetic modification.

37. One hundred per cent free?
(Mr Craddock) As is the case with Germany and Austria where they would go so far as to say that, for example, even an animal has not been treated with a veterinary medicine that has been derived as a result of some gene technology. Moving on to the question of the 1 per cent, the 1 per cent threshold for adventitious contamination exists in the current framework of legislation. It is not just a tolerance it is, in fact, linked to a parallel requirement that the manufacturer or supplier must be able to show that they have taken the necessary steps to ensure that they have done everything possible not to use GM, but recognise the reality that GM is unavoidable in some parts of the world. It is an allowance, if you like, that recognises that you will never get to that absolute zero with many of these commodity crops. Is 1 per cent the right figure? I think it is wrong to talk of one single figure, to be honest. I think the feasibility of achieving a minimum level will depend,

Countess of Mar *contd.*]

ultimately, on the crops themselves and of course we are at the very beginning, perhaps, of GM. We have got soya, maize and rapeseed but as you move into other crops then you have to start, perhaps, at seed purity level and then you have the feasibility of keeping the supply chain clean. That practicality will vary according to the nature of the crop. I think, in practice, many would be claiming already to be able to achieve considerably less than 1 per cent on a regular basis but by the very nature of the adventitious contamination (adventitious, accidental, whichever word you want to use) there will, of course, be the occasional hotspot—or glitch—in the system. It is that which the 1 per cent is aimed to accommodate. However, others in the chain say that it is already too tight.

Chairman

38. I wonder if I could bring you back to this issue of the introduction of rules on GM free labelling. I know it is something that you have discussed with the Food Standards Agency, and we will have the benefit of evidence from Sir John Krebs early in March. Could you, meanwhile, tell us whether you, the FDF, and the Food Standards Agency are as of one mind on how you would deal with GM free labelling?

(*Mr Wood*) If I may respond to that question, my Lord Chairman, I think we are. We looked with great interest at the paper that went to the FSA's Board and I think they analysed the situation very carefully. As my colleague Neville has said, it is very difficult to trace the materials through the supply chain. I think what the FSA have concluded is that the principal requirement is for legislation that protects the consumer but is also enforceable. What they have suggested is that any product that contains detectable novel material from a GM source should be required to carry a label to that effect. We would entirely agree with that. They have also suggested that if particular groups of consumers are concerned about consuming approved GM materials, then it should be possible for them to have choice in the marketplace. On those grounds the FSA has suggested that a strict, rigorous standard should be drawn up for "GM free". As my colleague has said that would need to be very strict, going back all the way through the food chain. We think that is probably the best approach because in that part of the market there would certainly be an on-cost in terms of auditing the raw material supplies and checking through the chain. We presume that the market would stand that on-cost in supplying a genuinely "GM free" product. I think the other point the FSA Board made, with which we fully agree, is the need for impartial consumer information, perhaps an education programme. We, as the Food and Drink Federation, started that initiative about seven years ago with our *Food Future* programme and details of that I have left with your secretary. We have tried to address the consumer debate by providing what we saw as impartial information that identified the benefits but also identified the disadvantages and concerns of many consumers about the application of this new technology to food production and manufacture. Because we are from the food manufacturing sector I think we have to accept we are not seen as objective or as impartial, although that is the stance we have been trying to adopt in bringing other stakeholders into our various debates on this issue. We think the FSA has identified the need, really, for a pro-active consumer information education programme—not something that the curious can just graze over but something that will try and explain a very complex technology to interested members of the public.

39. If I may say so, I hope you will not take it amiss if I say that when the food sector start talking about an education programme, it is not the sort of language that the stakeholders find very acceptable. They very much more would welcome your other reference to a stakeholder dialogue where, perhaps, it is the food sector as much as the consumer who has something to learn. One does not know how you get into a dialogue. I wonder whether you would like to comment on this concept of education programmes or a stakeholder dialogue?

(*Mr Wood*) Indeed, my Lord Chairman. We fully accept that we are seen as having an interest in this but I think, as my colleagues have tried to explain, we are the recipients of a lot of agronomic benefits through GM technology which do not carry benefits for the rest of the food chain. I think this is one of the difficulties that we are facing at the moment. If you look at the currently available GM technology there are no direct consumer benefits. A benefit to a North American farmer does not translate to a benefit for a UK consumer and that is the issue that we have to address. I agree with you that there needs to be a full stakeholder debate on this issue as to how we can tackle the very complex scientific issues and look at an EU regulation that provides for an expeditious and efficient procedure to clear all novel foods, including those from GM technology, and to increase consumer confidence in the application of that technology to the food supply chain.

Lord Crickhowell

40. Can I take up this point that has just been made about consumer choice and no benefit to the consumer? I can see the argument is being made that they do not see a direct financial benefit, but this is a difficulty about getting genuine choice. One of the reasons for growing a GM crop is to avoid the heavy use of chemicals in fertilizers to protect against environmental damage. In the question and answer session last week I cited a particular example of Llanos in Venezuela, where I have just been, which is a wonderful, environmentally free area. Some people are trying to grow rice and crop spraying heavily, causing great damage. If you say to the consumer "This crop has been modified so we do not have to use so many fertilizers and so many chemicals" they may take a different choice than if you simply say "It is GM free". I am not sure it is true that it is entirely for the benefit of the grower. I think there are wider benefits, and I do not know how you bring that choice to consumers.

(*Mr Wood*) I think, my Lord, that is the real conundrum. If we find there are environmental benefits in the UK, for example, if we can help

Lord Crickhowell contd.]

protect the skylark or the Norfolk Broads or something of that nature by growing GM crops in the UK, then we would have a local environmental benefit that, hopefully, would have appeal to UK consumers.

(Dr Schofield) If I may, my Lord, I think the point is that the agronomic benefits at the moment have been for rather large farming in the United States, which seems extremely remote from the European and British public. As you say, there are more benefits, for example, for the developing world and we know that they are developing their own GM crops—for example, in the Philippines in disease-resistant rice and disease-resistant sweet potatoes in Kenya—and if that information is provided openly from independent sources, then the public will change their views on these matters. Probably the information has not been provided as well as it could have been. Coming back to that information and education role, the food industry would be quite happy to support, for example where there are proposals from the Commission, having information lists of what GM foods are labelled, including some of the first generation derivatives, so that people can see what has been modified, and how important the reasons are for it. However, GM on a label, "produced with the help of", does not actually provide very much information. As you said, people might be quite enthusiastic if they realised it is helping some agronomic benefit as well as consumer benefit. That information has not been very well provided to the public,

Baroness Miller of Chilthorne Domer

41. In the Royal Society's recent report, which they published earlier this month, they have taken quite a tranche of what your customers would be when they say "infants, children, pregnant and lactating women, the elderly and those with chronic disease", and identified that group as vulnerable. They are suggesting that those people should have labelling that enables them to see that it is containing GM. Bearing in mind that might be almost half your customer base, is that not going to be a problem?

(Dr Schofield) No, I do not think so because, as you said, its recommendations come in line with existing regulations with which we already have to comply. So I do not think that is too much of a problem. Turning it around a little bit; there is a lot of research going on into foods which can actually benefit these groups and in which case you would have to go through first clinical trials. We are very happy to label them because we would hope that they would be beneficial to these groups. If you could actually get foods designed to help these groups of people you would want to put it very large on the label at the front and hopefully the technology can provide those consumer benefits for those particular groups.

Lord Crickhowell

42. Going back to this whole question of traceability, what commodities does Unilever use in food manufacture that the company believes are grown as GM somewhere, even if the company does not buy from such sources? I think, in an earlier answer, you suggested that the major one was soya. In that connection, is there not a slightly different situation between a company like Unilever, which perhaps is using very substantial quantities of a particular product and has a very large world-wide organisation and knows where it buys from, and other people in the food manufacturing chain who may (1) use a great variety of products and (2) find it much more difficult to produce a chain that takes them accurately back to sources?

(Dr Schofield) Yes, I think it would be. If you are going to, as the proposals mention, trace derivatives down to second, third and fourth generation the cost and the manpower of that would be very high and so for smaller companies who may not have the technical abilities to do that and who are not experienced in doing it, would find it very difficult. The other side is that for very large multinational companies it is also very difficult to supply all the needs from separate IP systems. Some small firms might be able to set up a very local IP system whereas if you are trading in very large numbers of derivatives from a large number of commodities, which are increasingly GM, it will be increasingly difficult to IP source those. So I think both sectors of the market, whether they are the large or the small company, are going to have problems with aspects of this traceability legislation.

43. Is Unilever using particularly large quantities of, say, soya, or other products? If more and more of that soya is, in fact, grown GM in the United States is there not going to be a problem for the company?

(Dr Schofield) Yes, it will be. The main one I mentioned is soya because the GM maize is mostly sourced from Europe from our own European enterprises. The soya that we use at the moment is mostly from the United States and Brazil but, increasingly, 54 per cent of the soya crop last year, it will be GM. It is now 90 per cent of the Argentinian crop and we know there are some illegal plantings in Brazil because we have been there to check them out. It is going to be increasingly difficult for those IP sources on the scale that we require.

Lord Palmer

44. What do you mean by "illegal planting"?

(Dr Schofield) The Brazilian government still has not approved the planting of genetically modified soya but some of the farmers, particularly on the borders with Argentina, have been using the seed for planting in parts of Brazil because they are finding it is to their advantage in the agricultural system that they are using. So we are aware of that.

Countess of Mar

45. In your written submission, you say that the proposal is excessively complex and appears to place a disproportionate burden on the food manufacturing sector, which is more or less what you have just said. I declare an interest here, as a small food producer. We are being encouraged in the agricultural sector to diversify. From my own point

Countess of Mar *contd.*]

of view, the only thing we buy in is the food that we give our animals. Do you think there is room for a differential to be made between gigantic users, like you are, and little tiny producers, like I am, in the requirements to prove that our product is GM free, or does not contain any genetically modified organisms?

(*Dr Schofield*) The IP supply will be easier in very small quantities. The problem, I think, will be animal feed prices. I am not such an expert to go into this, but the feed is a by-product of oil, so the prices are held down mainly because of the trading in oil commodities. Once you start to upset that market there could be increases for very small amounts of IP animal feed. That is a rather personal view.

46. As I understand it, there would also be difficulty with traceability. Animal feed producers are notorious for not telling us what is in their feed.

(*Dr Schofield*) I cannot comment on animal feed producers.

47. As I understand it, because I use milk from goats (and that is all I use) the milk would not show any sign of any genetic modification.

(*Dr Schofield*) Absolutely not.

48. This is where the difficulty would come in.

(*Dr Schofield*) You can trace into the crude animal feed from soya and maize. It is detectable. At that point the detectability is easy. Once you start to go further into derivatives for food processing the detectability is extraordinarily difficult, if not impossible. In most animal feeds the normal protein is detectable because it is obviously mostly protein. That would add an on-cost for small producers because the testing is not cheap. It is getting better, quicker and cheaper but it is still relatively quite expensive. The Royal Society report mentions that there is not a problem going through animal feed and so on but in products of animals you cannot detect the presence of GM.

(*Mr Craddock*) I think your question is, effectively, is it more difficult proportionately for you as a small manufacturer than for the big guys? I think the answer, at the end of day, is that we would face very considerable difficulties. We have left with your secretary some schematics about traceability. Although this regulation proposes that it is one up, one down, it seems to be based on the very, very simple premise that in actual fact what is done is that you buy one ingredient, you mix it with one other and you sell it to one customer. However, in actual fact, you may buy ostensibly the same raw material from two or three suppliers, there is an intimate mixing even within the manufacturer's own factory environment, and then of course you may use that raw material in perhaps 30 or 40 different types of finished product and you may sell those to numerous customers. So the actual spider's web of traceability is going to be extremely difficult to maintain. That is why we say it is disproportionate. Simple traceability for food safety purposes is already in train in many businesses and, basically, I think is working fairly well. There is a further level in this regulation which seems to be disproportionate. I think the issue that is key to why we say it will become disproportionate is not the fact that the regulation requires labelling

where there is knowledge or, indeed, implied knowledge that a material has been derived from genetic modification, it is the commercial consequences at the present time. As my colleague said right at the beginning, very few products, if any, are available in the UK or in Europe which are stating today that they have been derived from genetic modification. This is perfectly legal because we have taken enormous steps to remove these materials and their derivatives, probably 30, 35 different ingredients, from the food chain. The analogy I would draw, with a smile, is that it is labelling "avoidance". It is rather like the "tax avoidance/tax evasion" situation. We are doing everything possible at the present time to avoid using GM derivatives and see no prospect for a change in the near future or medium term unless or until there is a clear consumer benefit material that comes on to the market. This regulation will force the whole industry in Europe to avoid further use of an ever-increasing number of materials. That is why I think, at the end of the day, a small business will have its localised problems but the multinationals, who are not only sourcing ingredients but finished foods around the world, will have an even worse problem. We have already seen it in the last two years.

Lord Walpole

49. I am not sure whether you have answered this question. I feel you have skirted round it somewhat. What steps do your members, in fact, take to ensure that any claims that they make about the presence or absence of possible things are accurate?

(*Mr Wood*) If I may respond to that question and broaden it into the context of labelling as a whole. As my colleagues have implied there are very few claims or, indeed, labelling at the current time in the UK market that refer to GM, either its presence or "GM free". In a sense the issue now is, is the absence of a reference to GM accurate? That is the issue that we are facing. In order to address that, a couple of years ago with the British Retail Consortium (your next witnesses this morning) we decided that there would be merit in trying to combine the expertise of the manufacturing and retailing sectors in drawing up a standard for the identity preservation of conventional crops. We concentrated on soya and maize because those were the two principal crops of interest at that time. What we sought to do was to try and identify the practical steps that could be taken right the way from the seed producer all the way through to the retailer selling direct to the consumer, to try and ensure that the GM part of the crop was avoided, to try and reduce it to the practical minimum. What we hope to do is to develop a common understanding between the UK manufacturers and retailers and then broaden that to Europe and, hopefully, to the international trade so that we have a common understanding of what is meant by trying to obtain an identity preserved conventional supply of material. We hoped, in that way, that would provide confidence both to people in industry—of whatever size—and also to consumers as purchasers of products from whatever type of retail outlet. We hoped, in that way, that we could

Lord Walpole *contd.*]

establish what were the requirements in order to be able to give with confidence the statement that this is material from conventional supplies—ie non-GM, no GM label required—because it met the requirements of the new regulation. We avoided putting in the 1 per cent tolerance because we felt that that particular threshold would vary with time. As experience was gained it would drift down, it would probably vary with a particular crop, but the aim would be to try and avoid GM material and give confidence to the whole supply chain. That is what we are trying to achieve.

Lord Crickhowell

50. My Lord Chairman, I keep getting the impression that at the moment it is still relatively easy, and we are talking about, basically, relatively few commodities and the bulk of GM is coming from the United States. However, we have already heard that it is spreading, we have had references to South America and the Far East and other countries, and it is likely to spread to a whole range of other countries and other commodities. Furthermore, we are in a situation where many of the producers of those countries (and the American government is already talking in these terms) are saying "This is in breach of all the rules for international trade. There is no scientific grounds for banning these products and, anyway, they are traded in bulk in such a way that it is very difficult to actually trace them." Is it not likely that as the thing gets more complicated and the outside world gets more and more dominated by this block, and there will be so much manoeuvring in the trading markets of the world and products that it really will be impossible to trace where a lot of it comes from? Or do you think that is a pessimistic view?

(*Mr Craddock*) I would tend to agree with you that in the longer term that will certainly happen. One of our fundamental concerns about the regulation which is before us at the moment is that it drives beyond the detectability of the presence of any level of genetic modification into these refined derivatives, and we have mentioned earlier third, fourth and fifth generation. You can take it down so you separate some sugar from the crop and maybe you then process that further. You can convert some of it chemically, you can end up with vitamins, there is a whole family tree of derivatives that are potentially caught by this regulation. For the vast majority of these there is absolutely no known scientific method today and, as I understand it, nothing in the immediate pipeline likely to come in the next few years which will enable clear distinctions to be drawn between these derivatives—where they have come from and whether they are genetically modified or not. As the complexity increases, and as the cost of keeping a guarantee that what you are using is not genetically modified increases, so the potential for fraud—I use the word quite advisedly—will come into ever-increasing focus. We are relying on a paper chase and paper chases are notoriously difficult to prove in a court.

Baroness Miller of Chilthorne Domer

51. Is not one of the difficulties that consumers have with the whole concept that whereas for an industry such as yours minimal regulation and deregulation are very attractive, what consumers want is the precautionary principle? It is hard to see the industry investing, for instance, the same amount of money in research to prove ways of tracing things when, actually, your whole drive is to deregulate anyway, to make life easier.

(*Dr Schofield*) Industry, basically, is not against regulation which is for particular reasons, for safety or technical reasons, and if it also ensures consistency. For example, in Europe we would support a one level playing field in terms of regulation. The extent of regulation here is that we are not looking at it for any particular health or safety reason. The precautionary principle should be enshrined in the original risk assessment, whether it be a scientific risk assessment or the social dimension which is actually framed in the original risk assessment. I think that is the way it should be done. I do not think there is any reason that it should not be enshrined in the regulations. I think in this area we have great confusion between environmental issues and food safety issues. If you listen to the Food Standards Agency, the EU Commission and our own Government they are saying that in relation to the derivatives of these particular GM crops it is not a safety issue, whereas in the regulations it appears to be completely at odds with the sort of legislation for food safety reasons. The regulations are very heavy-handed and not commensurate with the risks. I think the risks and the precautionary principle have, in this case, overtaken need. These foods are being very heavily assessed and quite heavily regulated all the way through the various stages they have had to go through to be on the market. So I do not think it is regulation itself, I think it is the proportionality of regulation to the risk, which in the case of these foods I do not think it is, and I do not think the food industry would go against that. Where we are looking at foods which we know are not going to be substantially equivalent, which we know are going to be different, then one would expect to have to go through a fairly lengthy food procedure. Indeed, my own company has done that. I do not think there is a problem with that end of the market either. I think it is the proportionality in this case, in terms of health and safety.

Chairman

52. If I can follow up this point about proportionality, I am sure we all accept that the case for traceability of something which has modified DNA is very different from the one in which something is derived from GM material and where it may anyway be scientifically impossible to trace its derivation, but I think where the consumers have some concerns is where there have been cases of a breakdown in the traceability. I refer, for example, to one which is not the responsibility of your federation or UK regulators, but in Canada maize which had been designated for use for animal feed found itself in the food chain. Are you familiar with this story?

Chairman *contd.*]

(*Dr Schofield*) Yes.

53. This, of course, is a failure of the regulatory system. It immediately asks the question: if you cannot identify which food is designated GM and which is suitable for human use in Canada, what chances are there of getting it wrong in Europe? Would you like to comment on the relevance of that failure to us?

(*Dr Schofield*) First of all, in relation to the regulatory system, I think I mentioned earlier the Commission proposal where you have a one-tier system, "one door, one key", if you are going to approve this for feed and food use which I think is very valuable. I think, particularly with GM, there will be occasions when there will be small amounts as in all commodity crops, that come in unknown in terms of commodities. I think it is unfortunate in this case, and really it should not have happened, where there is the potential for food and feed crops such as maize to be intermingled at a very low level.

(*Mr Craddock*) I was thinking of your comments, really, about the detectability of the derivatives. My company goes to considerable extents to source some lecithin which of course we use in chocolate and is present in about 0.5 per cent. We have taken the decision that we will use identity preserved lecithin and we have a complex process in place whereby from Brazil we have checked all the way through the supply chain with periodic testing through the chain. It is very easy to test with lecithin in that you can detect the presence of genetic material when it has not been fully refined. Obviously that is part of our monitoring. However, it is also possible to start with known GM soya and extract from those beans—or the oil that comes from them—and then purify lecithin to a point where it is not detectable as GM. In other words you can spend a fortune generating identity preserved non-GM lecithin or you can buy an equivalent product from GM, refined and cleaned up to the point where you cannot tell the difference. Our concern is that these will become co-mingled at some point. This is part of the concern with fraud. You cannot tell the difference between them. I endorse what my colleague said about "one door one key", the single approval for GM in the future. I think that is a very big step forward.

Lord Palmer

54. Without, obviously, trying to break any commercial confidentiality, can you give an indication of the extent to which companies rely on the integrity of an audited supply chain and to what extent they use scientific testing?

(*Dr Schofield*) I think John can say a little more about the IP systems. I think I mentioned earlier, how do we claim on these? You either remove the ingredient, you have an identity preserved system— which we do—and I think Neville has alluded to things like lecithin, and scientific testing can be done at various stages. You can do it actually at the farm for protein detection testing and then at each ingredient step. Those are the tests that we expect our suppliers to do. We have facilities and we have the in-house capabilities to do all the scientific testing ourselves. We do not do it for the whole of the

companies but what we do do is to do ring-tests. We send samples and controls to various laboratories to test for their own competency, accuracy and the reliability of their test results.

55. Does this mean this is the only police force, as such, to stop this fraud?

(*Dr Schofield*) If we want to ensure the IP systems then we have to ensure that the paperwork and any scientific testing that is done is reliable. So we need to do that ourselves, and that is our own quality assurance systems. In terms of general enforcement in the EU, I think that is variable across the EU.

(*Mr Craddock*) If I may build very quickly on that, it is a series of steps that are taken. Firstly, ideally, you work with suppliers whom you can trust. That is the first step. Then you have your own internal policing which might include visits to the supplier or to Brazil etc and you have a clearly defined quality system and you will use in some cases third-party auditors, internationally recognised auditors. Then you have the analytical back-up. As my colleague has said, you do your own analysis in-house and you use third-parties and verify that everybody is getting the same results. The testing which is in place at the moment where we are looking for modified DNA or protein—leaving aside the undetectable plethora of materials of the future—is a highly sophisticated technique. It is not one that every laboratory can just switch on and switch off. I am sure your adviser can go into this much more than I can. The nearest analogy I can bring is that it is rather like getting signals from outer space; you home in on something and you magnify it, and magnify it and magnify it to the point where you think you have actually made some sense. You extract minute amounts of material from your test sample and then you have to replicate it with computer enhancing to determine, at the end of the day, plus or minus 30 per cent, is it there or is it not? It really is the cutting edge of forensic science being applied to food materials.

Lord Dubs

56. Is this not all a lost cause? Given the difficulties that you describe, and the fact that it is going to get more difficult in future, should we not say "Forget it, there is nothing we can do about it"?

(*Mr Craddock*) I think you lead us right back to the point that Mr Wood raised about consumer perception—education is not the right word— consumer information. There is I think in the medium term, but starting straight away, clearly a need for a programme which removes this myth about GM. GM is here, GM will stay, GM is global, the food business is global and, ultimately, it has to be accepted. We cannot avoid it. At the moment, you are absolutely right, we are almost chasing our tails to avoid using it for no logical scientific reasons. With the viable organism, just to qualify that: we have no problems about labelling where it is there in foods, whatever those foods may be, taking the point about the precautionary principle. This regulation is leading us into ingredients which are used in fractions of one per cent in foods. We have left you tables of derivatives and their usage. It is like over-meshing two spiders' webs.

Lord Christopher

57. Lord Dubs anticipated something I was going to say, but I want to take it a little further. Mr Craddock used a tax analogy earlier on. The papers this morning are full of VAT avoidance and evasion. You can solve that by abolishing VAT. In effect, you are saying that labelling will not matter because in five or ten years' time it will have no sensible meaning. The public will still be concerned. Do we really need to approach this from a different angle altogether? Do we need to assure people that GM in principle is safe, but there will be some which may not be, or may not be for old people or babies or whoever? Is there a different approach from labelling, if in fact labelling is not going to work?

(*Dr Schofield*) In terms of testing, nobody is going to put on the market something which is not safe. In fact with GM crops I suppose in many ways they undergo very much more testing than some conventionally grown crops. There is no argument with testing for safety at all. Once you have established the ingredients (and I am distinguishing between the environment and food ingredient safety) then I think this whole question of how you provide information is the most important one. As I mentioned earlier genetic modification, whether it is for an agronomic or a disease or whatever purpose, is not explained just on the label, you cannot do it. Once we get into genetic modification, perhaps for other benefits and nutritional benefits, we are going to want to explain that in a much more open way. I think we have to look at it from another way, that labelling will not fulfill all those purposes in providing information. I am sure with modern technology we ought to be able to put our heads together as to how to do that. One of the things is going to be perhaps a little more understanding of how some of the food chain works and certainly in terms of commodities, which I think is not terribly apparent.

Lord Palmer

58. Going back to one of your expressions "chasing your tail", it must overall be astronomically expensive for the entire food industry?

(*Mr Craddock*) The absolute cost is determined ultimately by the degree of purity that we are looking for. If the threshold that you are working to is, for the sake of argument, 1 per cent as opposed to 0.1 per cent or 0.01 per cent then the costs of segregation and the costs of identify preservation are determined by that level. A simple system of ordinary paper traceability such as we have in place for food safety purposes today, about what we bought and where we sell it without necessarily identifying specific properties about the ingredient, we estimate is somewhere between 1 and 2 per cent as an on-cost. If you move—and there have been numerous studies done on this—to a lower level of percentage impurity then the costs rise to 10, 15, 50, I have even seen figures as high as 200 per cent, as the premium for achieving the levels of segregation which some parties are calling for. So the cost is exponential depending on the degree of purity required.

Countess of Mar

59. You mentioned viable organisms, and presumably that is where the risk lies. If something with a viable part of it is released into the environment, or is fed to a human, then there is some risk. Are there any foods that are on the market now that contain viable organisms?

(*Dr Schofield*) Not genetically modified.

(*Mr Craddock*) There are foods containing viable organisms.

Countess of Mar: But not genetically modified.

Baroness Billingham

60. It is very difficult with the scientific evidence at the moment. The climate of public opinion of scientific evidence is pretty well on the floor. So, from the point of view of trying to persuade people and public opinion to be with us, it is an absolutely major problem. It is no good scientific evidence being so far ahead of public opinion that the two never engage. I take the point that you make, that we are talking about time-scales, and I think that is very important. I thought, when we started this debate a couple of weeks ago, that I had a fairly clear view as to what the problems were, what the potentials were, and I felt quite positively about it. Then, of course, you open your paper and you find something from the Royal Society and you fall flat on the ground again. As a non-scientific person, representing public views on this, I think we have got a huge task of educating and encouraging the public and yet, at the same time, being aware of our own responsibility for not, in fact, forgetting our duties for public safety. There is this double-axis here that we have somehow got to find in the middle of it. Somewhere there will be a time point where, perhaps, the two views will coincide. Who knows?

(*Dr Schofield*) It is the business benefit and the consumer benefit. One of the things we say is that we sell products, we do not sell the technology. That is part of the problem of explaining very complex science. I think we have to have the business case and the consumer case at some point, as you said, coming together.

Baroness Miller of Chilthorne Domer

61. Does Unilever use the same criteria as you explained for food for its cosmetic and personal care products?

(*Dr Schofield*) In terms of the food criteria, in terms of this it is safety, the business case and the consumer.

62. Do your products contain GM at the moment?

(*Dr Schofield*) In terms of wash products, detergents contain enzymes produced from genetically modified micro-organisms. In some countries, for example Switzerland, they are required to be labelled. So it is very clear.

Chairman

63. I am afraid we have run out of time. Thank you very much for having joined us this morning. You have given us a lot of helpful information. If there is

Chairman *contd.*]

anything further we would like to come back to you on, perhaps we can write to you, or indeed if there is anything that you feel you would have liked to have had time to put into the record, do please write in with further evidence. Thank you, once more, the three of you, for your help.

(*Dr Schofield*) Thank you, my Lord Chairman.

Examination of Witnesses

Mr John Longworth, Director of Trading Law and Business Affairs, Tesco Ltd, Ms Janet Nunn, Director of Regulatory and Consumer Affairs, and Mr John Morris, Executive, Regulatory and Consumer Affairs, British Retail Consortium, examined.

Chairman

64. Could I welcome the British Retail Consortium: Ms Janet Nunn, Mr John Longworth, who I remember giving evidence to an earlier Committee inquiry, welcome again, and Mr John Morris. Would you like to introduce yourselves and say anything by way of introduction?

(*Ms Nunn*) Thank you. Good morning. I am Janet Nunn, Director of Regulatory and Consumer Affairs at the British Retail Consortium. The BRC is the principal trade association representing retailers in this country and food retailers in particular. Virtually all the large multiple food retailers are in membership. Indeed, also certain trade associations like the National Association of Master Bakers representing the individual independent bakers.

(*Mr Morris*) I am John Morris. I work for Janet Nunn in the Regulatory and Consumer Affairs section specialising in the food area and more recently in biotechnology.

(*Mr Longworth*) I am John Longworth. I am Group Trading Law and Technical Director for Tesco. I am also Chairman of the Directors Technical Forum of the Institute of Grocery Distribution and a member of the Food Policy Advisory Group for the British Retail Consortium.

65. Thank you very much. I think you were sitting in during the last session so you will know that there is a list of Members of the Committee's interests on the table. Is there anything by way of introduction you would like to say before we ask you one or two questions, which will not necessarily be the ones that you are predicting?

(*Ms Nunn*) I do not really think so. We are eager to share with you what the retailers have been doing in recent years as the atmosphere in the UK has changed post-BSE with regard to science and food safety in particular. Clearly we have been warmed up already with what our manufacturing colleagues have said.

66. Can you start on that and tell us how you see the perception of the UK consumer at the moment, how it is changing and what is needed to meet the requirements you heard in the earlier evidence of a dialogue or possibly education, although that was a word I rather bridled at?

(*Ms Nunn*) If I can first of all draw your attention to ongoing consumer work done by the Institute of Grocery Distribution that John mentioned just now, which represents the whole of the food chain. They have in particular some work headed "Consumer Watch" which they conduct and publish three times

a year. That looks *inter alia* at consumer attitudes to food safety where genetic modification, BSE and the future of UK agriculture have figured consistently in there over the last couple of years. They have been saying that it is clear that consumers feel quite strongly about the genetic modification of food and that many people's views are evolving reflecting the different type of information and messages that they receive. Lady Billingham, I think your comment about how you feel you are on one line and then you read something from the Royal Society and revise your views again is true. John, do you want to amplify?

(*Mr Longworth*) From my experience we are obviously extremely interested in what our customers think and we constantly carry out market research and customer insight activity, which is a little more in-depth than market research, where we effectively examine what consumers think and how they will behave which is particularly important to us in understanding customer preferences. I would say that over the last 18 months there has been a decline in consumer concern about GM but not such a significant decline as to materially change the situation. For the most part consumers are still concerned about GM.

67. Are they concerned that they should know whether the food that they are going to eat is itself modified or are they equally concerned about whether it is derived from a genetically modified process?

(*Mr Longworth*) In all the research that we have done every time we have asked customers the question they have not made a distinction between the protein and the derivative. We, as a business, were the first retailer in the UK to label both GM protein and derivatives voluntarily quite a long time before the issue actually became an issue of public concern because we felt that it was important to provide customers with information on which they could make choices. There has never been a distinction made in our customer base between derivatives and protein.

Chairman: We will come to some of the practicalities of this. You will have heard the earlier evidence that it might be difficult to determine to what extent something is derived from a genetically modified process, but that is an issue you have to deal with at the moment.

Lord Fyfe of Fairfield

68. I think Mr Longworth has probably answered most of the points that I was going to make but you have talked quite convincingly, I must say, about the amount of research which your organisation has conducted into consumer attitudes and that, indeed, is an ongoing thing obviously, but you also referred to the fact that there seems to have been over the past 18 months a decline in concern by customers. I wonder what you would attribute that to. I wonder if you could tell us what would be the principal concerns of consumers who want to avoid food containing GM material. Some of this was covered by the witnesses we had just a few minutes ago but I wonder if people are as aware of the debate which is taking place on genetically modified food—the typical customer, whatever your typical customer is—particularly of the merits or, indeed, demerits of genetically modified food?

(*Mr Longworth*) It is very difficult to predict why people change their positions or why the level of concern may decline with any certainty. The sort of information we get tells us that customers first of all feel that the issue has been dealt with and, therefore, the level of concern tends to recede. The second point is that there are only so many things that people can be concerned about simultaneously and as other things become important in people's minds then the concern on issues that were once at the top of the agenda slip back a little. That is not to say that they would not be as concerned again if that issue went up the agenda. Obviously people get information from a variety of sources, from the media, the press, from public debate and so on, so that informs decision-making. One of the things that I want to emphasise is my feeling that it is customers who make perfectly rational decisions on risk. They make the same decisions I would make as an individual, notwithstanding the fact that I am a scientist and I have been in the regulatory field and so on and so forth. Even with all my knowledge, if you like, I would still make the same decisions that customers make because they are grown-ups and they make decisions on the basis of information they have available to them and they are perfectly rational decisions. I think that is an important point to make.

Lord Crickhowell

69. Just following that up, there seems to be a distinction. One recognises that if one goes into Tesco you have on the one hand a niche market for people who feel very strongly that they want to buy organic products, they do not like them covered in fertilizers or whatever, and it is a relatively small sector of the market; one usually identifies it quite early on when one goes into the supermarket and there is an area set aside for these products. I do not know what it is, ten or 11 per cent of the market, who are prepared to pay more for them, and you can concentrate quite a lot of effort on identifying these products, knowing where they come from and so on. Then you have this much wider and more complicated area of product, the bulk of the raw material, things like soya, going into a huge range of products, much more difficult to trace, as we have heard, and which may or may not have some label on it or next to it; people have to pick up the thing and

look at it pretty closely. There is a clear distinction between the choice of one niche sector which is clearly identified and this much more complicated one. How seriously are your customers looking at this issue? How much do you think it is affecting their purchases off your shelves?

(*Mr Longworth*) It is not affecting purchasing decisions today because Tesco brand as a range has no GM or GM derivatives in it. In a sense there is no measure of the way in which purchasing decisions are made today. Perhaps I should explain historically that we were the first people to provide information, and therefore choice, but we were probably the last major retailer to decide to provide non-GM products within our range when the public debate was at its height. That was not in any way an indicator of our preference as a business, we simply wanted to establish what it was that our customers actually wanted because we are guided by our customers, they are fundamentally important to us, we will deliver whatever they want effectively. It was a very uncomfortable decision for us, a very uncomfortable decision for me, because our normal approach to these things is always to provide choice and information. We do not dictate to customers what they should or should not have, it is their choice. In this particular instance the difficulty that we were facing was that we knew we had about 300 to 350 products in our range that had GM in and were in fact labelled as such and that by the end of that year there was a very strong possibility that more than 75 per cent of the products within the Tesco brand range would have GM in them. Clearly that was not going to lead to a situation where customers had any real choice so we decided to remove the GM from the Tesco brand in order to provide a choice between Tesco brand and the branded products which we sell in our stores as well. That was the only way we could provide choice. Customers showed their preference to the extent that the branded manufacturers then decided to remove GM from their products too. I think it was pretty clear at the time what the customer preference was.

Lord Crickhowell: So you now have eliminated all choice?

Baroness Billingham

70. Absolutely.

(*Mr Longworth*) The customer has chosen not to have GM. They were given a choice and they have chosen not to have it.

Lord Christopher

71. The choice would be another supermarket, and I will not name any in case I insult them, that does sell GM.

(*Mr Longworth*) I am not aware that there is a GM product, I am not aware that another supermarket is intentionally selling GM. I know there was a product in a supermarket that was not labelled as GM but I think the supermarket did not realise it.

Lord Crickhowell

72. Do you think your customers when they go on holiday to the United States are as concerned and go into the supermarkets and ask whether it is GM free, or is it just a psychological hang-up that we have got here?

(*Mr Longworth*) We have never asked the question.

Chairman

73. Do you have stores in the United States?
(*Mr Longworth*) No.

74. But your members do. Could you speak for the Consortium?

(*Ms Nunn*) The only company I am aware of that has stores in the US now is Sainsbury's on the eastern seaboard and I believe that they have a separate policy deciding centre in the USA based on their risk assessment, management and regulatory systems and their customers there as distinct from the customers here. It is not a case of having a J Sainsbury policy globally, there would be a separate policy there.

Countess of Mar

75. We heard earlier from Mr Craddock about lecithin and the lengths that Nestlé go to to make sure that GM lecithin does not go into their chocolates. My daughter mentioned lecithin to me a couple of years ago and she said "just look along the supermarket shelves and see how many products have it". Are your members able to guarantee that there is no modified lecithin in their products in view of the expense?

(*Mr Morris*) To a great extent they ensure that the lecithin they are using does not come from a genetically modified source. Yes is the answer to your question.

(*Ms Nunn*) It is true of all the ingredients because of the identity preserved standard, the IP standard that John referred to earlier, which we developed as retailers with manufacturers because we could see that we needed to have confidence in supply systems and their traceability. I think you have got a copy here, John. As John said earlier, it goes through from the seed suppliers, very early on, right the way through. It would work globally. It has been tested, it has been challenged back in October 2000 rather publicly. It was quite interesting to go through and see that it stood the test, it was very reassuring. It was iterative. We had put it originally on our website for free, people were accessing it and giving us feedback and the European Starches Association said "you are too focused on soya, you need to take the maize supply chain into account" and we changed it and reiterated and published it formally in October 2001.

Lord Dubs

76. Just to be quite clear, are you giving us a different view from the previous witnesses? In other words, do you believe that you can sustain the position of GM free products in the bulk of your members' stores?

(*Ms Nunn*) We do not have GM free, we do not say that. We agree with the former speakers that we are not in a GM free situation unless we were to be in a hermetically sealed greenhouse somewhere. We are quite consistent in the way that we say we are operating to non-GM supply chains. It is not GM free. Retailers are not comfortable with that terminology and we would be very unhappy if the Food Standards Agency or EU regulatory systems were to push for us to adopt that.

(*Mr Longworth*) To answer your question, I was finding it slightly difficult, listening to the Food and Drink Federation, to understand what they were saying in relation to whether they were predicting the difficulty, that it would be impossible to sustain. I suspect that they were directing us towards the view that it would be very, very difficult to sustain. I am not quite so pessimistic as that in relation to the sustainability question. My feeling is that the jury is out at the moment about which way that it will go. I know there are a number of Asian countries that are very keen not to have any GM in Asia because they are major oil exporters—not petrol; food oil and edible oils. In Brazil, for example, where we have one of my colleagues making visits regularly, every three months at the moment, it is very clear that there is a potential in Brazil for the maintenance of production of non-GM product for a very long time. You could drop the whole of western Europe in Brazil and have room to spare, it is a huge country. Even if in the bottom left-hand corner you have got a bit of contamination from Argentina seed production, it is just not going to affect the vast majority of production in Brazil for a very long time.

Lord Crickhowell

77. Can I ask a question that I was longing to put to Unilever, because Unilever is a company particularly well represented in the under-developed world and they have a lot of social products, but we ran out of time. Is there not a bit of a dilemma here? A lot of these countries are holding off at the moment because they are worried about losing the market, the major market; but if it comes to a choice between losing their market and having a starving population, and if you had some major series of droughts in that part of the world and put a rather different message to your customers, who are keenly concerned about starving babies across the world, "we are going to market products from this part of the world which are genetically modified because we are helping to avoid starvation", might you not get a different response from your customers, because at the moment, as we have heard, you are not giving them a choice?

(*Mr Longworth*) I must correct you on the last statement. In fact, we went out of our way to give customers choice and they made that choice. The moment customers tell us that they want a GM product we will provide it. We are not against the technology, we have never made any statement about the technology at all, we are for customers.

78. Has it ever occurred to you that you might positively market a particular product saying that it is coming from a certain country, it is genetically modified and it is greatly helping agricultural production in that country and avoiding starvation? It would be quite an interesting experiment to see what the reaction of the public was.

Lord Crickhowell *contd.*]

(*Mr Longworth*) There is not any product of that
nature at the moment. The countries in Asia that are
trying to preserve a non-GM status are not those
countries that are likely to be faced with starvation.
In relation to the products themselves, there is no
sign in the imminent future of a product that has a
sufficiently compelling consumer attribute to attract
customers in their decision-making between
perceived risk and attribute. If you are a customer, if
you are an individual looking at a product that has a
perceived potential risk for you and has absolutely
no benefit at all, the rational decision you would
make is not to buy it.

Baroness Billingham: I was glad that Janet and
other people raised the issue of the debate being
within a European dimension because I remember
sitting for a number of years in the European
Parliament hearing this debate and the only
difference between the debate there and the debate
here this morning is that it was in eleven different
languages, but there still was no consensus. I am very
interested to know how you are going to take this
debate forward. Look at how it is actually run. At the
moment we have a complete embargo, there is a
stalemate. We are not offering consumers any choice,
we have withdrawn, we are hiding behind the sofa
really. My question is how are we going to advance
this debate further? What is the next stage as far as
retailers are concerned? Is it that we are going to take
a European or a global dimension? I am going to
Florida next week, I am quite sure that I will not be
going into shops checking out and yet I will be
surrounded by GM food products there and however
many million people have been chomping their way
through GM foods not too many have taken legal
action as a result of it. There is a huge debate and we
have to broaden it.

Chairman

79. Let me bring this to a conclusion. The question
is what happens next in determining consumer
choice?
(*Ms Nunn*) I think that the OECD got it right at
their Bangkok conference last July in concluding that
governments must increase their support for
independent and publicly funded scientific research
into risks and benefits of GM foods and crops. You
are quite right, we cannot even afford to act on this
on an EU basis because essentially we trade globally.
Retailers source globally, manufacturers export
globally, and it is no good having a disagreement,
megaphone diplomacy, between the EU, the North
Americans or whatever. There needs to be a risk
assessment at global level in joining all scientists to
the debate and reaching a consensus about what
constitutes safe. I think the Phillips Report on BSE
said safe is what presents an acceptable risk to a
reasonable consumer.

80. Are you talking here about human health or
environmental risk or both?
(*Ms Nunn*) Essentially I am focusing on human
health since that is essentially what the customers are

interested in "what does it mean to me and my
family?". That is the prime motivator.

81. Are you aware then of the initiative of the
World Health Organisation in this respect?
(*Ms Nunn*) No.

82. If I can invite you to have a look at that as a
product of the Bangkok conference. The World
Health Organisation recognised that in America we
have had 350 million consumers who have been
doing, helpfully for us, a control for some time and
there must by now be some information coming out
as to what the risks are. The World Health
Organisation determined as a result of Bangkok to
put together this definitive statement as to how they
saw the developing issues in so far as they affected
human health. The environmental issues are quite
different because there we are dealing with gene
contamination. If those are not the issues that you
think your consumers are concerned about and it is
human health then clearly you have a duty to be
involved in dialogue and it must be the case surely
that you should be aware at least of questions the
WHO are asking and helping to inform the dialogue
about which we were talking earlier. I wonder if you
would comment on that.
(*Ms Nunn*) That is very interesting and thank you
very much for drawing it to our attention. Perhaps I
could make just a gentle point in that government
departments of all hue and colour are very good at
asking us for our views and our input and are not
necessarily always as diligent in feeding back out.
Clearly something like that is essential. We can all
look at the website and so on but the day-to-day
business may not allow us to stand back and look at
some of these big issues. You are quite right, that is
good to know and we will look at that.

83. Let us go on and anticipate things. I accept that
this is a pretty unscientific approach but nevertheless
given that we have 350 million in one country alone
consuming GM food it is quite possible, I think, to
predict that the World Health Organisation will say
that they have quantified such human risk as there is
and if there is it will be stated very clearly. Is there
then a requirement which could be identified to pass
this information on via the retail sector or is this
something that is not the responsibility of the retail
sector?
(*Ms Nunn*) It is also a responsibility of the retail
sector, together with governments, education
departments, the media, we all have responsibility to
inform the public in a responsible way about what
constitutes risk so that, as John said, they can take
their own decisions about whether they feel
comfortable with the risks they may be taking. I
think that the Food Standards Agency has it about
right now. It has gone through a process and is about
to embark publicly on a consultation on how to do
its scientific assessments and run its scientific
advisory committees. It is proposing there, for
example, to also invite international experts, not just
confining ourselves to British ones. I think that is a
good step. It is something that I am aware the
equivalent of the Royal Society in the USA did, with
which Dr Lyn Frewar of the IFR in Norwich was
involved. I think more of that needs to be happening,

Chairman *contd.*]

sharing between these key scientific risk assessment bodies internationally and that should mean eventually, I would hope, that we will be getting information out to the public in an informed way rather than this swings and roundabouts that we are having at the moment.

Baroness Miller of Chilthorne Dormer

84. Before I ask my other question, I wonder if I could just follow up that point you made about research being funded by governments and then the Chairman pointed out the WHO's work. Do you have any idea of the proportion of research into GM that is funded by the industry itself? It was a point that the previous witnesses did not take up. Do you know the proportion funded by industry, which the consumers would see as perhaps self-interest, and the proportion that is funded by governments?

(*Ms Nunn*) The short answer is no. To some extent it will always be slightly commercially confidential because companies want to see what they can do and not necessarily commit to explaining where they are intending to go next. My comment was really inspired more by what we saw as being the experience in the United States where, for example, a company then called Monsanto introduced the GM soya on to the market and I understand their system was that it shared its risk assessment data with the various bodies there, the USDA, the FDA and the EPA, but those bodies did not themselves conduct separate independent research. From where we are in Europe I do not think that would give that degree of reassurance and independence that our customers would be looking for. For Europe I think it would be right to have that independence and we are pleased to see that as an outcome of the Bangkok conference.

85. Thank you. If I might follow that with a different area of questioning, which commodities are used in food manufacturing that are grown as GM somewhere in the world? Then I would like Mr Morris to tell us why he has been guarding that tin of tomato purée.

(*Mr Morris*) Waiting for the right moment. According to the OECD, their debate on field trials which is the most relevant information that we like to quote, the food commodities that are being grown just now are sweetcorn, oilseed rape, potatoes, soya bean, tomato, sugar beet, wheat, rice and melon. Cotton and tobacco are being grown but I do not think that they are in the food chain.

Chairman

86. Can you tell us why you have got that tin of tomato paste?

(*Mr Morris*) Really to show how customers' perceptions have changed over the years. Not very many years ago, in 1996, this particular product was launched at two of Mr Longworth's competitors. It was a tomato purée labelled fully on the front "produced from genetically modified tomatoes". It was a larger size, it sold at the same price, was therefore better value, the colour was improved and the taste was meant to be very good indeed. It outsold the standard product. Customers can be led by their perception of a product. Unfortunately it is only since the commodity market has been taken over by a proportion of genetically modified goods that the problem has arisen. This is what our customers saw in the *Daily Mail* last week and if our customers read that they are going to avoid GM products.

87. I think this comes back to Lord Crickhowell's thesis which he has put to a number of witnesses that true choice means that you have to understand that the immediate reaction fuelled by irresponsible media headlines, and I think I can describe that one as irresponsible, is effectively determining how you provide choice. If it was true five years ago that people were prepared to buy the Flav'r Sav'r tomato but they felt let down by the inability of industry to deliver traceability of a commodity, which I think was the genesis of this lack of confidence. Then it would seem that a regulation such as the European Union is suggesting which restores confidence which existed earlier would in turn allow this choice of perhaps nutritionally enhanced products, perhaps products which help the producer in the Third World, perhaps products which might indeed, like the Flav'r Sav'r tomato, offer some benefit. Would this not be a true meaning of choice? I want to address this to Mr Longworth who says he is giving choice at the moment.

(*Mr Longworth*) I am not sure that the European regulation will actually help to reintroduce choice. The thing that will help to reintroduce choice is a product that customers actually want to buy. At the moment the situation is simply that there are in the food sector no products available on the market which provide a customer benefit that is sufficient to be attractive to customers. That is the real crux of the matter. In actual fact we did not sell the tomato paste at the time this was produced simply because our customers told us that they did not like the taste as much as the normal stuff.

88. Nevertheless, I think we have been told, or we have heard evidence, that it did actually sell in the two outlets perfectly well.

(*Mr Longworth*) It was cheaper.

89. Presumably you have a different consumer. It seems to me slightly surprising that if there was this record of a market, as Mr Morris reminds us, that fundamentals have changed so dramatically that there will never again be a market for it. It seems odd to me.

(*Mr Longworth*) I think it is just worth reflecting on the fact that there are a lot of biotech pharmaceutical products on the market which customers make no objection to at all because there is a clear benefit to customers from those products. Fundamentally it is an issue around perceived risk versus perceived benefit.

(*Ms Nunn*) I do think that the fundamentals have changed because what we had back in February 1996 was that the public did not know about the technology, it was a new technology, essentially they were neutral about it. The two companies that launched this did so in a very open way building up after Christmas with their media coverage, their articles and so on, they had leaflets at the shelf edge when it sold and that was an awful lot to do with why

Chairman *contd.*]

it did sell so well, quite apart from the attributes of the product itself and the price. What happened thereafter, of course, as we know, was in March the Government at the time had to do a U-turn on its messages about the safety of beef and the possible links with BSE and thereafter a long, slow undermining among the public psyche took place of what scientists, and government scientists in particular, were meaning when they said things were safe. I do think that we are going through a process now that we have the Food Standards Agency of rebuilding that. In trying to assess what the fundamentals are I think we are still not yet at the situation we were at in February 1996 when this tomato purée was being sold. It is not going to be easy to identify. Even if you say there is a product that has an advantage for the consumer, nutritionally enhanced products and so on, it ought to sell, we are already at a disadvantage as far as their confidence in science is concerned. It should be capable of being overcome but it is quite a challenge.

90. As Mr Longworth reminds us, there are many genetically modified products in the pharmaceutical sector which apparently do not have these obstacles.

(*Ms Nunn*) It seems from what we have heard through contacts with the pharmaceutical area that people have a different perception of what they want. If they need to take a medicine for their health because they are ill, or their family is ill, that is one thing. Because the foods they eat are generally to help them have a healthy lifestyle and a healthy body that is something else and they will make a different assessment themselves on what risks they are willing to take. They are two separate things and people take a different decision against that background.

91. Do consumers not act very rationally and say if there is a risk for the consumer and the risk is shared with the benefit then it is a logical decision to take, but if all the benefit accrues to the producer or the shareholder and any risks there might be, however residual, are carried by the consumer it seems a duff deal? Is that not the long and the short of it?

(*Mr Longworth*) I absolutely agree with that. That is precisely what our customers effectively tell us on these issues. If there were a strong benefit for the customers the product would sell. The perfect product is a viagra banana and it would sell like hot cakes, absolutely no trouble at all.

Lord Crickhowell

92. Has Tesco's policy not actually got it into the situation where if somebody produces a product which has a clear benefit for the consumers but you are at the moment saying "actually we are not going to put any of these genetically modified products on sale because there is a general perception against them", the product is not going to be put into your shops in order to test whether the consumer benefit is of real interest to the consumer?

(*Mr Longworth*) Not necessarily so. If there were a product that came along that we felt customers might perceive as being advantageous to them we would

experiment with that product, with customer panels and so on, in terms of research to see whether it would be acceptable or not, and if it were acceptable there is no reason in the world why we would not introduce it back into the market at some stage in the future.

Chairman: I am afraid that we are running out of time and we certainly have not stuck to the predicted list of questions, but I did warn you about that. You have led us into an interesting area and we have ended with the note that where consumers perceive something that is going to be of advantage to them through the GM route then the British Retail Consortium would certainly wish to test the market. That brings us back to the original requirement to try to meet the legitimate requirements of the consumer of traceability, labelling and information and the practicalities of an international market which is evidently becoming quite widely diffuse with GM products. Lady Maddock wants to ask one last question.

Baroness Maddock

93. I was going to ask the previous witnesses this question but we ran out of time. We have heard from the previous people giving evidence this morning that in the end they thought that GM foods would arrive and that because of the concerns and the discussion we have had this morning they thought the question of fraud would be difficult. My question was going to be about accuracy and so on. Do you have the same view that they have that if we are not careful and if everybody resists GM foods we are just going to get a whole lot of fraud in the markets?

(*Ms Nunn*) Not necessarily. We are going step wise into the water globally, it would seem, and from the soya experience, for example, I understand the premium that non-GM commodity varieties can get from the marketplace is of the order of £10 to £20 a tonne, so it is a premium but it is quite small. Of course by the time you break that down into the derivatives it is not something that pushes for an increase in the products sold on the shelf, the lecithin or whatever, it is of such small quantities. Looking forward as other countries grow GM crops, I cannot see that it will make any difference because when we go to Brussels to meet our colleagues from other Member States I do not pick up anything different there from what I hear mixing with the retailers in this country, that in essence European consumers have not yet got confidence in the technology and I am not aware of any products about to come on to the market to be offered that would change that. Clearly at the same time, as we have already discussed, there would need to be better information by all parties, government and industry, to address that consumer confidence and information that is necessary before the products can sell.

Chairman: Thank you once more for having joined us today and giving us most helpful information. Thank you.

Memorandum by the British Retail Consortium

INTRODUCTION

The situation in Britain, following the outbreak of *E.coli* 0157 in Scotland, BSE in cattle and the association with vCJD in humans and now the possibility of BSE in sheep, has left the majority of the population doubting advice from scientists and politicians on food related issues. These doubts have been fuelled by some sections of the media which have capitalised on the public's uncertainty over food containing GM ingredients. Currently we are not aware of any food products containing GM ingredients that are available through the retail sector. Neither are we aware of any food product containing a GM ingredient that offered a consumer benefit that is close to market.

1. *Do these proposals adequately address the requirements of European consumers for regulation, traceability and labelling of GM food and feed products derived from GMOs?*

Yes, BRC supports the current proposals for new legislation as we believe that they will meet the needs of the majority of consumers. We also support the widening of the scope to include all ingredients in food and feed which are derived from GM sources. We agree with the idea of incorporating both food and animal feed legislation together as a package. BRC believes that by making the legislation clear and coherent, and at the same time giving informed choice, consumer understanding of genetic modification and their confidence when purchasing food will be improved.

2. *Do they make sensible distinctions between the requirements of animal feed and those of food for human consumption?*

Yes, BRC supports the removal of distinctions through the extension of the requirements to cover both food and animal feed. By introducing one system for both, it should not be possible for a repeat of the "Starlink" fiasco happening in the EU ie human food chain contaminated with product only approved for animal feed. BRC is pleased to see that the harmonisation of authorisation procedures and risk assessment will be centralised at the European Food Safety Authority.

3. *How effective are the proposals likely to be in ensuring full traceability of GM material at all stages of the chain from producer to consumer?*

BRC believes that the best way of ensuring that products do not contain GM ingredients is by having a robust identity preserved system in place right up the supply chain. To this end BRC has published, in partnership with the Food and Drink Federation, a Technical Standard based on best practice to assist in the supply and traceability of non-GM material. We understand that this new Technical Standard is becoming widely accepted throughout Europe as the benchmark for the supply of non-GM soya and maize. Even when it was in draft form in November 2000, it proved robust when a number of retailers audited their supply systems when they needed to show that their products did not contain traces of an unapproved GM material.

Another suggestion, that BRC has already put to the Food Standards Agency, is an alternative to the sampling and testing of food ingredients for the accidental presence of GM material. This is based on the EC Directive on the Hygiene of Foodstuffs (93/43/EEC) which includes a provision for industry guides for good hygiene practice to be produced to assist compliance. The "BRC/FDF Technical Standard for the Supply of Identity Preserved Non-Genetically Modified Food Ingredients and Product" that was published in September 2001 is such a guide to good practice and we expect that it will be widely adopted throughout the EU on a voluntary basis. Based on risk analysis, it lays down operational standards for all sectors of the supply chain from the seed supplier through to the end user. If this Technical Standard could be officially recognised, it could provide food retailers and manufacturers with a working document that would provide an alternative system that would minimise the possibility of GM material entering the food chain. Food manufacturers and retailers could then demonstrate compliance with regulatory requirements by voluntary adherence to the Technical Standard as opposed to mandatory sampling and testing.

4. *Are the proposals likely to be enforceable in practice, particularly where no novel genetic material is contained in the food or feed?*

As it is impossible to test all food and feed, traceability will need to be based on evidence from the audit of the supply chain, supplemented by a sampling regime based on established risk. Once again the BRC/FDF Technical Standard will provide guidance on best practice and will assist enforcement officials in their work.

5. *A threshold level of one per cent or lower for the accidental presence of GM material in food and feed has been proposed, below which there would be an exemption. Is a threshold of this level, common to both food and feed appropriate?*

Yes, BRC feels that with the current testing techniques available, the level of detection for accidental presence of GMOs in both food and feed should stay at one per cent. However, as testing techniques improve, the level of detection should be reviewed.

6. *Is the role proposed for (a) the European Food Authority and its scientific committees and (b) Member States in the authorisation process for GM food and feed appropriate?*

No, BRC believes that for the purposes of labelling, it is essential to continue with the one per cent threshold for adventitious presence of EC approved GMOs. A move to allow lower ranking EC Scientific Committees to assess and approve GMOs that, in their opinion "did not pose a danger to the environment or health", could undermine consumer confidence. From a practical point of view, retailers who must conform with the legal requirements, need to be working with the legal certainty that would only exist after full EU approval.

7. *Are the proposals likely to be compatible with the requirements of the Cartagena Protocol on Biosafety and with other international commitments, including OECD programmes?*

Yes, BRC believes that the requirements of the Cartagena Protocol on Biosafety have been addressed by the Commission in the drafting of these proposals. This is acknowledged in recital 38 on page 17 of the proposal and dealt with in detail in Article 43.

8. *Are the proposals compatible with obligations towards non-Member States seeking to export food and feed to the EU?*

BRC is not aware that any aspects of the proposals that could further restrict trade.

9. *Should the present EU-wide moratorium on approving GM food and crop product applications be maintained until the issues concerning traceability and labelling of GMOs have been resolved?*

No. The EU should be encouraged to re-start the approvals process for GM materials. The current moratorium is running the risk of building up an approvals backlog.

10. *What other aspects of the proposals require further consideration before the UK Government can sign up to them?*

BRC is concerned that the Food Standards Agency, in its role as the UK representative in Brussels on this new legislation, is pressing for the establishment of a "GM free" status which we believe is unattainable for commodity crops. The only exception to this would be where crops are grown in a controlled environment, possibly in secure greenhouses. BRC believes that the description "non-GM" should continue to be used.

March 2002

WEDNESDAY 27 FEBRUARY 2002

Present:

Christopher, L	Mar, C
Crickhowell, L	Miller of Chilthorne Domer, B
Dubs, L	Palmer, L
Fyfe of Fairfield, L	Selborne, E. (Chairman)
Maddock, B	Walpole, L

Memorandum by Friends of the Earth

INTRODUCTION

Friends of the Earth very much welcomes the enquiry by the House of Lords into the labelling and traceability of GMOs. In July 2001, the European Commission tabled its proposals for new EU Regulations on both GM Food/Feed and Tracebility/Labelling of GMOs. Whilst these are two separate pieces of legislation they will go through the EU at the same time and are naturally closely connected with each other.

GENETICALLY MODIFIED FOOD AND FEED

The GM Food/Feed Regulation (COM(2001) 425) will replace the authorisation for GM foods and food ingredients currently covered by the Novel Food Regulation (Regulation(EC)258/97). It will also introduce, for the first time, authorisation procedures for GMOs used in animal feed which are currently unregulated by EU legislation. The existing Novel Food Regulation will remain in place for the placing on the market of "novel foods" other than those produced from genetically modified organisms.

Many EU citizens, as well as environmental and consumer NGOs, welcome the fact that the proposed GM Food/Feed Regulation would involve more stringent procedures for approving GMOs in food than the current Novel Food Regulation which allows for simplified notification procedures under which companies can seek approval for GM foods on the basis of "substantial equivalence" with conventional foods. Also welcome are the proposed new rules for labelling of the GM Food/Feed Proposal which would extend labelling to cover all GMO derivatives such as oils and other products which currently escape labelling because DNA/foreign protein from GMOs can no longer be detected after processing. Finally, the extension of authorisation and labelling rules to cover animal feed is a welcome and long-overdue addition to the EU's regulatory framework, since these products are subject to neither authorisation nor labelling at present, although most of the GMOs imported into the European Union actually end up as animal food.

There are, however, many negative aspects to the Commission's Proposal. As in the case of the proposed Traceability/Labelling Regulation, it effectively "legalises" contamination by unapproved GMOs by setting a threshold of one per cent for the "adventitious" or "technically unavoidable" presence of GMOs. The Commission defends this concession on the basis that it would only be permissible if the unapproved GMOs "have been subject to a scientific risk assessment made by the relevant Scientific Committee(s) or the European Food Authority". This means that, for example, if the EU's Scientific Committee on Plants has deemed a GMO to be safe, the presence of that GMO would be tolerated regardless of the fact that it has not been authorised under EU legislation. In other words, the 1 per cent contamination threshold would allow unauthorised GMOs to enter the food chain; furthermore these GMOs would not have to be labelled.

To make the above concession possible, the GM Food/Feed Proposal requires the amendment of the new Deliberate Release Directive which stipulates that thresholds for "adventitious" or "technically unavoidable" presence should only be allowed for authorised GMOs, and that any releases of unauthorised GMOs should be terminated. The adoption of the proposed GM Food/Feed Regulation in its current form, therefore, would weaken the new Deliberate Release Directive, which only entered into force in April 2001 and will become law in the Member States on 17 October 2002.

Including this exemption in the proposed Regulation clearly does not ensure consumer choice (nor for that matter guarantee consumer safety) since it allows the presence on the market of GMOs which are unauthorised, not subject to traceability and are also exempt from labelling—providing that the GMO producer can demonstrate that their presence was "adventitious" or "technically unavoidable". It effectively means that one in 100 tomatoes, 10 out of 1,000 salmon, or 500 tons of a 50,000 ton shipment of soya could be transgenic, yet exempt from any EU legislation. The consumer, therefore, faces a lottery when, for example, buying a tomato as to whether it may be 100 per cent transgenic or not.

Rather than take pro-active steps to avoid GMO contamination, the Commission has unfortunately proposed legislation which would open the door for contamination of the food and feed chain by unauthorised GMOs. Instead of taking measures, which would oblige GMO producers to ensure that their products do not pollute conventional and organic production, this proposal legalises such contamination and puts all the burden of avoiding unwanted or unauthorised GMOs on the shoulders of those who seek to avoid it.

FoE's assessment of the GM Food/Feed proposal

On the positive side:

— the EU would at last have an authorisation procedure and labelling rules for GMOs used in animal feed;

— the simplified procedure for placing GM food on the market under the concept of "substantial equivalence" would be discontinued;

— all GMO-derived foods should be labelled, regardless of whether processing and heat treatment make the detection of foreign DNA/protein in the finished product impossible.

On the negative side:

— animal products such as meat, milk and eggs from animals which have been fed on GMOs are not subject to labelling although they have been produced with GMOs (despite the fact that consumer organisations have called for such products to be labelled, and despite the fact that a traceability system would make that possible);

— the authorisation procedures set out in the Proposal would undermine Member States' decision-making powers by giving total responsibility for risk assessment to the future European Food Safety Authority (EFSA) which "may" ask appropriate agencies in EU countries to carry out food safety assessments;

— the Commission splits risk assessment and risk management between the EFSA and the Member States respectively;

— it would be possible for companies to file a single application for both placing a GMO on the market and for authorisation of that GMO as food and/or feed, thus by-passing the Deliberate Released Directive 2001/18/EC;

— emergency measures which currently exist under the Deliberate Release Directive for EU Member States to take action should they feel that a particular GMO poses a risk to the environment or human health would be considerably watered down—countires would lose their right to take unilateral action and could only "inform" the EFSA and the European Commission about their concerns;

— exemptions from the Regulation are made for the "adventitious" or "technically unavoidable" presence of GMOs up to a threshold of 1 per cent, such GMOs need neither be authorised nor labelled;

— The above exemption requires the amendment of the new Deliberate Rellease Directive 2001/18/EC which stipulates that thresholds for "adventitious" or "technically unavoidable" presence should only be allowed for authorised GMOs, and that any releases of unauthorised GMOs should be terminated.

TRACEABILITY AND LABELLING OF GMOS

When the revised Deliberate Release Directive was adopted by the European Parliament in February 2001, several Member States reaffirmed their intention to maintain the Moratorium on GMO approvals until new provisions were in place to ensure traceability and labelling of GMOs and GMO derivatives. Some Member States have even said that the question of liability should also be addressed before more GMOs enter the market place.

Although the new Directive 2001/18/EC requires EU Member States to ensure traceability of GMOs at all stages of placing on the market, it does not itself provide the legal basis to do so. The European Commission, therefore, had to propose new legislation in this regard. Although this was originally promised for March 2001, it was July when the Commission finally presented its Proposal for a Regulation of the European Parliament and of the Council concerning traceability and labelling of genetically modified organisms and traceability of food and feed products produced from genetically modified organisms (COM(2001)182).

The purpose of the Regulation is to ensure traceability of GMOs from operator to operator in order to facilitate comprehensive labelling of GMOs, and to put a system in place which would enable withdrawal of GMOs from the market should problems such as harm to the environment or human health occur.

The final version of the Proposal is somewhat better than earlier draft texts which contained worrying provisions such as allowing for the "adventitious" presence of GMOs authorised in third countries (such as the United States and Canada). However, the Commission's final proposal is nevertheless considered by some as a concession to the biotech industry in that it effectively "legalises" contamination by unapproved GMOs by setting a threshold of 1 per cent for the "adventitious" or "technically unavoidable" presence of GMOs. The Commission's argument for this concession is that this would only be permissible if the unapproved GMOs "have been subject to a scientific risk assessment made by the relevant Scientific Committee(s) or the European Food Authority". In other words, if, for example, the EU's Scientific Committee on Plants has deemed a GMO to be safe, the presence of that GMO would be tolerated regardless of the fact that it has not been authorised under EU legislation. In other words, the 1 per cent contamination threshold would allow unapproved GMOs to be released and to enter the food chain. In addition, GMOs which would be tolerated under this concession would not have to be labelled either.

Furthermore, the Proposal requires the amendment of the new Deliberate Release Directive, which stipulates that thresholds for "adventitious" or "technically unavoidable" presence should only be allowed for authorised GMOs, and that any releases of unauthorised GMOs should be terminated. Thus, the adoption of the proposed Traceability/Labelling Regulation, in its current form, would weaken the new Deliberate Release Directive, which only entered into force in April 2001 and must be transposed into the legislation of EU Member States by 17 October 2002.

FoE's assessment of the Traceability and Labelling proposal

On the positive side:

— the EU would have a traceability system that ensures, in theory, that GMOs can be identified and labelled throughout the food and feed chain;

— the tracebility regime would facilitate monitoring of health and environment effects of GMOs and the withdrawal of harmful products.

On the negative side:

— complete traceability from operator to operator is restricted to GMOs not used for food, feed or processing—it would, in fact, only apply to live GMOs, ie seeds;

— medicinal products for human or veterinary use are not included in the scope of the proposed Regulation, leaving open the issue of traceability of GM plants grown for the production of pharmaceuticals;

— animal products such as meat, milk and eggs from animals fed on GMOs are also excluded from traceability;

— the Proposal does not cover traceability of non-food GMO derivatives, although several GM plants are intended for non-food uses such as oilseed rape (fuel), cotton (fibre) and tobacco;

— traceability is dependent on the assignment of unique identifying codes which have not even been developed yet;

— exemptions from the Regulation are made for the "adventitious" or "technically unavoidable" presence of GMOs not authorised for market release under the Deliberate Release Directive up to a threshold of 1 per cent (The exemptions are made by reference in this Proposal to the parallel GM Food/Feed Proposal, Article 42 of which foresees the amendment of Directive 2001/18/EC).

13 February 2002

Examination of Witnesses

MR PETER RILEY, Senior Real Food Campaigner and MR ADRIAN BEBB, Real Food Campaigner, Friends of the Earth, examined.

Chairman

94. Gentlemen, could I welcome you here. I am sorry, I gather you had to run here because of the train difficulties. I realise that you are hot but I hope not too bothered. Could I first of all draw attention to the declaration of interest which is on the table which explains the interests of different Members of the Committee. Could I say that we have until 11.15. We may not get through all of the questions which we indicated we might wish to ask, and we will quite certainly wish to add or subtract from that list, so please do not think that there is anything predictable about what is likely to happen. Would you like to introduce yourselves and say anything by way of introduction?

(*Mr Bebb*) Sorry for the almost lateness because of the trains. My name is Adrian Bebb, I am the GM Campaigner for Friends of the Earth. We have been running a campaign on GM foods for five years. That campaign started through pressure from our local groups but also from the general public who wanted us to take a bigger look at GM crops and foods. This was at about the time when the first GM foods had just been put into the food chain without any labelling, without any public consent, so there were lots of irate members of the public at the time who asked us to get involved and have a closer look at GM foods and crops.

(*Mr Riley*) My name is Pete Riley, I am the Senior Campaigner for Friends of the Earth's Real Food and Farming Campaign which includes our GM work.

Chairman *contd.*]

95. Thank you very much. Shall we go straight into questions unless you would like to make a statement to begin with? I think you are familiar with the nature of our inquiry looking at these two proposals from the Commission. I would like to start the questioning by asking if you would give us the basis on which you are running the campaign in Friends of the Earth. Is it that Friends of the Earth object to the technology on the grounds of safety or on the grounds of lack of choice? Do you believe, in so far as you wish to see food containing genetically modified ingredients and food derived from genetically modified processes labelled, that this should extend to all systems of production or is it just to GM food that you wish to see this displayed?

(*Mr Bebb*) I will make a start and then my colleague will probably interrupt me and correct me if I am wrong. Friends of the Earth, as I said, has been running this campaign for five years. Originally we ran the campaign because of public pressure that was asking us to have a closer look. It was quite clear that there was a huge choice issue for consumers, that they had not been informed that they were suddenly eating GM foods and that new proteins had been put into the human diet without their consent or with very little public knowledge. Friends of the Earth took a closer look and it became quite clear that no-one had asked any long-term questions about the environmental safety. We questioned English Nature, the Government's advisers on environmental and wildlife aspects, and we found out to our dismay that they had called for a moratorium, behind the scenes, on the commercial growing of GM crops. We also looked at the health aspects and we looked at what research had been done into health impacts and saw that Government had only just started commissioning research into the long-term impacts of eating GM foods. It was quite clear that even though the technology was rushing ahead and products were being put into the marketplace the basic research and some of the basic questions into long-term impacts had not been addressed and had only just been asked. Friends of the Earth has been campaigning for the last five years for a moratorium on the commercial development and selling of GM foods and crops until some of the long-term impact questions can be fully assessed. It is quite clear that the public has gone through quite a few food crises throughout Europe over the last ten years and it is becoming increasingly clear that the public are starting to ask more about how their food is produced. The GM issue is a perfect example where they have made it very clear that they want to know if they are eating GM foods and they have asked for a lot more information. Although we are specifically campaigning on GM here, it is a rising issue with the public; they want to know how their food is produced and they certainly indicate that they want their food to come from a greener form of agriculture.

(*Mr Riley*) The only other thing I would add is that it was also very clear when we started the campaign that animal feed had been excluded from the thinking at that point. We are pleased animal feed is now firmly on the agenda and we are going to get some legislation on it so there is clear information for farmers. It is pretty clear that farmers need information about what is in the animal feed so that they too can make informed judgments and that traceability down the animal feed chain is going to be available to the retailers and food manufacturers who are increasingly demanding it. I do not think it is only the customers who are demanding it, the demand for traceability is coming also from the food industry as well.

96. Mr Bebb referred to the ingestion of food but of course we are dealing here with the risk assessment on two levels, one the environment and the other human health. If we stick for a moment to the ingestion of food, we are meeting representatives of the American Embassy later this morning and I have no doubt that they will remind us that the Americans have been consuming genetically modified food for some years now and this is, therefore, by any accounts quite a large experiment, if that is what it is. Is there any evidence here to be drawn from the health risks of eating genetically modified food in the light of the American experience?

(*Mr Bebb*) I think the word "experiment" is the right word. There is very little research, from what we can see, looking into the overall health impacts. Also the way the Americans have introduced the food makes it almost impossible to detect any problems. For instance, there are over 40 GM foods now in American diets and you have to ask the question, if one of those foods caused allergens how would you track that down to a specific GM food? The whole issue of post-release monitoring is that it is very difficult to pinpoint any problems in society down to a particular GM food. This is why Friends of the Earth is campaigning to make sure that the actual regulations in the first place are much tighter and the testing is much tighter, because once the food is put out into the general marketplace it is very, very difficult to detect any ill effects because where do you start to look in the first place? The biggest example of things that have gone wrong in the States has probably come about because of the crop called Starlink which was a maize that was only approved for animal feed. Two years ago Friends of the Earth tested some corn products in America, I think it was some taco shells or something similar, and found that they contained Starlink even though that had not been approved for human consumption. It had not been approved for human consumption because there was a general concern that it could cause allergies, there certainly have been cases of allergies from it. It is difficult to say whether or not it is because people have seen it in the news so they had an allergic reaction and said, "yes, that is definitely the taco shells I have eaten", but there was a product recall of over 300 different products in the States. It has cost Aventis millions of dollars to try and rectify the problem and even they have admitted that it is very difficult to get it out of the food chain now even though it was never approved for human consumption in the first place. That shows a problem when you have not got traceability in place as to how you rectify the problem when it does go wrong. This is one of the reasons why we need proper traceability in Europe, so if something does go wrong, if a crop got in that was not approved for food use, did get into the food chain, we need to set up some sort of system

Chairman *contd.*]

to try and trace that back and get it out of the food chain as soon as possible.

Lord Crickhowell

97. Could I come in on this one? Clearly the Americans say, and surely you would agree, no food of any kind is safe, whether it is GM or not; a great many foods may have reactions and create allergies. Is it not remarkable that in a country where this experiment, as we call it, has been going on on a huge scale for a long time, in a country which is very litigious and very effective in tracing through the courts any consequences, there has not yet as far as I know been significant success in the courts in proving ill-effects of the genetic modifications to which we are referring?

(*Mr Riley*) We go back to the word "experiment". My idea of an experiment is that you have some control. You have a group of people to whom you give one treatment, a second group of people is given another treatment and possibly a third group of people are given a completely different treatment. That is not what is happening in America. Everybody is exposed to genetically modified food and, I might add, a whole new range of other additives and chemicals that have come on to the US market both in food manufacture and food growing, and also in chemical exposure through the home and through work. We are not dealing with a controlled experiment and if any new health effect emerged in America it would be virtually impossible to point that to a particular cause; it could be chemical, it could be related to GM, we do not know because we have not got a controlled experiment. I take a particularly moral viewpoint on that, that it is not ethical to carry out large-scale experiments on the entire population of a nation, which is what the Americans are doing.

98. Whether it is an experiment or not, there are very, very large numbers of people who will be affected by it for a very long time and in a way we have the opposite situation in Europe where there has been some pretty tight control. Have you any evidence that there have been effects in America which we have avoided in Europe because of controls?

(*Mr Riley*) I think the question pre-supposes that the Americans have got a system for looking at public health in a way that could identify potential health impacts of any new part of the diet. I am not sure that they have. If they have, then I would say that it would be very difficult for them to actually pinpoint a particular cause to a particular effect. We do have legal action taking place in the States at the moment regarding the lack of scrutiny of two crops. One is to the Food and Drug Administration (FDA) and one is to the Environmental Protection Agency (EPA). There is a challenge going on at the moment. There were warnings about the level of safety assessment that should be required for a new GM crop coming on to the market which were ignored by the FDA. As far as I know that is still before the judge so we will see whether the American courts agree that the American system is robust or not.

(*Mr Bebb*) If I could quickly add a tiny point to that. The National Academy of Sciences came out with a report just last week; they looked very closely at the approval of GM foods and crops in America and were quite scathing about the approvals process and how GM foods are given the go-ahead. I think the tide is turning in the States now academia is waking up and looking at it at a much closer level. I think it is also worth making the point that Friends of the Earth do not say that all GM foods are dangerous and we are all going to die if we eat them. What is clear is that this is a very new technology: we are introducing new proteins we have never eaten before into the diet, we have got to make sure that the regulations and the testing carried out is to the highest standard so that nothing goes wrong, and if a GM food comes along which does have problems for the human diet, or for that matter for the environment, then it is picked up by the regulations and by the testing that is carried out. We do not want to have a case where one of the foods goes wrong, it is out there, and it has got through the safety system that we have in place. I think that is what this legislation is a part of—increasing the traceability so we can make it fully accountable. This is a new technology, this is a new science, it is not going to go away, the stakes are very high and we have got to make sure if something did go wrong we have got it right.

Lord Fyfe of Fairfield

99. Good morning, gentlemen. Following on from the Chairman's questions and remarks, would you maintain in your organisation that each product should be viewed on the basis of its individual merits and risks or that generic legislation should be applied on a uniform basis?

(*Mr Riley*) I think the first thing we want to see is to make sure that the system we have in place is actually robust enough to pick up unexpected impacts of genetic modification of food and crops. Once we have got that system in place, and we do not believe we have got that system either in the States or in Europe or anywhere else on the planet, we will then be happy that that system be applied to each individual food coming into the market and it would be judged on its individual merits. Having said that, because some people take an ethical stance about genetic engineering, they regard it as unethical completely to move genes between species, and a lot of other people take a view about other aspects of GM which means that they would want to avoid it in their diet, I think we should respect that wish. That is one of the reasons why traceability and labelling is an essential part of this process in addition to the ability to trace anything back if anything goes wrong in the system.

Lord Dubs: May I follow on from that because I just wonder how you believe that the proposed legislation should be enforced in the absence of accepted scientific tests to distinguish between identical products? In other words, if there are not scientific tests to draw that distinction between GM and non-GM containing products, how can you enforce the legislation?

Chairman

100. You were talking about new proteins and I think Lord Dubs is drawing attention to the fact that they may not be new proteins; there may be nothing that has changed.

(*Mr Bebb*) My colleague just said that people have ethical viewpoints on whether or not they actually approve of that method of production. I think the whole purpose of this legislation is to have full traceability from the farm to the fork, which is the expression that is being used. Currently we do have limited labelling legislation but it is only for products which have DNA protein in the final product. What is clear is that consumers across Europe, not just in this country, want more than that and this is the idea of having traceability. That is what this legislation is all about, that we do have a paper trail so that we can track foods all the way down the food chain. We have that already, we have set up systems for beef, we have it for organic produce, we have it for Fair Trade foods, we have it for kosher meat. Traceability is not new, the food industry uses traceability all the time and even though the DNA analysis or the chemical analysis of the final product may be the same, it is tracing it down to the means of production. That is what this legislation is about, to ensure that the consumer can have choice if they want to avoid GM crops or if they want to eat GM crops for that matter.

Lord Dubs

101. I understand that, but the point is we do not always have scientific tests to identify GM elements and if you have not got that how can you achieve the choice that you are talking about?

(*Mr Bebb*) At certain levels of the process you can do tests. When it is still viable, when it has not been heavily processed, you can do the tests and from there what this legislation sets out is some form of paper trail.

102. I understand that, but what if it is not possible? Were it possible everything you say follows and that is fine but I am putting it to you that it is not always possible scientifically to do that, and what then?

(*Mr Riley*) I think our viewpoint would be if the biotech company brought the food on to the market without an analytical method available which hit the thresholds that were required by legislation then it should not get approval. It is a bit like a pesticide being brought on to the market and approved without any means of it being analysed as a residue in food, we would find that equally unacceptable.

Lord Crickhowell

103. In your evidence you say that by setting a threshold of one per cent for the technically unavoidable presence of GMOs the Commission is opening a huge gate, of which you disapprove, and you then rather helpfully suggest some questions that we should put to the American Embassy. You elaborate on that point and you challenge the US view that a one per cent threshold cannot be reliably tested. You adduce as a piece of evidence some recent work from the UK Food Standards Agency on one particular product, bread, and you argue that it is

possible to test down to very low thresholds. However, the evidence that we are getting from a number of other distinguished sources does not agree with your view. I have got in front of me the evidence from the BBSRC, the Biotechnology and Biological Sciences Research Council, for example, which entirely rejects the view that you can get down to very low levels. It points to the nature of the spread, unintentional perhaps, of GM material from one crop to another, about the way in which the whole products are traded around the world, and it simply declares that for practical considerations you cannot get reliable systems below one per cent. We have had similar evidence from the Royal Society of Edinburgh which elaborates in some detail on this. Why do you think that all these other people, who are very clear that you cannot get absolute certainty and that you have got, therefore, for practical reasons to accept the one per cent, are all wrong and you are right? You seem to be out on a limb on this one.

(*Mr Bebb*) The testing for the presence of GM material is as new as the technology itself and we will see improvements, we have seen improvements just over the last couple of years. The Food Standards Agency has just carried out research into the testing; they tested bread products and they made it very clear in their press statement that it showed very clearly that one per cent was working and they could detect very small quantities of GM material. That is what the Food Standards Agency is saying.

104. You are picking on one particular product and there is a wide variety of products—there are oils and other products, where all the evidence is that you cannot trace in this way. Are you wise to base your case on one particular test for one particular product when all the evidence for other products is that you cannot reliably test?

(*Mr Riley*) The testing depends on there being modified DNA present in the food. The point we made earlier is . . .

105. But you cannot trace scientifically in some cases.

(*Mr Bebb*) You can trace paper.

(*Mr Riley*) If you go to the processed foods, such as oils, where there may be no traceable DNA at that point you ask the company to provide evidence on paper back to a point in the chain where they can show that their analysis shows that their raw material did not contain modified DNA. That is what the large retailers operating in this country at the moment do and they tell us that they are quite happy that they are going down to 0.1 per cent and they are not finding any traces of DNA where they are measuring it at the appropriate point in the chain. Beyond that you have to rely on paper chains and we need to be very tight on that regulation.

106. Do you believe that in an increasingly complex world in which large quantities of materials in the majority of products around the world are now genetically modified in some way and as trade develops around the world in all its complexities you can actually maintain an accurate paper chain and a reliable paper chain?

(*Mr Riley*) I think increasingly companies will be looking to go to particular farmers to supply them with what they want because of the uncertainty that the commodity market provides. This is exactly what

Lord Crickhowell *contd.*]

companies like Tesco are doing, they have gone down to the farm level in Brazil to get their soya at the moment. If farmers see that there is a business to be made by providing European consumers with what they want and not with what they do not want, they are shrewd businessmen and they will provide the companies with the assurances that the companies are looking for.

Countess of Mar

107. You have made some very firm assertions about the need for legislation to be enforced. Have you made an estimate of the costs of such enforcement? Who do you believe should pay? Should it be the ultimate consumer or the Government or the companies in the food chain from the farmer to the retailer by reducing their profits? I must declare an interest as a farmer and a cheese maker.

(*Mr Bebb*) I think if there are costs you have got to force the costs up the food chain to the people who are causing the problem in the first place and that is the biotech companies and the farmers who grow the GM crops. We were told four or five years ago when soya first came in that there was no way we could have consumer choice, it is a commodity crop, and the supermarkets were saying it would cost an awful lot if they segregated the GM soya from the non-GM soya. Of course, the public made their view very clear and the supermarkets now ensure that the soya they take is segregated without additional cost to the consumer. In that particular case it was solved by the supermarket. I think it is outrageous that the Food Standards Agency have proposed a GM free label (and we have got a letter from Sir John Krebs) which would force up the cost of food and make it very specialised. We then have got serious questions about low income families. Are we saying that they are not going to have any choice about whether they eat GM foods or not? I do not believe it is going to get through the other Member States, I think they will shoot it down straight away because they will see the downside of it. It seems the Government's position on this is that it should be made more expensive to the consumer and Friends of the Earth does not support that: we believe it should be forced up through the food chain to the biotech companies and the GM farmers in America who are producing these foods and causing the problems in the first place.

Chairman

108. Are you familiar with the American system of supplying identity preserved lines, IP lines? What is your conclusion as to whether this is effective in the traceability of these lines from the farm straight through to the consumer and what is the implication for the consumer?

(*Mr Riley*) From what we can gather from the people who are using this system, it is reliable at the moment. We have concerns at farm level concerning cross-pollination: whether the US authorities are prepared to look at what separation distances are needed to enable people serving the non-GM market to achieve the levels of purity that companies in

Europe would require. From the evidence we have before us from the retailers, who we talk to quite a lot, they seem to be quite happy with the way things are working at the moment. Whether they are going to be able to keep that up, given that the American authorities appear to be completely intransigent on this issue, is another matter of course.

(*Mr Bebb*) I think one of our big concerns about this legislation is that it allows for a one per cent contamination of varieties that are unapproved and also the general one per cent threshold. The words that are used are "technically unavoidable". I think the question that it would be good to ask the US Government later on today, perhaps, is: are the non-existent separation distances in America technically avoidable or technically unavoidable? I would say that was avoidable. If American farmers made more effort and if the American system put in place separation distances to keep the crops apart then you might see the one per cent threshold come down because of that. That is a question that needs to be asked of the Americans.

Lord Crickhowell

109. It is not only that particular form of contamination that arises. It is extremely difficult if you have got shipping and large bulk transit systems and so on to get absolute purity. Unless you are then going to have complete separation of bulk crops all the way down the chain on international markets you are bound to get some contamination. This is what some of the evidence we have suggests. If you try to break down that system completely are you not going to add substantially to the costs, even if you can achieve it?

(*Mr Bebb*) This is the idea of identity preserved food chains.

110. I am asking about the practicality.

(*Mr Bebb*) There are areas where you could have contamination all the way down the line, that is for sure, and that is why it is impractical to say that you have a complete zero per cent threshold at the moment. We need full traceability, which this legislation starts pointing toward, where we can have proper identified preserved food chains all the way down the line. At the end of the day it comes down to how the crops are grown in the field and cross-pollination is a big issue. We had the incident here two years ago with Advanta when they sold contaminated seeds unknowingly to UK farmers and also other farmers in Europe and they were saying that contamination took place over four kilometres and this seems to point to an inadequacy in the technology. If they have produced technology which they cannot control, and they cannot allow to grow without contaminating neighbouring crops, then I think serious questions need to be asked about it and they should be told to go back to the laboratories and come back with something that they can control.

(*Mr Riley*) I think what the biotech industry has done is that they have created more commodity crops and that is how we have to view GM soya, as a commodity crop on its own and non-GM soya as a commodity crop. The fact that that does not fit with the existing trading system is their problem and they

Lord Crickhowell *contd.*]

have to come up with a way of providing people with what they want. It seems to me that the Americans are stuck in some sort of 1930s ghetto when they think that people will take what they provide; but that is not going to happen any more—people want what they want, and the Americans have to remember that trade is about providing people with what they want, not with what they don't want. It is the Americans who have got to change on this and not the Europeans, because the Europeans, in a sense, are well ahead of the Americans in the whole approach to this issue of traceability of food. Because of our history in the last 20 years we are very, very conscious of it.

Chairman

111. Let me bring you back to the identity preserved lines. Accepting for the moment Mr Bebb's point that we must ensure that contamination rules are internationally acceptable in terms of isolation, the US farmers favour the approach of identity preserved lines; they clearly are more expensive because there is the cost of maintaining integrity throughout the scheme, but nevertheless this does provide exactly what you are suggesting, Mr Riley, that the consumers should be entitled to have identification throughout. Is this a system that commends itself to you?

(*Mr Riley*) I think it also needs to apply to GM crops, they need to be traceable because of the problems we outlined earlier and, of course, traceable for other reasons as well, for instance, micotoxins and pesticide residues. People need to be able to say "where does that crop come from?" I think we are moving towards more of a contract-based system where people are buying whole crops from farmers rather than the old-fashioned commodity system as that is the way the European market is going.

112. So you are really suggesting, therefore, that we impose on consumers a cost whether it is GM or not?

(*Mr Riley*) That would make it fairer but once we have got the systems up and running the evidence from what we have at the moment is that there does not appear to be an excessive additional cost on consumers from IP systems.

Lord Walpole

113. Do you accept that in this particular area consumer surveys are not always accurate predictors of consumers' actual actions?

(*Mr Bebb*) I think you can say that in some cases but I think as well that the GM issue is the complete reversal. When we saw that GM was a very big issue in the public domain a couple of years ago the public made it very clear with their actions, they stopped buying GM foods and that was why they were taken off the marketplace. We saw the sales of the Flav'r Sav'r tomato, tomato purée and products like Unilever's Beanfeast plummet overnight. Shoppers actually voted with their purses and perhaps that does buck the trend of what people say and what people do. In this case it seems that they have made

their views very clear. I do not know if you are aware of the Eurobarometer poll that was carried out just before Christmas. This is an annual poll carried out across all Member States that looks at science and people's acceptance of science. Quite clearly consumers and the public come to accept scientific developments when they get to know more about the issues. The one issue that bucks that trend is GM foods. The more people knew about it the more concerned they got about it and the more they wanted to have a say. That resulted in 95 per cent of people who said they wanted a choice whether or not to eat GM foods. Again, this comes back as to why this legislation is needed.

Baroness Miller of Chilthorne Domer

114. Not all consumers presumably have the same concern about it. It seems to me to fall into two categories, one is about their own health and the other is about the health of the environment in this country, so they might have those two different reasons. Would you agree with that?

(*Mr Bebb*) Yes, exactly. There is a whole wide range of views. You have got views from religious people as well who think it is playing with God, to people who think it is an unsustainable form of farming and do not want to support it. All the way down the line there are different views and I think that is why we need a system that respects those views. We think this legislation is certainly a step in that direction.

115. Can I just check a matter of detail? In the answer to our first question you said that originally English Nature had behind the scenes called for a moratorium.

(*Mr Riley*) Yes.

116. Why did it do so behind the scenes and not in public, and how do you know?

(*Mr Riley*) I think you should ask them that question. The information came out because we wrote them a letter and asked them their opinion and they replied to that letter and we published the letter. That was how the information came out. Obviously they had held that view for some considerable time and presumably they felt by talking privately to civil servants that they would be able to move the situation along and get proper research in that respect.

Chairman

117. Just for the record, it is in the public record that English Nature have asked for a moratorium, there is no secrecy about it.

(*Mr Riley*) No.

118. You may have anticipated them going public but they went public some years ago.

(*Mr Riley*) They did indeed. The first instance of their going public was when we wrote to ask what their opinion was.

119. I did not want the Committee to feel that there was still some air of secrecy about this.

(*Mr Riley*) Absolutely not.

Lord Christopher

120. Do you distinguish at all between one GM product and another depending on the purpose of the modification, insect resistance, herbicide resistance?

(*Mr Bebb*) Yes. Each one needs a different risk assessment as there are different potential impacts, both environmental and health, so they have got to be looked at individually. At the same time we have got to ensure that we have got this umbrella legislation which provides choice if that food is allowed to go into the food chain. We do agree that there is a difference between different GM products and they need different risk assessments. We have been working for the last five years at a European level to improve legislation for those risk assessments.

121. Some people have been arguing that genetic modification has been going on for generations.

(*Mr Riley*) It is certainly the view of the Americans and their evidence to the World Trade Organisation (WTO) on this particular legislation is that they seem to indicate that all foods are genetically modified and it is all a matter of definition. It is quite clear that what we have been able to do over the last few years is very different from what we have been able to do over the plant sciences and plant breeding over the last few thousand years, where we can extract DNA from one species and insert it into another one. This is where the public wants to know more and they want to have a choice because they are not happy as to whether or not that process will have long-term impacts.

122. How would you suggest that one attempts to distinguish between all of this? If the ancient hybrids, as it were, are acceptable and have been eaten for many years and so on, is it going to be true in your opinion that once everybody gives the green light to GM that everything that happens in the GM field is perfectly safe?

(*Mr Bebb*) No. At the moment we have very simple forms and very crude forms of genetic engineering used in herbicide resistant and insect resistant crops. The next generation which the industry is developing will have more than one modification and I think this raises even bigger headaches for the food authorities who have got to try and find a way of testing for long-term safety. There was a recent paper from the Royal Society on this and they raised the issue that the next generation of crops are going to cause even more problems in trying to work out the long-term safety of it. At the moment we have got this proposal called substantial equivalence which the Royal Society has now come out quite firmly against. This legislation is in two parts, the GM foods and animal feeds and the labelling, but they have now dropped the requirement to use substantial equivalence as a safety threshold, which is something that Friends of the Earth has been calling for some time because it has been a very dubious approvals process.

Countess of Mar

123. Going on from what you have just said about double changes, if people are testing they have got to know what they are testing for, have they not? They cannot just test and find it, they have got to have some idea of what they are looking for before they start testing?

(*Mr Bebb*) Yes.

124. Is this not an enormous hurdle that has got to be leapt over before we can be absolutely sure about the safety?

(*Mr Riley*) I think this is one of the fundamental problems with the substantial equivalence approach, that substantial equivalence assumes similarity whereas if you are really going to be diligent about safety you have to assume the unexpected. What we have not got at the moment is any system for screening these new foods for unexpected consequences of genetic transformations. There are plenty of examples where the unexpected has occurred in the laboratory. We do not think that the current system of food safety assessment is robust enough to actually prevent one of those getting on to the market. If it did then the whole industry would be in serious trouble. If it was in America we simply would not know which of the 40, 50, 60 GM foods on the market had caused the problem, so the Administration would have to effectively withdraw the lot and everything would have to go through that proper safety assessment before we could be sure which one had caused the problem. In a sense it is in the interest of the biotech industry to get this right and we do not think they are anywhere near getting it right at the moment. We need to spend much more time thinking about it and less time trying to sell it to people.

125. What worries me is that we are altering proteins which are basic building blocks and although they may be there in tiny, tiny quantities the effects may be subtle and cumulative. We do not know what will be happening to the next generation. I am particularly worried about the young and children whose immune systems and central nervous systems are not properly developed.

(*Mr Bebb*) This was one of the issues raised by the Royal Society in their recent report. They questioned whether or not GM foods should be fed to young people and babies. They were particularly focusing on baby milk products and whether or not they would contain GM ingredients. That could make up a large proportion of a baby's diet, maybe 100 per cent of a baby's diet in the first few months. What would the implications of that be if you fed that to children? One of the crops we have looked at very closely is the GM maize, which is the first crop that the Government wants to commercialise in this country. The Government's advisory committee held a big public hearing into it last week and there were statistically significant differences between the GM line and the non-GM line. That had gone through all the approvals process, it had been checked by every committee in Europe and it still got through and no-one picked it up. We showed some of the research to independent scientists we had never met before, we asked them to look at it and they said within five minutes that it was obvious it was very poor research. This comes back to our statement saying we are not sure that the current system is good enough to weed out any GM products if they were deemed unhealthy or pose a health risk.

Baroness Maddock

126. I think that Friends of the Earth believe that possibly there is an additional health risk when people ingest high fructose corn syrup as a sweetening agent made from GM maize compared with conventional maize. Is this the sort of thing that you have just been referring to?

(*Mr Bebb*) Slightly, but I think it is a wider question. The public has made it very clear that they want choice on GM foods and GM ingredients. I think you have taken evidence from the National Consumer Council who did some quite extensive surveys just before Christmas which backed up the opinion that the consumers want to know all the way down the line where the ingredients come from. People do have a huge objection to the growing of GM crops *per se*. Talking about the fructose, that would be one part of the plant, the rest of the plant could be fed to cattle, it could be going into the food chain as sweetcorn or whatever, I do not know. The public have made it very clear that they want to have a choice on GM ingredients and whether or not they eat them and this is what this legislation is about and that is why we welcome it. We think it has got loopholes and we are not happy about issues like the one per cent contamination by unapproved varieties but at least we are starting to get towards a traceability system for GM foods which has got to be welcome.

127. My question was really is there an additional health risk and is that what you were talking about in answer to the previous question?

(*Mr Bebb*) In that particular example, which was one crop we have really looked at in detail, the jury is completely out. The science was done so badly any scientist we showed it to—and the Government even had their own expert witnesses at this hearing last week and they basically agreed—said you cannot tell from this research whether it has a negative effect or not. There was a chicken study where they fed the corn to chickens and twice as many chickens died which ate the GM corn but they said the research was done so badly you could not tell if it was the GM that caused the chickens to die or because the research was carried out so badly. The jury is out.

(*Mr Riley*) Can I pick up the question of the fructose? What I said in my answer to Lady Mar was that the food safety assessment does not look for the unpredictable. There is absolutely no reason why an unpredictable event as a result of GM could not transfer into a processed product and if you do not look for the unexpected in the raw material then you are not likely to find it. That is our fundamental problem with the whole system, that it assumes everything is hunky dory when it may not be. Because we are feeding this potentially to everybody on the planet, and every farm animal on the planet, so we think we have to be very, very careful before we launch into this in a big way. That is just a sensible, precautionary approach from our point of view.

Lord Dubs

128. Could I just ask about the position in developing countries compared with the Western World? Let me ask by way of an example. Farmers in countries such as China are now able to grow boll weevil resistant cotton without using organophosphates as insecticides. Obviously this has reduced the cases of severe poisoning for peasant workers in the cotton fields. Does your organisation consider it proper or moral for a country such as the UK or Western Europe that does not grow cotton to attempt to influence China to revert to what was previously a dangerous practice?

(*Mr Riley*) I should start by reminding you that Friends of the Earth has been campaigning about what we consider to be dangerous pesticides for about 25 years now, so this is not a new area to us. On GM cotton we need evidence that it is a sustainable system, that it will work and deliver what we want in terms of environmental impact and quality of the product. Equally, we do not regard the use of insecticides as a sustainable system, so we are comparing two unsustainable systems. We need to have a much broader look at available solutions to deal with these serious pest problems. In the end the Chinese will decide whether they want to go ahead and grow GM cotton or not and it will be based on their risk assessment of their environment and the risk to workers, and that is fine. Equally it would be equally fine for us to ask for them to tell us what methods of production they used in that particular type of farming so we could make informed choices as to whether we buy that particular cotton or not. The same applies to foods as well. I think in the end it will be the Chinese who decide whether they go ahead with it or not, and not us, and that is right and proper. That is why we want strong international agreements, such as the Biosafety Protocol, to enable individual nation states to bring in laws which they think are appropriate for their particular environments and societies.

(*Mr Bebb*) I think it is worth just adding on briefly that the Chinese have just brought out new legislation on the imports of GM crops and you might want to ask the Americans about that, they are not very happy about it, they are threatening it as a barrier to trade. Even the Chinese authorities are looking at GM safety and GM licensing in a lot more detail now and they have just brought out new legislation which I think comes into play pretty soon, I think in March.

Lord Palmer

129. To what extent do you believe that the UK should interfere with agronomic practices of a foreign country, especially if that country was prepared to accept any theoretical environmental hazard?

(*Mr Riley*) As I said in answer to Lord Dubs, it is up to the individual state to make decisions without any pressure from any country, including the US which I have to say is far more prominent in pressurising countries than the UK is at the moment or even the EU. It would be reasonable for us if we take the view that we want to know that the crop is traceable and the methods of production are quite transparent. That is the way the market in Europe is going and increasingly that is the way I think the global market will go because in some ways it is in the interests of farmers to go that way because they might get reasonable contracts from companies to supply at a reasonable price and that might reflect the

Lord Palmer *contd.*]

work and input that people put in a bit better rather than the uncertain prices they pick up on the commodity market.

Chairman: I am afraid that we have run out of time. In fact, we have exceeded our time. You have given us some very helpful answers. If there is anything further that you would have liked to amplify in your evidence do please write to us. You have already give us some helpful written evidence but if you wish to write, it is not too late. Thank you for joining us today.

Memorandum by the United States Embassy, London

The United States thanks the House of Lords European Union Committee, Sub-Committee D, for the opportunity to comment on the inquiry into the European Commission's proposed regulation, COM (2001) 425, *Genetically Modified Food and Feed,* which lays down a Community procedure for safety assessment and authorisation of biotech food and feed as well as comprehensive labelling requirements for these products, as notified to WTO members in G/TBT/N/EEC/6 and on proposed regulation, COM (2001)182, on traceability and labelling, which is closely related to COM (2001)425. The Sub-Committee's questions are italicised in the text below.

1. *Do these proposals adequately address the requirements of European consumers for regulation, traceability, and labelling of GM food and feed and of food and feed products derived from GMOs?*

The United States is not in a position to determine whether the proposals adequately address European consumer requirements, but is able to provide the following views on the proposals. The United States recognises the Commission's objective of protecting health, the environment and consumers, and preventing deceptive practices through the adoption of the Food and Feed regulation. Nevertheless, the proposals raise a number of questions as to the feasibility of their implementation and the actual attainment of those objectives. The proposed Food and Feed regulation fails to distinguish between considerations of health, safety and the environment on the one hand, and those of perceived consumer desires on the other. As a result, the United States is concerned that the design of the regulation may be flawed and certain burdens imposed on suppliers will be more trade restrictive than necessary to achieve the desired objective.

Among the stated "general objectives" of the proposed Food and Feed regulation is that of providing ". . . the basis for ensuring a high level of protection of human life and health, animal health and welfare, environment and consumers' interest in relation to genetically modified food and feed . . ." (Article 1). Considering that any biotech foods allowed on the market will have had to be demonstrated to be safe and the EU has not shown that bio-engineered foods are unsafe, how will mandatory labelling help the Commission achieve its objective as stated in Article 1? Specifically, it is not clear to the United States what risks the proposed labelling requirements are attempting to address.

The Food and Feed proposal indicates the objective of the "comprehensive" labelling requirements is to respond to an overwhelming need for consumers to make individual choices, thereby fostering increased public confidence and acceptance of products of biotechnology. If consumer choice is truly the objective of the proposal, the United States would argue that a more crucial element would be to give guidance as to what would constitute a food that has not been produced through biotechnology. Would it not be more informative and less trade disruptive to publish guidance or impose requirements that would assure that products labelled, "non-GMO" are in fact, non-biotech?

The US is concerned that the Traceability and Labelling proposal will continue to undermine the EU's efforts to establish a credible food safety regulatory regime. The proposal will weaken European consumer confidence in the safety of its food supply. The proposal does nothing to ensure food safety and it encourages fraudulent labelling claims by requiring labelling of biotech-derived processed products that have no detectable biotech content. This outcome is not in the country's interest of the EU or its Member States.

Without further description of the type of unforeseen effects anticipated, it is unclear how the proposed traceability and labelling measures would meet the stated objectives.

In the United States, products are assessed for safety before release on the market. The United States understands that under Directive 90/220 and 01/18, products are not allowed on the market unless they are determined to be as safe as conventional counterparts. However, unforeseen effects are not solely relegated to biotech products but are also possible for other products. The EU has acknowledged in a recent report (*A Review of Reports: EC-Sponsored Research of Genetically Modified Organisms*) released by DG Research that these biotech products are as safe or even safer than conventional products. It is accordingly unclear to the US why the EU would seek to impose additional traceability/monitoring requirements, and to do so only with regard to biotech products.

The United States would note that the term "genetically modified" applies to all breeding methods, and indeed, to all food crops. The United States continues to believe that the use of this term by the EU and Member States fosters the mistaken belief that only the techniques of modern biotechnology modify genes. The United States also believes that perpetuating such mistaken beliefs impedes public acceptance of bio-engineered foods and crops. The United States, therefore, recommends the use of a more accurate term to describe the products the EU wants to capture under the regulation.

The United States has also asked the Commission to clarify how the additional labelling requirements for undefined ethical and religious issues, contained in Article 14.2 of the proposal, will inform a consumer who may prefer to avoid a biotech derived product. Specifically, the United States would like to know why these issues are specific to foods produced through biotechnology and not to foods produced through other means? Is this information also required for conventional products? If not, why not? And finally, who determines what additional labelling requirements will be and on what basis?

2. *Do they make sensible distinctions between the requirements of European consumers for regulation, traceability and labelling of GM food and feed and of food and feed products derived from GMOs?*

Article 4.1 in the Food and Feed proposal establishes, among other things, a requirement that biotech foods "must not present a risk for human health or the environment". Article 17.1 requires that biotech feed "must not present a risk for animal health, human health or the environment." This level of assurance is wholly unobtainable for *any* food or feed product, regardless of the production method, as the absence of risk can never be proven. Virtually every food or feed carries some level of risk if not properly handled. What kind or degree of evidence does the EU envision would be necessary to demonstrate that this standard has been met? How does this relate to 2000/286's proposed food and feed safety standard, and/or existing standards established for food additives, or pesticide residues in food, and what is the basis for any difference?

Article 30 in the Food and Feed proposal advocates the establishment of a register of "authorised genetically modified foods and feeds." Could the text of the regulation, rather than the Explanatory Memorandum, please clarify whether, if an event is approved, all food and feed derivatives will automatically be included in the registry? Which DG will be responsible for maintaining the registry?

3. *How effective are the proposals likely to be in ensuring full traceability of GM material at all stages of the chain from producer to consumer?*

Imposing such traceability requirements without the means for testing the veracity of documentation can lead to fraudulent practices and fuel consumer distrust in the regulatory regime. How does the EU intend to detect fraudulent claims in documentation?

The proposed regulation on Food and Feed would expand mandatory labelling of biotech food and feed to require the labelling of all food and feed products according to the biotech content of each ingredient, whether or not those ingredients are detectable in the end product and even when test methods do not exist to confirm their presence. In these cases it will be impossible to verify, by testing, a claim that product ingredients are non-biotech. The United States is greatly concerned that this regulation will, therefore, invite fraud and a further weakening of consumer confidence in EU food safety delivery systems.

The traceability requirements may be problematic for developing countries, particularly for those importing from many sources for further processing and re-export to third countries. When will the EU provide importers with guidance on sampling and testing for bulk commodities so that they can determine the identity of the biotech events in products where this information is not available?

US experience shows that traceback systems for human health or food safety, and traceability systems for consumer information, lead to significantly different approaches and policy decisions. The traceback system used in the United States is part of a food safety system. The US traceback system was developed largely by the private sector to recall food in response to a public health or food safety concern. In the United States, lot numbers, batch codes and/or processing plant indicators appear on virtually all processed food packages to satisfy the various business needs of food producers and for traceback purposes. Such measures are also widespread in Europe. This less burdensome and less costly system has worked effectively for years and enjoys a high level of public confidence.

The proposed regulation on Food and Feed would impose labelling requirements on products that have already been approved for use and for which no specific handling, usage, safety, or compositional distinctions have been identified. The result of the foregoing could be a further erosion of consumer confidence in the EU's regulatory system, because the consumer is left without truly accurate information about the product. Furthermore, the United States does not believe that expanding mandatory traceability and labelling requirements to animal feed is justified nor will it enhance public health.

4. *Are the proposals likely to be enforceable in practice, particularly where no novel genetic material is contained in the food or feed?*

The United States believes that the proposal on Traceability and Labelling is not workable or enforceable, would be very expensive to implement, and would not achieve the stated objectives. The proposal is not workable or enforceable because it would require products (for food, feed, or processing) containing or consisting of biotech events to be accompanied by a listing of the biotech events that they may contain along with their unique codes. In the absence of expensive identity preservation systems, suppliers will be forced to list all biotech events approved by the EU. The difficulty and complexities in accurately identifying all of the biotechnology events that could possibly be in a shipment creates enormous liability and risk for the shipper/trader.

As more biotech events and products are approved and used worldwide, tracking these products through the distribution system and/or testing will become more complex, if not impossible. The result is added expense and liability risk for shipping products without any corresponding increase in consumer and environmental protection. Already, EU food processors have shifted away from foreign sources of food ingredients to meet the extremely low 1 per cent threshold for labelling. This is only possible because the approval process in the EU is blocked and planted acreage of biotech crops is minimal.

In the proposal on Food and Feed the US understands that operators will be required to demonstrate that they have taken appropriate steps to avoid the adventitious presence of biotech material. Given difficulties encountered with the implementation of similar documentation requirements in other circumstances in the EU (such as in the case of organic products), the United States is concerned about the potential for uneven application and enforcement of this requirement across Member States or even local governments. For example, in the case of organic products, the absence of a harmonised EU procedure for issuing import authorisations and the lack of EU-wide oversight of the approval and enforcement process has resulted in varying Member State procedures, policies, and approval rates causing a great deal of uncertainty and administrative burden on organic exporters and certifiers, thereby blocking trade.

5. *A threshold level of 1 per cent or lower for the accidental presence of GM material in food and feed has been proposed, below which there would be an exemption. Is a threshold of this level, common to both food and feed, appropriate?*

In the proposal on Traceability and Labelling articles 6.3(i) and 19.3(i) require the applicant to supply a method for sampling and detection of each event in foods and feeds. The United States is concerned that reliable methods for quantifying biotech material within the low levels established as tolerances by the EU are not yet available. Furthermore, detection methods and limits of detection vary depending on the method and degree of processing. Experience has shown that a 1 per cent threshold also cannot reliably be tested and consistently be met. In many cases, no trace of the event will be present in the final processed product. When the margin of error is so low, inconsistent test results will increase the level of uncertainty for shippers, thereby discouraging trade for some and increasing liability for others despite best efforts. To establish consumer confidence in any system, claims must be achievable and readily verifiable.

The United States posed the following questions to the Commission, which underscore the complexity of the issue: Please clarify the responsibilities of the Community Reference Laboratory (CRL) (Article 7.3 (f); Article 33 and Annex) and the national reference laboratories with regards to the testing for biotech events, data evaluation, and dispute settlement. How frequently will these laboratories test? Will they test only products originating within the Community as well as from third countries? Who will oversee the activities of these laboratories and ensure that their tests are carried out in a uniform and timely manner? What legal standing do tests run in one Member State have in other Member States? What will be the role of the CRL in dispute settlement between Member States? What will be the role of the Commission? What will be the impact, if any, of testing results that may be provided from non-EC or Member State sources?

6. *Is the role proposed for (a) the European Food Authority and its scientific committees and (b) Member States in the authorisation process for GM food and feed appropriate?*

(a) The United States applauds the creation of the European Food Authority and its involvement in the approval process. However, we note its limited role. Decisions will still be made through a political process. How will the EU ensure that the authorisation is based on science and not politics, given that the Member States will vote on the approvals by qualified majority and neither they, nor the Commission, which is responsible for drafting the proposed decision on authorisation, are bound by the opinion of the EFA?

The proposed regulation on Food and Feed foresees that a new European Food Authority (EFA) will be required to undertake scientific risk assessments for both bio-engineered foods and feed, yet final approval decisions will be taken by Member States in committee, rather than by the EFA itself, whose opinion appears designed to be limited to scientific and technical considerations. The process allows the Commission to take into account unspecified "other legitimate factors" and to propose a decision regarding approval inconsistent with the outcome of the risk assessment and other safety and technical information already considered under the responsibility of the European Food Authority. This decision-making structure leaves substantial room for political interference of the type that has led to the current moratorium on agricultural biotech product approvals. In addition, the legislation sets a standard of "no risk" as the basis for regulatory decision-making, which could ultimately block the authorisation process since it is impossible to guarantee "no risk" for any product, biotech or conventional.

The EFA may ask a "food assessment body" [Article 7.3 (d)] or "feed assessment body" [Article 20.3 (d)] in a Member State to do a safety assessment, or a "competent authority" to carry out an environmental risk assessment. What criteria would be used by the EFA to determine if safety and/or environmental risk assessments were required beyond the initial information provided by the applicant? Could the EU provide more guidance as to the role that these bodies will play in individual regulatory decisions?

(b) While the introduction of a new European Food Authority into the process could be a helpful step toward improving the predictability of the authorisation process, the new Food and Feed proposal fails to address the core problem facing the European Union in biotechnology—individual Member States will continue to be able to hold the approval process hostage to political concerns with complete disregard for science and sound regulatory decision-making. Furthermore, the United States remains concerned that individual Member States will continue to flout EU regulations by maintaining their own restrictions on biotech products.

Article 44 in the Food and Feed proposal allows each Member State to establish rules for penalties on infringement. In the absence of available, accessible and standardised testing methodology, the United States is concerned that the Member States, which will be responsible for enforcing the legislation, will not be able to do so consistently, raising uncertainty for operators throughout the chain.

Under the Food and Feed regulation, the Commission needs to clarify how it will ensure that the risk management decisions of the individual Member States are consistent and transparent? Will the regulation strengthen the Commission's ability to enforce EU regulations currently being flouted by several Member States?

7. Are the proposals likely to be compatible with the requirements of the Cartagena Protocol on Biosafety and with other international commitments, including OECD programmes?

Work is still ongoing within the ICCP, the Intergovernmental Committee on the Cartagena Protocol, on the procedures and processes that will need to be in place before the Biosafety Protocol enters into force. It is unclear at this time how closely the new EU proposals on traceability and labelling will align with the detailed implementation provisions of the Protocol.

8. Are the proposals compatible with obligations towards non-Member States seeking to export food and feed to the EU?

As the leading developer and producer of agricultural biotech products, the United States has significant interest in how the Traceability and Labelling proposal will affect US suppliers. The United States would also note the potential burdens imposed by the new requirements would be substantial for suppliers in developing countries as well. This is particularly troublesome given that it does not appear that some of these new requirements are addressing identified risks or hazards. The burdensome documentation and labelling requirements leave room for rampant fraud without affordable, accessible testing for implementation or enforcement, and increase issues of liability for all operators on the marketing chain. The United States urges the EU to assess the feasibility of implementing the proposed Traceability and Labelling regulation, to identify and evaluate less trade distorting alternatives to achieve its objectives, and to analyse and evaluate the regulatory impact.

9. Should the present EU-wide moratorium on approving GM food and crop product applications be maintained until the issues concerning traceability and labelling of GMOs have been resolved?

The United States believes that the moratorium on biotech crop product applications should be lifted and approvals restarted. It is noteworthy that Commission members have said that the moratorium is illegal.

10. What other aspects of the proposals require further consideration before the UK Government can sign up to them?

Given the stated objective of the proposed food and feed regulation, it would be our understanding that the proposed regulation is therefore, in whole or in part, a measure defined as a sanitary or phytosanitary measure under the WTO, ie, one applied, among other things, "to protect human or animal life or health within the territory of the Member from risks arising from additives, contaminants, toxins or disease-causing organisms in foods, beverages or feedstuffs." While the United States welcomes the notification to WTO members under the TBT Agreement, we question why a parallel notification was not also made to WTO members under the SPS Agreement. The United States has encouraged the Commission to also evaluate the proposed regulation in light of the disciplines of the SPS Agreement. We have asked the Commission to explain its rationale for not notifying the proposed regulations to the SPS Committee or otherwise to provide a notification to that Committee.

The United States urges Her Majesty's Government to encourage the Commission to: (1) assess the feasibility of implementing the proposed regulation reliably and accurately; (2) to identify and evaluate less trade restrictive alternatives to achieving its objectives; and (3) to analyse and evaluate the regulatory impact.

15 February 2002

Examination of Witnesses

MR PETER KURZ, Minister-Counsellor for Agricultural Affairs, MRS DEANNA AYALA, Agricultural Attaché, and MS ALYCE TIDBALL, Environment, Science and Technology Officer, United States Embassy, London, examined.

Chairman

130. Ladies and gentlemen, thank you very much for joining us today. We are very pleased that we are going to benefit from evidence from the United States as major producers of genetically modified food. We are well aware of the interest you have in the proposed EU legislation. Mr Kurz, would you like to introduce yourself and your colleagues by way of preamble? I should incidentally report that on the table there is a declaration of the interests of Members of this Committee.

(*Mr Kurz*) Thank you. I am Peter Kurz, I am the Minister-Counsellor for Agricultural Affairs, US Embassy, London. This is Mrs Deanna Ayala who is Agricultural Attaché. This is Alyce Tidball who is the Science and Technology Counsellor at the US Embassy.

131. Thank you very much. Could I invite you briefly to outline the United States Government's current position on the EC proposals for traceability and labelling of GM food and feed?

(*Mr Kurz*) Thank you very much, I would like to do that. In our opinion these proposals raise a number of questions as to the feasibility of their implementation and the actual attainment of their stated objectives. The proposed Food and Feed Regulation, for example, fails to distinguish between considerations of health, safety and the environment on the one hand, and those of perceived consumer desires on the other. As a result we are concerned that the design of the regulation may be flawed and that certain burdens imposed on suppliers will be more trade restrictive than necessary to achieve the desired objective. To be specific, among the stated general objectives of the proposed Food and Feed Regulation is the objective of providing "the basis for the assurance of a high level of protection of human life and health, animal health and welfare, environment and consumers' interest in relation to genetically modified food and feed". Considering that any biotech foods allowed on to the market will have had to be demonstrated to be safe in any case, and that the EU has not shown that bioengineered foods are unsafe, how will mandatory labelling help the Commission to achieve its objective as stated in Chapter 1, Article 1? Frankly, it is not clear to us what risks the proposed labelling requirements are attempting to address. The food and feed proposal indicates that one objective of the comprehensive labelling requirements is to provide consumers with a real choice, as stated in the introduction, thereby fostering increased public confidence and acceptance of products of biotechnology. If consumer choice is truly the objective of the proposal, how will this regulation increase consumer choice, given that even under less stringent EU labelling regulations, processors and retailers are re-formulating rather than labelling due to perceived concerns about the customer reaction and market share? The United States would argue that it is equally important to give guidance as to what would constitute a food that has *not* been produced through biotechnology. Would it not be more informative and less trade disruptive to publish guidance or impose requirements that would assure that products labelled non-GMO are indeed non-biotech? In fact, we are concerned that the labelling and traceability proposal will serve to undermine EU efforts to establish a credible food safety regulatory regime. The proposal will potentially weaken European consumer confidence in the safety of its food supply. It does nothing to assure food safety. Indeed, the proposal encourages fraudulent labelling claims by requiring labelling of biotech derived processed products that have no detectable biotech content. This outcome is not in the interest of the EU or its Member States. The traceability and labelling proposal refers to a "safety net" which traceability would provide "at all stages of the placing on the market" for GMOs and products produced from GMOs "should any unforeseen adverse effects be established." US experience shows that trace back systems for human health or food safety and traceability systems for consumer information, lead to significantly different approaches in policy decisions and are less burdensome and less costly systems that have worked effectively for years. The trace back system used in the United States is part of our food safety system. The US trace back system was developed largely by the private sector to recall food in response to a public health or food safety concern. In the United States lot numbers, batch codes, or processing plant indicators appear on virtually all processed food packages to satisfy the various business needs of food producers and for trace back purposes. In the United States biotech products are assessed for safety before release on the market. We understand that under Directive 92/20, and its revised version 2001/18, biotech products are also not allowed on to the market in the European Union unless they have been determined to be as safe as

Chairman *contd.*]

conventional counterparts. However, unforeseen effects are not solely relegated to biotech products but are also possible for other products. The EU itself has acknowledged in a recent report released by DG Research that these biotech products are as safe as, or even safer than, conventional products. It is accordingly unclear to the United States why the EU would seek to impose additional traceability and monitoring requirements and to do so only with regard to biotech products. Here, if you do not mind, I would just like to note that the term genetically modified or GMO does apply to all breeding methods and, indeed, to all food crops. We continue to believe that the use of this term by the EU and Member States fosters the mistaken belief that only the techniques of modern biotechnology modify genes. We also believe that perpetuating such mistaken beliefs impedes public acceptance of bioengineered foods and crops. We would recommend, therefore, the use of a more accurate term to describe the products the EU wants to capture under the regulation, such as "produced with biotechnology" or simply "biotech".

132. That would include cider and cheese, that is produced with biotechnology?

(*Mr Kurz*) Yes, that is correct. I say this by way of explaining why the US use that term as opposed to GMOs. Finally, we have also asked the Commission to clarify how the additional labelling requirements for undefined "ethical or religious concerns", which are contained in Article 14.2 of the proposal, will inform a consumer who may prefer to avoid a biotech derived product. Specifically, the United States would like to know why these issues are specific to foods produced through biotechnology and not to foods produced through other means. Is this information also required for conventional products, and if not why not? Finally, who determines what additional labelling requirements will be and on what basis?

133. Thank you very much. I interrupted you just to ask you why you were referring to biotechnology as opposed to GM, and I understand why you do not like the term "genetic modification", but perhaps I should have used the example of bread. If you are using yeast to make a product, that is biotechnology, it is a living organism being used in a technology. I think really what you are saying, therefore, is a product which embraces new technology, which can be genetic modification, can be using a process of genetic engineering. Is this what you mean rather than just biotechnology?

(*Mr Kurz*) Yes, I would say so.

134. I really do not think you are asking us all to put on a loaf of bread that this is using biotechnology, are you?

(*Mr Kurz*) Well, biotech is the preferred term that we use in relation to agriculture.

Chairman: Perhaps it is the usual example of divided by a common language. I think we would describe it as new biotechnology.

Lord Crickhowell

135. I have got in front of me the paper which describes what the United States Under-Secretary of State, Alan Larson, had to say at the Washington International Trade Association on 8 January. He then cautioned Europe on the potential consequences for world trade and on the development of this technology posed by the recent proposals. He went on to say some quite interesting things about the need for co-operation in research and so on and other aspects. My particular question is: which is the Administration's greater area of concern at the moment, the existing approvals moratorium or the traceability and labelling proposals, or do you take them equally as problem areas?

(*Mr Kurz*) We would say that both issues are extremely important, and the United States will continue to pursue both the lifting of the moratorium and a sound scientifically based approach to biotech product approvals and issues such as labelling and traceability regulations. Let me address the moratorium issue. Since 1998, 13 agricultural biotechnology applications have been stalled by the Commission's *de facto* moratorium on approvals. This lack of action has halted almost all US maize exports to Member States costing the industry at least $200 million annually. Furthermore, some Member States have not acted on registrations for biotech applications which have already been approved by the Commission. As you know, on 25 July last year the College of Commissioners proposed regulations on labelling and traceability of food and feed which are under consideration in the Council and the European Parliament. The United States has provided extensive comments on these proposals to the EU, after they were notified to the WTO's Technical Barriers to Trade Committee last August. A number of other countries have also provided similar technical barriers to trade comments. We would also like to note that a number of amendments have been proposed in the European Parliament committees that reflect our concerns and on 14 February the EU notified its biotech proposals to the World Trade Organisation (WTO) Sanitary and Phytosanitary Measures (SPS) Committee. The United States plans to provide the EU with comments in response to these notifications as well. As the world's leading producer of agricultural biotech products the United States is very concerned that the Commission's proposals are not workable and could unduly impair trade. We would sincerely like to work with the European Parliament and its interested Member States to ensure that the benefits of biotechnology reach everyone. These benefits include food choice, agricultural innovation and increased trade. The failure to approve new biotech events over the past three years has resulted in a flight of the technology from Europe. During this past year field trials in the EU have numbered 44 compared to more 2,300 in the United States. Restrictions on agricultural biotechnology in Europe, however, are already resulting in less research and development for this new technology which has great potential for improving food security in developing countries and demonstrates an ability to reduce environmental

Lord Crickhowell *contd.*]

degradation through decreased use of agricultural chemicals and improved agronomic practices. As I mentioned earlier, the EU has acknowledged that the biotech products which have been developed to date are as safe as, or even safer than, conventional products. The fact is, as more biotech events and products are approved and used world-wide, tracking these products through the distribution system and testing them will become more and more complex, if not impossible. The result will be added expense and liability risk for shippers without any corresponding increase in consumer and environmental protection. We believe that the labelling and traceability proposals are unworkable as they are now written. We think that they need to be re-worked and we would much prefer to see sensible approaches explored which share our view that agricultural biotech regulations should be science based, workable and not disruptive to trade. In the meantime we think it is important to move ahead with the approvals process and we think that is something that ought to happen now. We have noted that the EU Commission has WTO obligations to have a transparent and timely approval process. Indeed, within Europe it has been acknowledged that the present moratorium is illegal. In other instances where states have failed to comply with Commission decisions, as with respect to resuming the trade in British beef, the Commission has taken steps to compel states to comply.

136. Just one follow-up question if I may. You laid a lot of emphasis—and I understand it—on the possible environmental and other benefits from GM products. You emphasise that as being an important issue just as much as the world trade issue. One of the things that has struck me very much as I have listened to evidence is the problem of giving people genuine choice. If you simply refer to GM products in labelling you are not actually able to tell them always what the other benefits might be. There is a tendency in Europe to think that the benefits have all gone to the producers. I know of many cases where there are enormous environmental benefits to be obtained as well. Very often in the world of environmental regulation one has to make difficult choices. I used to be an environmental regulator and had to make those choices. There is clearly a different reaction in the United States from the reaction there is in Europe. Have you been more successful in creating genuine choice by getting over messages about what the benefits are? Is that something we ought to learn? Do the American public, apart from having assurance on safety, get to receive more information on the possible benefits of the particular modifications? I am, I know, rather wide of my original question but there is the whole issue of choice in this as well so that actually seeing what the benefits are does seem to me to be a key issue.

(*Mr Kurz*) I certainly agree with you. We do have a relatively small percentage of our population of consumers who are interested in those kinds of questions but, by and large, somehow the consumption of biotech food products seemed to become a pattern of everyday life almost as if it came in through the back door. These products have been around for some time now and they do not seem to have raised an awful lot of concern, and I do not really know what the reason for that is.

Lord Walpole

137. Is it because people did not know about them?
(*Mr Kurz*) I remember the first one which was what they called the Flav'r Sav'r tomato and this was a tomato that could stay longer on the vine and be picked later without spoiling. There was quite a bit of interest about how this was done. This was back in the late 1970s, early 1980s. People decided basically that they did not want it because it did not taste good. The taste was a disappointment. It seems to be an area where these questions that you are raising just never caught on with the general public. I do not really know what to say to that other than that our Food and Drug Administration does have a very high approval rating among the general public, and a lot of confidence and trust that if they approve a product it is going to be okay to consume it. However, I do not believe that is an entirely satisfactory answer, so I do not know. I guess often in questions of food safety you see populations in one part of the world getting excited about an issue that does not concern people somewhere else.

Baroness Miller of Chilthorne Domer

138. With regard to the moratorium, one of the issues that has concerned consumers here very much is the environmental issue. Do you think that the difference perhaps for us is that we have a very small land base and if there are going to be problems as opposed to benefits then because agricultural land is so linked with areas that we regard, for example, as sites of scientific interest or our national parks, it is almost as if we are introducing GM crops to our entire land base, whereas you have huge areas that are just agricultural and then huge areas that are national parks. How would Americans feel if GM crops were grown in their national parks?
(*Mr Kurz*) That is certainly a good question. It is true that our major production areas, at least for arable crops, tend to lie far from major population centres. It is certainly understandable that the population density and relatively small size of the land mass in the UK are going to heighten people's concern with the environmental aspects of biotechnology. I do think that similar concern exists in the US and that it is also growing. It may be that there is more of a realisation that in addition to possible ill effects of biotech crops there are potentially good ones too. Of course, the one that comes to mind is in the case of what we call the Roundup ready soya beans where the application of herbicides is significantly reduced using biotechnology.
(*Ms Tidball*) I would agree with Peter that you can certainly understand, because of the size of the land mass, the closeness of the crops and so on, that there might be some reticence and why it is very important to continue, as you are doing, with your trial crops. But that really does not have any effect on the safety of the food or the need for labelling and traceability. That is a question—is there a danger of gene flow to

Baroness Miller of Chilthorne Domer *contd.*]

your national parks, for example? I would also point out that even though our national parks are in huge areas and we have large farms, we have interspersed among all those farms city parks, county parks, state parks, federal forests, federal protected areas. It is not as if we have huge blocks of each thing separately. They are interspersed also.

(*Mr Kurz*) Maybe also, just giving this a little more thought, there is some perception in Europe that these products are fairly new and that they are new in the US as well as in Europe whereas in fact they have been around for a while and there has been an awful lot of testing done before they were approved. We not only have the Food and Drug Administration to monitor the human health side, but also in particular we have the Environmental Protection Agency which looks almost exclusively at the environmental side of new biotech events as they are called. Again, I think there is a fairly high level of confidence in the testing that has been done before these products were approved. Maybe what we need to do is a better job of telling people about the work that has been done so that they perhaps would share some of the confidence that we have.

Chairman

139. Would you accept that in Europe and, for that matter, in the United Kingdom in particular, the biotechnology industry went to some time and trouble to assure consumers in the market that there would indeed be labelling and traceability and that indeed was true at the time Flav'r Sav'r tomatoes were marketed in the United Kingdom? However, the European consumer was suddenly presented with what appeared to be a *fait accompli* of imports from America and elsewhere of soya and maize which had been genetically modified, which the consumer was suddenly told, against all assurances which had been given previously, that there could be no traceability or labelling because it was a commodity which could not be separated. That immediately caused the reaction, which had not been there at the time of the Flav'r Sav'r tomato, and which of course is now setting the agenda and perhaps is the reason why these proposals are coming out of the European Union.

(*Mr Kurz*) That would suggest that this was in part a marketing issue perhaps.

140. It is a matter of consumer confidence, I suspect, and we have heard earlier today that there is certainly evidence that European consumers do indeed ask for labelling and traceability and this directive seeks to meet that requirement. I do not think we can be in any doubt that consumers are asking for something of that order. Whether it is practical or not is an issue we have to address. I am asking you whether you recognise that there was a quite fundamental shift in the European perception on this issue and suddenly being presented with imports, particularly from North America, on which apparently traceability was no longer going to be achievable and indeed we were told it was not feasible. This was contrary to the assurances which the European biotechnology industry had carefully

given with the Flav'r Sav'r tomato and earlier new biotechnology products.

(*Mr Kurz*) I see. I would think that that is a very plausible hypothesis. I am not as familiar with the history of those kinds of assurances that you were given by the European biotechnology industry earlier, but I guess you could certainly say that products that were introduced to Europeans with the same expectations for their reception that they had in the US, maybe there was some homework lacking in that area, some more studying that should have been done to realise that a different situation prevailed here. As a result it is requiring some effort on our part to right that.

Baroness Maddock

141. If the EU Member States could arrive at a compromise substantially based on the proposals from the Commission and so unlock the approvals process, how far do you think that would remove the concerns of the US and other major exporters of food and agricultural products? What scope do you see for such a compromise and basically what could you live with?

(*Mr Kurz*) The proposed EU labelling requirements would be imposed on products that have already been approved for use and for which no specific handling, usage, safety or compositional distinctions have been identified. The result could be a further erosion of consumer confidence in the EU's regulatory system because the consumer is left without truly accurate information about the product. The regulations would set a precedent that could also be applied to non-agricultural industries. The EU is advocating adoption of its policies on traceability and labelling in a number of international fora, such as the Codex Alimentarius and the Cartagena Protocol on Biosafety. These policies could have serious implications for trade and on the adoption of biotechnology products, particularly in developing countries, many of which do not have the infrastructure to support or enforce these policies and yet would benefit economically and environmentally from the use of these new product varieties. Frankly, we do not see any ground for compromise in these proposals. We agree with the United Kingdom's Food Standards Agency Chairman, Sir John Krebs, who has said that he views the proposals as unworkable.

Lord Palmer

142. Just following on from Lord Crickhowell's question about choice, do you agree it is right that consumers should have the ability to choose between GM and non-GM products, irrespective of whether they accept the GM safety assessments? If so, what is the best way of ensuring that consumers can make an informed choice?

(*Mr Kurz*) Every company in the retail business knows that it will fail unless it gives the consumer what they want. Consumer choice lies at the foundation of every successful modern economy. If consumers want to avoid biotech ingredients in their foods we believe that this can be done through the use

Lord Palmer *contd.*]

of voluntary labelling. Manufacturers label their products for many traits that they feel are desirable in the market using such voluntary systems. The EU is already using voluntary labelling in the case of their organic regime. Consumers who wish to buy these specialised products can make that conscious choice. On the other hand, in the case of mandatory biotech labelling as proposed by the Commission, distributors have made it clear that they are not likely to carry biotech products. In effect, products containing biotech material will be cleared from the shelves seriously limiting rather than improving consumer choice. In Europe the proposal is to label everything that has been produced with biotechnology processes except for wine and cheese produced from biotech enzymes, which is a curious exception from our point of view, when there is no scientific evidence that the resulting product is in any way different. This approach could lead to the consumer having no choice because every product will have to be labelled "contains GMOs" or, as we are seeing on the market now, retailers will re-formulate away from biotech ingredients at substantial cost to meet the needs of the few. It is unrealistic to expect food processors to carry both biotech and non-biotech lines if they are forced to trace all products regardless of content. The best way to ensure that consumers can make an informed choice is to allow labelling of products as having been produced without the use of biotechnology.

Chairman

143. If I could just follow that up? I understand that United States farmers have been supplying identity preserved foods for clients for many years and indeed it is a system which they favour, and that includes some IP non-GM lines. As I understand it—correct me if I am wrong—these are generally in smaller quantities, kept entirely separate from the usual bulk distribution system at all stages of harvesting, transport, processing, etc, and that IP lines command a high premium on the market to cover the additional costs. Is that what you are recommending? In other words are you suggesting that those who want GM-free foods should pay a higher premium in order to be assured that they have got just that?

(*Mr Kurz*) Hopefully it will not be such a high premium. Presumably if the demand is there the process can be made more inexpensive. It is certainly a fact that IP (identity preservation) costs extra money; there is no doubt about that.

144. So you are suggesting that the IP route is the route that should be followed if people want to have food which is not GM processed?

(*Mr Kurz*) Yes, and the reason we suggest that is because it is the only way to assure that the consumer really gets biotech-free foods. There is no point in devising a system that is not really foolproof where in fact the product will be shown not to be biotech-free.

145. But it has been put to us by a number of organisations in written evidence, and indeed in oral evidence this morning, that the onus perhaps should be on those who have produced the new biotechnology crops to provide the information which is required by the consumer and not the other way round. By requiring the consumer of non-GM lines to pay a premium you will effectively, they would say, reverse the onus of "polluter pays". I accept that "polluter pays" may not be the way you look at GM; you may see it as an improved product.

(*Mr Kurz*) Thank you for that.

146. But nevertheless that is a representation which has been put to us by several of our witnesses. I would like you to comment on it.

(*Mr Kurz*) I guess this would bring to mind the model of organic foods where organic foods are in the market and labelled as such under one scheme or another. We have one here and there is one in Europe and we are beginning to talk about how we can have equivalence between the two systems. In other words, if the US Department of Agriculture (USDA) certifies a product as organic, this will be recognised within the European Union instead of the system we have now which involves various government and non-governmental agencies and offices and certifying organisations and all this of course raises the cost. Hopefully with organics we will move to a point where, if the demand is sufficient, the premium that has to be paid will be relatively modest and then hopefully that would serve as a model for biotech foods as well. We are also dealing with the marketplace here and the realities of production of grain and foodstuffs, and to ask producers to take the onus on themselves in view of the fact that this is only a relatively small percentage of the world market asking for biotech-free foods, frankly is not going to happen. Let us face it, let us be realistic about that, except for producers who see this as a specific business opportunity and as a specific market niche, as in the case of the IP soya that you referred to.

Lord Christopher

147. I think the comparison with organic production can only be taken so far because there is a significant difference between organic food, and some people prefer it, and the genetically modified materials. You have been very confident in your approach but it seems to me that when you said it came through your back door I think what Europe is saying is that it wants it, if it is going to come, through the front door. There is a significant difference. What I would like to put to you is that you said yourself at the beginning that first of all you were not quite clear what risks we were worrying about in Europe. Then in your answer I think to our second or third question you indicated that in your judgement it was going to be in practical terms impossible to do a great deal about this as you moved into second and third generation forms of genetic modification. What is your feeling about that? How do you expect Europe to respond to that even if America goes along with it?

(*Mr Kurz*) Curiously, when our Department first published their proposed regulation they did not specify that organic foods in the United States would have to be biotech-free. They were inundated with comments from the public on this regulation, more comments than we have ever had on any proposed rule. As a result they changed that in the re-writing of

Lord Christopher *contd.*]

the regulation and in the final rule as approved organic foods in the US must be free of any biotech content. Ironically consumers who want to buy organic foods will also be getting biotech-free foods. That seems to be the way that we dealt with it and it was in response to an unforeseen percentage of the public who were demanding this. I do not know whether it was because they felt that in theory organic foods should be biotech-free or because there were a number of consumers out there who do not want biotech foods and they saw this as a good way to ensure that they would be available on the market. In any case that is what they got.

Lord Dubs

148. Was this in response to consumer pressure? Where did this come from? What you say is very interesting because having, I thought, taken the position that this labelling and traceability for biotech foods was not really on the cards, you have now said that there is another way of doing it and your organisation is already doing it. Was it in response to consumer pressures or was it an Administration view?

(*Mr Kurz*) I would say so. There was a movement to have an organic programme, a national organic programme, as opposed to one conducted by the various States or independent certifying bodies, and so the US Department of Agriculture wrote out a proposed rule and put it out for public comment. They really were astounded at the response they had to this. I think it was 300,000-400,000 written responses complaining about this proposed rule. In addition to allowing use of biotechnology in organic production there were some other things that were not popular too, one of which permitted use of sewage sludge or something like that. There were three or four things, and one of them which was quite prominent was biotech, and so they simply had to re-write it. It was in response to public pressure.

149. I am a little surprised, quite pleasantly though,—and please, if I am putting words in your mouth you will throw them back—but are you not saying that yes, although you do not like the expression GM and all this sort of stuff and you do not accept the thrust of British or western European policy on the latest proposals, in fact you are doing something very similar in response to a large degree of consumer pressure in the States? You may be calling it organic but under that label you have got a number of things, including, in our terms, GM-free products. You have really come a long way towards meeting the European position, have you not?

(*Mr Kurz*) I would maybe re-shape that to say that the primary interest was only part of the organics community. It is not so much that there were hundreds of thousands of people out there who were concerned about the availability of biotech-free foods as that there were hundreds of thousands of people who wanted a strict organic standard. In other words, the number of Americans who are more interested in the organic question greatly exceeds the number who are interested in biotech.

150. Sure, but the effect is similar, is it not?

(*Mr Kurz*) The effect has been similar.

Baroness Miller of Chilthorne Domer

151. Under-Secretary of State Larson is on record recently as saying that EC proposals were unworkable and discriminatory and disadvantageous even for Europe. If that is the case then why do you think the European Commission is taking such a strong stance, if it is so disadvantageous to them?

(*Mr Kurz*) First of all, the United States questions whether the European Commission has taken a strong stance given that these proposals barely squeaked through the College. As we understand it, the Directorates of Trade, Research, Enterprise, Agriculture and Internal all have very serious concerns with the proposals. To expand upon Under-Secretary of State Larson's statement, the United States believes that this proposal is not workable or enforceable because it would require products (for food, feed or processing) containing or consisting of biotech events to be accompanied by a listing of the biotech events that they may contain, along with their unique codes. In the absence of expensive identity preservation systems, suppliers would be forced to list all biotech events approved by the EU. The difficulty and complexities in accurately identifying all of the biotechnology events that could possibly be in a shipment would create enormous liability and risk for the shipper or trader. As the leading developer and producer of biotech products the United States has significant interest in this proposal and its potential impact on US suppliers. The United States also notes that potential burdens imposed by the proposals would be substantial for suppliers in developing countries as well, both as potential producers of biotech crops or as intermediate suppliers of processed goods. This is particularly troublesome given that it does not appear that the proposal is attempting to respond to identified risks or hazards and is being implemented on product that has already undergone a risk assessment and has been approved for use. The burdensome documentation and labelling requirements leave room for fraud without affordable, accessible and reliable testing to ensure compliance. The proposed regulation would impose labelling requirements on products that have already been approved for use and for which no specific handling, usage, safety or compositional distinctions have been identified. The result of the foregoing could be a further erosion of consumer confidence in the EU's regulatory system because the consumer is left without truly accurate information about the product. Furthermore the United States does not believe that extending mandatory traceability and labelling requirements to animal feed is justified, nor would it enhance public health.

152. Clearly people in Europe do feel dissatisfied at the moment with the safety issues. Can I just ask you the same question but a different way round from what we asked Friends of the Earth earlier? We asked them if morally it was right that the UK should take a view on whether China, for example, should grow GM cotton. Can I ask you whether you feel it is morally acceptable that the United States take a view on whether Europe, if it is not satisfied with safety issues, should or should not label such produce?

Baroness Miller of Chilthorne Domer *contd.*]

(*Mr Kurz*) From a moral point of view?

153. Yes.

(*Mr Kurz*) Certainly we are not in the business of taking moral points of view. What we look for, I guess, is the science of it and whether there is any, as we call it, sound science behind some of these proposals or not. As far as the moral side of it goes, that would be an issue of individual choice.

154. But they can only have that choice if it is labelled.

(*Mr Kurz*) That is why we are recommending that the label says "does not contain biotech".

Countess of Mar

155. You have used the term "sound science". You have also used on a couple of occasions the phrase that GM products are safe, that they are as safe as or are safer than existing products. Can you understand the doubts and perhaps the scepticism that the European consumer has in the light of the activities of the companies who are now producing all these GM seeds and GM products, given the chemical record of these same companies? I have had a lot to do with organophosphates and we were initially told that organophosphates were safe, and it is interesting that the United States in fact is trying to get rid of OPs as quickly as they possibly can. We have seen the same with organo-chlorines. We are very conscious of history in the United Kingdom and in Europe. Maybe you are not quite so conscious of it in the United States. We have I think tended to learn from it. Can you understand the concerns about the use of this word "safety" in the light of the past use of the word "safety" in relation to our food?

(*Mr Kurz*) I certainly think we can. I think it is interesting that you have identified the fact that numerous naturally occurring substances also present risks or threats to human health, and we can think of many examples in the chemical world or in the whole world of food processing. We have a great deal of sympathy for the idea of a viable European food safety agency and would like to work in any way we can with the European Union to try to bring that about, any sort of organisation that will include accountability and gain the confidence of consumers. There is probably no better way to serve our interests than to see this come about. Any of us who have been in Europe for any length of time are certainly aware of past problems and I think you are absolutely right. There is no question that these have a very large bearing on this particular question in the public mind, and justifiably so, and it is our job to explain how our system works and why we think these products are safe and why we have approved them for use in the United States.

Chairman

156. But could I ask Lady Mar's question in a slightly different form? I am sorry if I am being repetitive. You make the point that regulation should be based on sound science. There is equally the role of social scientists who would I think recognise that risk perception, where it may differ from risk assessment, is nevertheless an equally valid basis for regulation. That is why, for example, when we fly the Atlantic there are many more safety requirements than going by sea, though actually the safety records may be comparable. Would you accept therefore that if perception of risk varies from what the science might say, the regulators and the policy makers in Europe are not only entitled but required to reflect the agenda of their constituents and if they say that they require a different degree of regulation then that is a reasonable basis, even if it is not necessarily supported by the sums?

(*Mr Kurz*) I do not think you would find many people in the US who would agree with that. I think the answer would be that the authorities have a responsibility to educate the public about risk.

Countess of Mar

157. Has the European problem with GM products in practice affected US exports of soya and maize to the UK and to the rest of Europe? Can you provide figures for the years 1995 to 2001? What percentage in each year was sold as GM-free?

(*Mr Kurz*) Thank you, Lady Mar. I do have some figures for you. As I mentioned earlier, it is estimated that the United States is losing in excess of $200 million in maize sales to the EU each year that the moratorium on biotech approvals remains in place. Prior to the *de facto* ban on biotech imports Spain and Portugal had been significant buyers of US maize and as a result of Spanish and Portuguese accessions to the EU, the EU agreed to establish tariff rate quotas for US maize imports into Spain and Portugal to compensate for the market share that we lost when these countries joined the Union. This worked as intended and US exporters sold maize against those quotas up through August 1998. Since that time the EU has not approved any new biotech maize varieties so for the remainder of 1998 and since then US exporters did not offer maize for sale into any EU Member State because several of the maize varieties grown in the United States, the biotech varieties, had not been approved by the EU. Both shippers and importers were unwilling to risk the chance of having a shipment rejected upon testing at port of entry and finding that they had an unapproved variety. Our data shows that US maize exports to the EU have fallen from a peak of roughly 3.5 million metric tonnes in 1995 to 400,000 tonnes in 1998 and subsequently to 100,000 tonnes in 2001. Of that the majority is for feed use. We do not have any knowledge of maize coming into the UK as non-biotech. There is, it appears, a small amount of maize showing up in the trade data but we are not clear about how that is getting in. As for soya beans, likewise we do not have any knowledge of product coming into the UK as non-biotech although we know that there have been discussions among US suppliers and potential UK buyers of identity preserved non-biotech soya for human consumption. As we have said, this product is

Countess of Mar *contd.*]

readily available in the US and is exported quite extensively to Japan. Currently the EU imports in excess of 26 million tonnes of soya beans, predominantly from the United States and South America. Nearly eight million come from the United States with a value of around \$1.1 billion for each of the years over the period since 1995. It is interesting that a single boat load—and this harks back to some of our earlier discussion—of commodity soya beans can contain 50,000 tonnes, each of which consists of more than seven million individual beans. Such a boat load of soya beans from the United States will have been collected and co-mingled at every point of a ten-stage handling system from several thousand different farms. Each farm would typically have grown between six and ten different varieties of soya beans, biotech and non-biotech, according to whatever the on-farm practice is. All these from several thousand different soya bean varieties which are commercially available to farmers in the United States. You can understand that it is impossible to tell what percentage, even of any one load of soya beans, might be biotech-free, for this kind of system to work. As a matter of fact the United States is in the third position and it has been for a number of years, behind Brazil and Argentina, in supplying the EU market with soya products, and this has to do with the enormous acreage increases in Brazil and Argentina and the investments in processing capacity which have gone along with that. It is fair to say that the United States, while still the world's largest soya producer, has major problems of competitiveness compared to these two countries, particularly when you take into account the labour costs and currency values. In 2001 approximately 70 per cent of our acreage and 95 per cent of the acreage in Argentina was planted with two biotech varieties of soya beans. In Brazil authorities estimate that at least 30 per cent of their acreage is planted to biotech varieties, although these have not yet been commercially legalised. Thus you can see that the major exporting countries have moved decidedly in the direction of biotech plantings. On soya beans, as compared with corn, my understanding is that once farmers begin with biotech varieties of soya beans they stay with them because in the case of soya beans the use has to do with resistance to herbicides, which need to be applied every year, and if you do not have to make as many applications you save money, whereas in the case of corn the incentive for biotech production has more to do with the presence or absence in any given year of the corn bore insect and the biotech events are designed to protect against this pest. Therefore it gets back to the earlier question about where the onus should lie for providing biotech foods. When you see these kinds of figures, 95 per cent of the planted acreage in Argentina, you can see where the future is going. Clearly there is no way to reverse that trend.

158. We get back to this business of choice. Farmers in the USA and Brazil and Argentina have chosen to plant GM seeds. We have chosen through our democratically elected European governments not to have them. For you to cry "unfair trade" seems to us to be unreasonable. We feel that you are dictating to us what we must buy. I as a consumer may not wish to buy GM foods. I as a producer do not want to use them because my customers do not want to buy them. Should I not be allowed to have the choice and should I not be allowed to know what is in the food, because it has got a label on it, in order to make that choice?

(*Mr Kurz*) I understand that and I think frankly, regardless of what you hear me say or what government officials may say, we are talking about a free market economy and in the end we have to supply what consumers want. There is no question about that. That is the way our system works. I have heard that statement made by the Director of International Marketing for Wal-Mart a few years ago at the Anuga Food Show in Cologne. I will always remember that. He said, "We operate around the world and everywhere we go we give the consumer what she wants." If they do not want biotech foods they are not going to buy them. The fact of the matter is that Europe is still buying large quantities of soya beans and these are not GM-free soya beans.

159. We do not know whether they are not.

(*Mr Kurz*) Some of them are not.

Chairman

160. Could I refer to the previous Administration, the Clinton Administration, which set up with the European Union a Consultative Forum which produced its final report, you will remember, in December 2000, and of course I accept that the Administration has since changed. I would be interested to know to what extent you could still sign up to the recommendations which were made by that Consultative Forum. Incidentally, if the European Union and the United States were going to be in confrontation on this issue a Consultative Forum seemed sensible, and if I could quote under "Traceability and Monitoring" in the report, which both parties agreed to, it said that "the capacity to trace these products"—that is GM products—"is essential to ensuring consumer choice, understanding the causes and establishing liability in cases of unanticipated negative effects." Then, in a further recommendation, it says that "consumers should have the right of informed choice regarding selection of what they want to consume. Therefore, at the very least, the EU and the US should establish content-based mandatory labelling requirements for finished products." Do I understand from what you have told us that you no longer go along with those recommendations?

(*Ms Tidball*) I do not know if I can specifically comment on that, but I did want to mention something in respect to what you said.

161. I would be quite interested to have an answer. Are you saying you would like to write to us with an answer?

(*Mr Kurz*) That might be a good idea.

Chairman *contd.*]

162. What I would like to ask you in very simple terms is, we have the recommendation of the EU-US Biotechnology Consultative Forum. Does America still stand by what it said then?

(*Mr Kurz*) Fair enough. We will write.

163. You wanted to refer back to what Lady Mar said.

(*Ms Tidball*) I just wanted to say that nobody would ever force a consumer to buy something they did not want, but if it is not on the shelf they cannot choose to buy it. The moratorium does not provide them with the opportunity even to choose to buy it.

Countess of Mar

164. But what we are talking about here is labelling.

(*Ms Tidball*) If there is a label that says, "This product is GMO free" that would provide the information for people who want to avoid any biotech product.

165. On the other hand they might want to know what modifications had been made to the food if it is not GM-free.

(*Ms Tidball*) I do not know but if they do not have the opportunity to buy it there is no choice. They may choose not to buy it if they do not have the information they need but if it is not even on the shelf they cannot make that choice. Believe me, if it cannot be sold it will not be imported.

Lord Walpole

166. I was just wondering where does the US Environment Protection Agency stand in all this? I ask that and I have other things in the back of my mind like jumping genes and stacking genes and all the rest of it. They must be beginning to be worried, surely?

(*Ms Tidball*) The Environmental Protection Agency's legal mandate in the regulatory process for agricultural biotechnology is at this time only for pesticide resistant crops because they regulate pesticides.

167. So they do not have anything to do with the creeping genes and jumping genes and the static ones that are getting into things that are herbicide resistant? They do not have anything to do with that?

(*Ms Tidball*) Not at this point.

168. So all they do is look at pesticide equivalent ones, equivalent to genetic modifications?

(*Ms Tidball*) Yes.

Countess of Mar

169. Does the Food and Drugs Administration have any role to play in this?

(*Ms Tidball*) Not in that part of it. The Department of Agriculture and perhaps the Department of the Interior would look at the aspects of the gene flow, gene stacking and things like that.

170. So what you are saying is that there is no overall body that has complete oversight of what is going on?

(*Mr Kurz*) There are basically three agencies: the EPA, the Food and Drug Administration and the Department of Agriculture.

Lord Walpole: But there are problems, are there not, because you cannot deny the fact that there are problems in Canada?

Countess of Mar: And Mexico.

Lord Walpole

171. And Mexico. I cannot believe that countries either side of you have problems and you do not have them.

(*Ms Tidball*) Nobody is saying that gene flow does not exist.

172. But who is responsible before these things stack up and escape, if you like, because they will, will they not?

(*Ms Tidball*) There is no doubt that, for example, if you are referring to rape-seed in Canada . . .

173. Yes.

(*Ms Tidball*) And it happens in the United States too. The concern is another question.

Lord Walpole: As an ex-farmer I would find it a very distinct concern, yes, I would.

Chairman

174. We have brought this to a conclusion. We are all most grateful to you for the patience with which you have answered our questions. We have covered a lot in the hour or so that we have had you available to help us. Thank you very much. If you would give us your written answers to that thought about the EU-US Consultative Forum we would be most grateful.

(*Mr Kurz*) Thank you very much.

Supplementary Written Memorandum by the United States Embassy, London

The United States again thanks the Sub-Committee for this opportunity to comment on proposals related to labelling and Tracability of products of modern biotechnology. At a 27 February 2002, hearing at the House of Lords, Sub-Committee Chairman Lord Selborne submitted a question on behalf of the UK Consumers' Association to the US Embassy delegation to which the United States agreed to respond in due course. Following is the point under consideration and the US response.

The Sub-Committee requests that the United States provide "the current Administration's position on the conclusions of the EU-US Biotechnology Consultative Forum" as reported in December 2000. Specifically, the Sub-Committee asks that the statement cover two recommendations from the forum:

> "Governments should undertake to develop and implement processes and mechanism that will make it possible to trace all foods derived from GMOs, containing novel ingredients or claiming novel benefits. Before such new products are approved for marketing or when there are significant environmental questions, a detailed plan for mandatory monitoring should be established on a case-by-case basis." (Recommendation 8)

> "Consumers should have the right of informed choice regarding the selection of what they want to consume. Therefore, at the very least, the EU and US should establish content-based mandatory labelling requirements for finished products containing novel genetic material." (Recommendation 15)

The EU-US Consultative Forum on Biotechnology provided an opportunity for EU and US private citizens to discuss issues related to products of modern biotechnology. At the conclusion of its work in December 2000, the Forum presented its report to the USG and EU.

In the course of drafting the report, Forum participants laboured over divisions in approach, and the United States recognises that, as a result, there are varying interpretations of the report's recommendations.

Recommendation 8 calls for a traceability system for biotech food products. The United States does not support this recommendation. The United States has had in place for almost 100 years strict and effective trace back procedures which ensure that public health concerns can be quickly and decisively met. In the United States, lot numbers, batch codes and/or processing plant indicators appear on virtually all processed food packages for trace back purposes and to satisfy the various business needs of food producers. The trace back system applies to biotech products as well as conventional products. The United States would note that to date not a single approved biotech product has been recalled due to a public health concern resulting from the genetic makeup of that product.

Recommendation 8 also touches on the need for strict environmental controls prior to release in the marketplace. Again, the United States has in place regulatory procedures through the US Department of Agriculture and the Environmental Protection Agency, such as extensive field testing, pre-market examination and credible risk assessment, which must be met prior to release and commercialisation. These procedures enable the US Government to establish beyond a reasonable doubt the environmental safety of biotech crops. These tests are conducted on a case-by-case basis as the report recommends. Thus, the United States is already meeting the goals set forth in this recommendation.

With respect to consumer right to know, it has always been the position of the United States that consumers have a right to know whether a food product has been altered in such a way as to impart allergenic properties or negate substantial equivalence with its parent. This position leads to the practice of treating substantially equivalent products the same with respect to their labelling. The United States also recognises that there will be consumers who want to avoid certain products such as those produced through modern biotechnology. In that case, the United States submits that those consumers should be able to purchase products that are "non-biotech" by seeking out products labelled as such. This position is consistent with the recommendations laid out by the Consultative Forum.

12 March 2002

WEDNESDAY 6 MARCH 2002

Present:

Crickhowell, L
Dubs, L
Fyfe of Fairfield, L
Maddock, B
Mar, C

Miller of Chilthorne Domer, B
Palmer, L
Selborne, E (Chairman)
Walpole, L

Memorandum by the UK Government

INTRODUCTION AND SUMMARY

The Government's main concerns with the issues raised by the proposals stem from its regulatory responsibilities for the authorisation of the placing on the EU market of genetically modified organisms (GMOs) and of GM foods. The system for such authorisations is based on a generic EU Directive (2001/18) that lays down common principles for the safety assessment of any genetically modified organism (GMO). GM foods are controlled by the EC novel foods regulation (258/97). GMOs used as human and veterinary medicines are controlled by EC regulation 2309/93. At present there are no specific rules for GM animal feed.

The Commission's proposals have a significant political dimension because a blocking minority of Member States are reluctant to re-engage in the decision making process for GM crops and food. The Commission has stated that its proposals are aimed at improving consumer confidence in the regulation of GM food and feed and increasing consumer choice thereby contributing towards unblocking the authorisation process for GM crops and food. They nevertheless have important implications for food production costs and enforcement, and will impact on the EU's trade partners, including developing countries.

In summary

— The Government is supportive of real consumer choice and agrees that there are many positive elements in the Commission proposals. However, the Government does not consider that the requirement in the proposals to label ingredients where no GM material is present to be enforceable, practical or proportionate;

— The proposals make a sensible distinction between requirements for food and feed;

— The Government has real doubts that the traceability of food and feed will be effective, particularly when the requirements would only apply within the European Community when almost all GM crops are grown outside the Community;

— A common threshold for food and feed is considered appropriate;

— The role of the European Food Safety Authority (EFSA) is to be welcomed, although the practical consequences will require clarification;

— The lighter traceability requirements for commodity crops intended for food, feed or processing and the use of unique identifiers are compatible with the Cartagena protocol;

— The European Commission has notified their proposals to the WTO, although there are concerns that they may create barriers to trade particularly with developing countries;

— The Government has never been in favour of the *de facto* moratorium on decision making of GM products; and

— The Government is urging the Commission to consider the potential impact of their proposals on developing countries.

RESPONSES TO QUESTIONS IN THE CALL FOR EVIDENCE

1. *Do these proposals adequately address the requirements of European consumers for regulation, traceability and labelling of GM food and feed and of food and feed products derived from GMOs?*

1.1 The Government's priorities in relation to GM food and feed are to ensure safety and consumer choice. The existing EC novel foods regulation (258/97) introduced a mandatory pre-market approval process for GM foods. All GM foods are subject to a rigorous safety assessment.

1.2 The Government considers that the current safety assessment procedures, using the framework of substantial equivalence as a tool, are sufficiently robust and rigorous to ensure that approved GM foods are as safe to eat as their non-GM counterparts. However, the Food Standards Agency is funding a major research programme looking at the application of new and emerging safety assessment techniques to ensure that the assessment process keeps abreast of the development of more complex GM foods. Having been assessed for safety before approval there is no reason to expect GM foods should give rise to long-term effects although, as with other foods, such effects cannot be completely ruled out, but would be difficult to detect. The post-market monitoring of any GM foods approved in the future will need to be considered on a case-by-case basis. Nevertheless the Food Standards Agency is funding research looking at the feasibility of setting up a mechanism for post-market monitoring.

1.3 The current labelling rules (described in Annex 1) require foods to be labelled if they contain genetically modified material (novel DNA or protein). The current labelling rules, by applying to foods that are different to conventional ones in a clearly definable way, have the advantage of being practical and enforceable.

1.4 The current approval procedures for GM foods are not operating in an efficient or predictable manner. Since the regulation came into force in 1997, 13 applications for approval of GM food have been submitted, yet to date no decisions on these have been made.

1.5 The Government believes that placing the European Food Safety Authority at the centre of the approval process will improve the efficiency of the process and make it more predictable. However, as explained in the answer to question 6, further work is needed on the detail of how these new arrangements will work in practice.

1.6 The extent to which the traceability proposals add value to existing arrangements is debatable. Directive 2001/18 recently updated generic EU measures applying to the placing on the market of any product consisting of or containing a GMO. These rules have to be implemented by all Member States by 18 October 2002.

1.7 Directive 2001/18 introduces new detailed measures for monitoring the safety of GMOs after they have been placed on the single EU market. It also contains mandatory provisions for the labelling of GMOs and for Member States to ensure their traceability at all stages of their placing on the market. The safety of individual GMOs must be assessed on a case-by-case basis and Member States must agree the specific conditions that should apply in any particular case.

1.8 The Commission's proposals firstly seek to make clear that the rules on traceability in Directive 2001/18 apply not just in individual Member States but are harmonised across the Community. This seems redundant so far as products that contain or are themselves GMOs, such as maize crops, are concerned since the case-by-case rules founded on Directive 2001/18 will apply.

1.9 Secondly, the Commission seeks to go beyond the scope of Directive 2001/18 by also applying traceability and labelling rules to products that are not GMOs, but are derived from GM sources, such as highly refined maize oil. Such products are identical in all respects to their non-GM counterparts. They therefore present no different risk to those produced by conventional means.

1.10 The Food Standards Agency conducts regular surveys of consumer attitudes on a wide range of food issues. The most recent study, published in September 2001, found that two thirds of consumers have confidence in current food safety measures, while price is the main concern for almost half of all consumers. In relation to GM foods, 11 per cent of the consumers expressed concern about GM foods, reflecting a continuing decline in the levels of concern seen in 1999.

1.11 By extending the current labelling rules based on the presence of GM material to include the labelling of products derived from GMOs, the new proposals appear to give consumers increased information and choice regarding GM foods. However, for those consumers who wish to avoid foods produced using GM technology completely the requirements are unlikely to go far enough as they exempt foods produced using GM derived processing aids such as hard cheeses, the majority of which are currently produced in this way, as well as meat, milk and eggs from animals fed GM animal feed. In addition, unless the rules are enforceable they will be open to abuse so that consumers will not know to what extent they can rely on the information about their origin that is given on the label.

1.12 The Government is therefore concerned that the current proposals to extend the labelling rules will not be practical or enforceable and could mislead the consumer. The Food Standards Agency is nevertheless committed to informing consumers of the full extent to which GM technology is used in food production. One way of achieving this would be to supplement the existing labelling rules with a GM free labelling option. In this way clear standards and terminology can be agreed.

2. Do they make sensible distinctions between the requirements of animal feed and those of food for human consumption?

2.1 Many crops used as a source of food ingredients can also have animal feed applications. In some situations the by-products from the production of food ingredients are used as feed material, in other situations a crop can be used interchangeably for food or feed. The Government has been pressing for specific provisions for the approval of animal feed products and welcomes their inclusion in the food and feed proposal. The proposal makes a sensible distinction between the data requirements for food and feed purposes. A welcome feature of the proposals is that the authorisation procedure will require a single application to market a GMO as a food and a feed. Many lessons have been learnt from the "Starlink" incident in the USA. "Starlink" is a variety of maize that received approval in the USA for feed use only but was later identified in foodstuffs on sale in the US supermarkets. By introducing a common procedure for the authorisation of both GM food and feed, the proposals ensure that a similar incident could not be repeated under EU procedures.

2.2 In the case of compound feeds (feeds consisting of more than one ingredient) the proposals do not contain a provision for indicating which specific ingredients are produced from GMOs. Such a provision already exists for foods and should be included for compound feeds.

3. *How effective are the proposals likely to be in ensuring full traceability of GM material at all stages of the chain from producer to consumer?*

3.1 The Commission proposals will only apply from the point of entry into the European Community. GM crops grown in the EU account for only a few thousand acres of the 130 million acres of GM crops cultivated worldwide.[1] The supply chain for the considerably greater volume of imports, such as maize or soya bean, will be longer and more complex than for crops cultivated in the EU. The effectiveness of the traceability arrangements for such imports will therefore depend to a large extent on the integrity and reliability of traceability systems in third countries and thus the ability of importers to secure reliable procedures and systems for accounting for the origin and destination of GM material across the entire food chain. As well as being difficult to achieve, particularly in the case of commodity crops, this could have cost and other implications both for the developed and developing country exporters of agricultural commodities, with possible consequent implications for world trade. The proposals would not require the traceability of non-GM crops, even though they may contain low levels of adventitious GM material.

3.2 The provision in the proposals for the EU to agree a system that will enable the GMOs present in a product to be uniquely identified in documentation accompanying shipments of agricultural commodities is welcome in principle, although there are limitations to the use of such unique identifiers. However, the development of such a system is required for the purposes of Directive 2001/18 as well as to give effect to international obligations under the Cartagena Protocol on Biosafety.

3.3 Unique identification codes are of limited use where final food ingredients derived from GMOs contain no GM material and are indistinguishable from their conventional counterparts. The proposals recognise this by not requiring such codes to be applied to derived products.

3.4 The utility of unique identification codes as a tool for tracing GMOs is significantly determined by the practical realities of world trade in commodity crops. The traceability measures proposed would be intended to apply both to commodity crops grown in the EU and to those imported from abroad. However, there are limitations to the extent that unique identifiers can be an effective tool for the traceability of commodity crops which are traded on the open market worldwide and passed through a complex supply chain.

3.5 Supply chains in developing countries, in particular, typically lack formal contractual arrangements, are based on simple cash transactions, and with commodities sourced from hundreds of small producers. Traceability from producer to exporter could only be assured in cases where a few large producers grow a commodity crop specifically for export.

3.6 The proposals seek in part to deal with these complexities by specifying that, for commodity crops, importers need only declare the unique identity codes of GMOs that bulk shipments may contain. This is compatible with the requirements of the Cartagena Protocol on Biosafety. However, the burden of proof will be on importers to declare whether any shipment contains GM varieties. This will mean that EU importers of conventional varieties, to which traceability rules will not apply, will have to be able to show that GM varieties are not present or that they are only present at or below an agreed threshold in the case of GM varieties that meet the criteria for importation.

4. *Are the proposals likely to be enforceable in practice, particularly where no novel genetic material is contained in the food or feed?*

4.1 For products consisting of, or containing, novel genetic material, claims relating to GM content can be tested by scientific analysis.

4.2 Where no novel DNA or protein is present in the food or feed enforcement will depend on a paper trail which could be open to fraud. The proposals as drafted do not indicate how the origin of food or feed should be verified in such circumstances. It is therefore difficult to envisage how such labelling can be enforced to ensure that consumers will not be misled.

4.3 The proposals would have implications for all foods, as retailers would need to be confident that their supplies were accompanied by reliable paper work to comply with the labelling requirements, regardless of whether there was any intention to include GM ingredients. The fact that the majority of GM crops are grown

---

[1] The US grows 68 per cent of the world's GM crops, Argentina 22 per cent, Canada six per cent and China three per cent. In the US alone 70 per cent of its soya bean crop is GM, 75 per cent of its cotton crop is GM, 50 per cent of oilseed rape and 25 per cent of maize.

outside the EU would exacerbate the problems of verifying information. This would be a particular problem for small manufacturers and retailers who did not use a consistent supply chain.

4.4 With respect to developing country exports many small farmers and producers could not provide a reliable paper trail to satisfy requirements and meet the contractual and documentary standards of importers.

5. *A threshold level of 1 per cent or lower for the accidental presence of GM material in food and feed has been proposed, below which there would be an exemption. Is a threshold of this level, common to both food and feed, appropriate?*

5.1 Existing GM food labelling rules contain a 1 per cent threshold for the accidental presence of GM material in non-GM sources below which labelling is not required, although this only applies to ingredients from EU approved varieties. Several other non-EU countries have also introduced thresholds, which vary from 1 per cent to 5 per cent. Many GM crops are used for both food and feed purposes. It is therefore sensible that any threshold is common to both food and feed.

5.2 Current detection methods for GM material are capable of supporting a legal threshold of 1 per cent. This also reflects what suppliers are at present reliably able to secure through the supply chain. Studies show that although lower levels of detection are possible, the technology is not reliable enough to support a threshold below 1 per cent, particularly when testing final food products or compound feeds. The Food Standards Agency held a meeting with stakeholders to consider the implications of low levels of GM ingredients in foodstuffs. Taking into account the views expressed there, the Government has decided that the threshold should remain at 1 per cent for the time being, but should be kept under review pending improvements in detection methodology.

5.3 The proposed 1 per cent threshold also applies to non-EU approved GMOs. While it may not be practically possible to achieve a zero threshold, this aspect of the Commission's proposal is unsatisfactory as it stands. For example, the proposal is not clear on exactly how GMOs not approved in the EU would be assessed for acceptability.

The best means of overcoming the problem of non-approved GMOs is to clear the backlog of decisions required on outstanding applications for approval within the EU.

5.4 As regards developing country exporters, even a tolerance threshold of 1 per cent would be difficult for them to meet as the costs of segregation between GM and non-GM varieties will be significantly higher in such countries.

6. *Is the role proposed for (a) the European Food Safety Authority and its scientific committees and (b) Member States in the authorisation process for GM food and feed appropriate?*

6.1 At present applications for approval of GM foods are submitted to the Member State where the product is first to be marketed. Other Member States then have the opportunity to comment on or object to the initial assessment. Under the proposal all applications would be submitted to the European Food Safety Authority (EFSA), rather than individual Member States.

6.2 The regulation establishing the EFSA agreed unanimously by Member States was adopted on 21 January. The primary responsibility of the EFSA is to provide independent scientific advice to support EU action on food safety. The EFSA covers all stages of food production and supply from primary production to the safety of feed and through to the supply of food to consumers. The EFSA can carry out scientific assessments on any matter having a direct or indirect effect on the safety of the food supply. It can also give advice on non-food and feed GMOs.

6.3 It is possible that the Authority will ask a Member State to carry out the risk assessment on its behalf. However, it is unclear how Member States will be selected and whether the same Member State will carry out both the environmental and food/feed assessment.

6.4 It is essential that there is no reduction in the standards applied in the current approval process as regards information to the public. Current UK policy is that in the case of all applications made to the UK authorities complete dossiers (except commercial in-confidence data) are made available for public comment. The Government supports the establishment of the proposed Community register of GM food and feed. However, the proposal implies that the information included on the register will be limited to a summary of applications for authorisation and authorisations granted. The Government would like to see more information placed on the Community register.

7. *Are the proposals likely to be compatible with the requirements of the Cartagena Protocol on Biosafety and with other international commitments, including OECD programmes?*

7.1 Two aspects of the Cartagena Protocol on Biosafety are particularly relevant to the proposals. Firstly, the Protocol implies a need for a system of unique identification codes, to enable individual GMOs to be identified and for further information about them to be obtained from the Biosafety Clearing House under the Protocol. Secondly, the Protocol contains specific identification requirements for bulk commodities of GM crops for direct use as food, feed or processing.

7.2 The successful delivery of the system proposed by the Commission depends on agreement to a system of unique codes. Since imports of GMOs into the EU are largely from third countries, the EU system should be consistent with mechanisms being developed under wider international organisations, including the work on unique identification codes being undertaken by the Organisation for Economic Co-operation and Development (OECD). In this respect, the Government welcomes the recent adoption by the OECD of "Guidelines for the designation of the OECD's unique identifier for transgenic crops" and will argue for this work to form the basis for the EU system of identification.

7.3 Regarding bulk shipments of agricultural GMO commodities directly for use as food feed or processing, the Commission's proposals allow operators importing to list the unique identification codes for the GMOs the consignment potentially contains, as opposed to the GMOs the consignment actually contains. This is compatible with the requirements for the identification of bulk shipments of agricultural commodities contained in the Cartagena Protocol and therefore in line with our international obligations.

7.4 Commitments as regards international trade agreements are dealt with in the answer to question 8.

8. *Are the proposals compatible with obligations towards non-Member States seeking to export food and feed to the EU?*

8.1 Exporters of GM products, such as the USA and Canada, and including developing countries such as Argentina and Brazil, have argued that the wide scope of the proposals, if adopted, will cause unnecessary restrictions on world trade. It is for those countries to make appropriate representations on the issues of particular concern to them.

8.2 In general terms, however, although international food standards are necessary and desirable, they should not be used arbitrarily or set up additional barriers to other country's exports, particularly those of developing countries. Standard setting should take into account the circumstances of developing countries and their capacity to meet developed country standards.

8.3 The UK and the EU are committed to improved market access for developing countries. However, the Commission's proposals will potentially set up new barriers to developing countries who might intend either to export GM food and feed, or their products, to the EU. In addition to the burden on GM exports, a country growing a GM crop might find its exports derived from a non-GM variety of the same crop rejected because of difficulties in meeting thresholds for contamination. Such problems could deter developing countries from adopting otherwise beneficial crops even for purely domestic consumption.

9. *Should the present EU-wide moratorium on approving GM food and crop product applications be maintained until the issues concerning traceability and labelling of GMOs have been resolved?*

9.1 No. The UK has never been in favour of the *de facto* moratorium on decision-making on GM products that is carried out in accordance with the law. Existing Community legislation sets out a timetable within which decisions on applications to place GM products on the market must be reached. Under this legislation, the initiative for proposing decisions on the currently outstanding product applications rests with the Commission. The Government believes the Commission should use its power of initiative. The UK will then consider each case on its merits and voting in favour of those applications which meet the current high biosafety standards and propose appropriate traceability and labelling conditions for GMOs in accordance with Directive 2001/18.

10. *What other aspects of the proposals require further consideration before the UK Government can sign up to them?*

10.1 The potential implications of traceability and labelling in terms of bureaucratic requirements for developing country exporters are significant, and need further consideration in multilateral fora. Retailers in Europe will need to be confident that their suppliers are providing a reliable paper chain in compliance with the proposed GM labelling requirements. Developing country agricultural systems are characterised by mainly small-scale farms, with limited access to advice and information on, or any supporting infrastructure for meeting, agricultural export requirements. These circumstances will make it extremely difficult, if not impossible for developing country exporters to provide the necessary paper trail to comply with the requirements.

10.2 The UK Government will urge the Commission to look at the potential impact of this proposal and consult with developing country representatives about their ability to meet the standards proposed. The EU will also need to consider the provision of capacity building and technical assistance to help developing countries comply with the legislation.

10.3 Some of the international tensions surrounding the proposals could be reduced by early entry into force of the Cartagena Protocol on Biosafety, which the Government supports.

Annex 1

CURRENT GM GOOD LABELLING RULES

1. Rules for the labelling of GM foods are currently provided by four EC Regulations.

— EC Novel Foods Regulation (258/97) (NFR) provides labelling requirements for novel, including GM, foods coming onto the market in the future (Article 8(1)). The requirements provide for labelling only for the final consumer. In practice, Member States would agree on a labelling regime for the GM food as a condition of approval.

— EC Regulation 1139/98 requires the labelling of foods and food ingredients containing ingredients produced from GM soya or maize. This Regulation was amended by Regulation 49/2000, which provides a 1 per cent *de minimis* threshold for adventitious contamination.

— EC Regulation 50/2000 requires the labelling of foods and food ingredients containing additives and flavourings from a GM source. The Regulation applies to additives from all GM sources, and not just soya and maize. There is no *de minimis* threshold similar to that for soya and maize ingredients. It is understood that GM additives sold as such will require labelling under the proposed amendment to the additives framework Directive.

2. The trigger for labelling under these provisions is the presence in the final food of novel DNA or protein resulting from genetic modification. Labelling is not required for derivatives where no GM material remains. With the exception of foods approved under the NFR, labelling is required where the food is sold to the final consumer or to catering establishments. As such, there are currently no specific requirements for traceability or labelling of GMOs that are sold between manufacturers further up the supply chain.

3. Domestic legislation, enforcing the EC regulations, consolidates the rules into a single Regulation. The Genetically Modified and Novel Foods (Labelling) (England) Regulations 2000 applies in England. Similar legislation operates in Northern Ireland, Scotland and Wales. The Domestic regulations go beyond EC requirements in applying the labelling requirements to foods sold loose or pre-packed for direct sale. This includes foods sold from restaurants, cafes etc, as well as some bakers and delicatessens. The domestic regulations provide a degree of flexibility for the way in which businesses selling foods in this way may provide the information.

4. At present, there is no legislation specifically covering the labelling of food as "GM free". Any food product on sale in the UK labelled "GM free" would be subject to the normal requirements of food law. The Food Safety Act 1990 makes it an offence to describe a food falsely, or in a way likely to mislead a purchaser to its nature, substance or quality. Also, the Trade Descriptions Act 1968 makes it an offence for a trader to supply a product (including a food product) to which a false trade description has been applied, or to which a trade description has been applied which is misleading to a material degree.

LABELLING IN CATERING ESTABLISHMENTS

5. When the labelling rules for GM soya and maize were introduced, the UK chose not to exempt catering establishments from these rules on the grounds that consumers wished to make informed choices wherever they bought food. Recognising the practical difficulties faced by the catering sector, flexible arrangements were introduced. These have continued to attract criticism from the catering sector on the grounds that very few people ask for information on the GM content of food when eating outside the home.

6. In September 2000 the Board agreed to retain the UK's national requirements for catering establishments to convey information on the presence of GM ingredients. In reaching this conclusion the Board drew on independent research, conducted in June 2000 by MORI on behalf of the Agency, which looked at consumer information needs for foods sold in catering establishments. Of those respondents who had eaten in a restaurant in the last six months, 29 per cent said (when prompted) they would like to know about the presence of GM ingredients. Conversely, 25 per cent of the sample said they were not interested in such information. Around three per cent of people said they had actually asked about the presence of GM ingredients when eating in a restaurant in the last six months.

15 February 2002

Examination of Witnesses

THE RIGHT HONOURABLE MICHAEL MEACHER, Member of the House of Commons, Minister for the Environment, DR LINDA SMITH, Head of GM Policy and Regulation Unit, Chemicals and Biotechnology Division, MR DAVID STEELE, Head of the European and International Branch, GM Policy and Regulation Unit, Chemicals and Biotechnology Division, Department for Environment, Food and Rural Affairs, examined.

Chairman

175. Welcome, Minister. Thank you for joining us today. I know that you are travelling later in the day, so we are very grateful to you for being able to fit this in. I also welcome your colleagues who have joined you.

(*Mr Meacher*) Linda Smith is Head of the Policy and Regulation Authority Unit; and David Steele is responsible for the International and European Branch.

176. Minister, would you like to say anything by way of preface before we go through one or two questions? You know very well, having attended our Committee before, that we are not always likely to stick rigorously to the list.

(*Mr Meacher*) I have not anything to say that is not already very well known. This is a much cultivated area—if I can use that word in respect of GM—a much covered area, so I suggest you go straight to the questions.

177. We are trying to stick specifically to the Traceability and Labelling Draft Regulations, although inevitably we find that we do wander into the wider ethical and other issues. Lord Crickhowell wanted to ask the first question about the responsibility within Government for this area.

Lord Crickhowell

178. We note with interest that the evidence on behalf of the Government has been submitted by the Food Standards Agency. We have had a note of explanation about the relationships between your Department and the Food Standards Agency. In the days when I chaired the National Rivers Authority, which later became part of the Environment Agency, I would rather have liked to give evidence on behalf of the Government, but I think that that might have been strongly resisted at the time. I am a little puzzled about the complexity of government relationships because, clearly, the Department of Trade and Industry will be interested in world trade issues, and then there is the question of international development policy. There clearly could be tensions and disagreements about priorities in these areas. We would like to know exactly how these are sorted out and how it is that the Food Standards Agency is the appropriate body to give evidence on such matters.

(*Mr Meacher*) I think that is a fair statement. It is a very complex and very contentious area, and of course there is expression of different views, and one would entirely expect that. The pivotal body on biotechnology, as I am sure you know, is the ministerial committee SCI(BIO). It is a sub-committee of the Committee on Science Policy. It includes the relevant interests, not just DEFRA, which now combines Environment and Agriculture, but it also includes DTI, and DfID with regard to the international angle. Sir John Krebs, who I know you

are seeing later today, and the technical committee give expert advice on food safety issues; and any evidence which is given to this Committee is agreed by the ministerial committee, SCI(BIO). Therefore, it is not a partisan or sectoral provision of evidence: whoever provides it, it has been agreed by the Government collectively. Indeed, the Government's position on the Commission proposal on labelling and traceability has also been agreed by the ministerial committee on European issues. I think that whoever has submitted it, you can take it that it is collectively agreed across Government. There are differences of interest, and different dimensions of interest feeding in to this issue. The Food Standards Agency leads on food and feed issues; its particular concern is provision of consumer information, carrying out attitude surveys regarding consumer opinion. DEFRA has wider responsibilities under the generic Directive 2001/18, which is concerned with deliberate release and the placing on the market of GMOs. DEFRA, given its nature, has the responsibility for food chain issues and wider agricultural production issues. That, I think, expresses the different interests, but hopefully they combine with a united and agreed view.

179. That is very helpful. You are clearly indicating that these issues have been thrashed out in advance of the statements that we are getting and are agreed by all concerned. We have heard evidence from the representatives of the American Embassy, who are acutely concerned about the world trade aspects and think that the health and safety aspects are being overplayed. I have given perhaps an over-simplified summary, but, presumably, if one later got into strong dispute about world trade issues, then the balance of who says what and who leads the battle might change in that the Department of Trade and Industry would become more involved in those issues. It is helpful to have a clear understanding that these have been thrashed out by committees in advance, and that the Food Standards Agency is therefore stating the current collective joined-up Government view. That is what we are seeking to ascertain.

(*Mr Meacher*) That is perfectly true. You referred to the issue that is probably the most contentious in this area, which is the so-called moratorium on further approvals in regard to the applications that have been made over the last several years. The last one was approved in 1998, so it has been three or four years now. There is agreement in the UK Government that we are not part of and do not share the view of the seven states that take the view that there should be such a moratorium until the labelling and traceability provisions of Directive 2001/18 are in place. Our view is that there should be an agreement between the Member States that we would resume the process of giving approval where appropriate for GM applications, and that we would agree that we would apply the provisions of Directive

Lord Crickhowell *contd.*]

2001/18, including in regard to labelling and traceability, before they were transposed and actually became legal. That seems to us to be a very fair and reasonable compromise. We had a significant discussion about this at the EU Environment Council—not the last one which was three days ago but the one before that—and there seemed to be very little change; there is still a blocking minority. Obviously, this is a serious matter. There are obviously questions of referrals to WTO, and there is one that you are aware of; but I hope that our American friends also realise that this is not just perverse intransigence on the part of certain Member States, and that there is very genuine and real concern about consumer attitudes to GM, and questions of health and safety. Even if some people take the view that they are misconceived, they are nevertheless a political reality, and it is very difficult, given the degree of feeling and lack of public acceptability at this point in many Member States, to proceed. The UK does not believe that the moratorium is the way to deal with it.

180. Those points were very much brought out when we discussed them with the American representatives, not least because their evidence had been preceded by Friends of the Earth. We did ask them those specific questions, whether they were more concerned about the moratorium than the labelling or *vice versa*, and they made it very clear that they were concerned about both aspects, not just the moratorium. They were very concerned about the labelling aspects.

(*Mr Meacher*) That is an issue on which all the EU Member States are very clear, that there should be labelling and traceability in the interests of providing the fullest information that we can to promote consumer choice. There is no difference in any Member State about that.

Baroness Miller of Chilthorne Domer

181. Thank you for your explanation of how the joined-up government bit works, but given the political reality, as you have said, it is a very sensitive area. Can you clarify where ministerial responsibility for this Government view stops? Which Minister is responsible? I heard what you said about the committees, but I am not certain of your reply. Who would answer those questions to the House, and who would represent that view to the Council of Ministers?

(*Mr Meacher*) It would depend exactly on the issue. If it was a WTO issue, this certainly involves trade issues and the DTI in particular, and there would have to be a decision reached in Government as to who was the appropriate minister. I would expect that to be the Secretary of State for DEFRA, unless it was a particular angle on the trade issue where another secretary of state may be more appropriate. Now that Environment and Agriculture are in a single department, that is the main focus within Whitehall for these issues. Obviously, we would look at each issue as it arises, to decide its appropriate *locus*.

182. The FSA questions are usually answered by the Minister of Health.

(*Mr Meacher*) FSA questions which are to do with food safety and health are properly a question for the Department of Health, just as trade is for the DTI. It depends on the issue.

Lord Dubs

183. We know that GM foods are grown in countries outside the EU, and not just in North America; and it is increasingly likely that developing countries will grow GM crops. That would give rise to materials intended for consumption in the EU. How does the Government intend to approach that? Do you see that there is a difficulty that can be overcome?

(*Mr Meacher*) We certainly have to because, as you say, the level of cultivation of GM across the world is growing. It is heavily concentrated in half a dozen or so countries, but it may well grow in the future. Our response to the question of the regulation of GM seed or production of crops that are grown outside the EU is exactly the same as those cultivated within the EU, namely that our concern should be the promotion of protection of human health and the environment, and providing product information in order to promote consumer choice. I entirely accept that if a GM product is assessed as safe outside the EU, the view might be taken—and this may be what lay behind your question—that we should simply accept that as justifiable for import into the EU; or should we impose any additional tests ourselves? We are certainly not in the business of deliberately creating barriers or imposing additional tests, but the fact remains that measures that are necessary to manage risk do depend on differences between the environments of the exporting and importing countries, and it has to be carried out on a case-by-case basis; for example, whether it is a cultivation, in which case the issue of separation distances is all-important, as opposed to whether it is being imported simply as a feed for animals. We have to take into account those kinds of considerations in deciding how to apply these criteria.

Chairman

184. Can we follow up the question about importing from a third country, for example a developing country where the scientific facilities are likely perhaps to be less sophisticated than in North America, and where there will be a requirement, if this traceability regulation is enacted, for there to be full traceability at the point of entry into the European Union. This, I assume, will cause some logistical problems to many third world countries that may have decided, for their own reasons, which I do not think we could quarrel with, that GM production might be appropriate in order to meet their own needs for sufficiency in food supply. Is it realistic to think that we can impose traceability on third-world producers, where they might amass crops that will go ultimately to animal feed in Europe, to the degree that the draft regulation at present suggests?

(*Mr Meacher*) That is a very fair question, and I think we are right to seek that; and indeed the

Chairman *contd.*]

Cartagena Protocol on Biosafety, which regulates international trade in GM products, tries to meet that problem by an improvement in capacity-building in developing countries. There are provisions in the Protocol that are designed to assist developing countries in taking decisions, and equally to provide traceability. Your question is a good one because there is no doubt, I think, that in many countries that level of capacity is simply not there. The UK has a good record in providing for an increase in capacity-building. If I recall, we are giving something like £38 million at the present time for capacity-building of one kind or another to developing countries, which is quite considerable. I do know that UNEP is concerned over the fact that so many multilateral environmental agreements (MEAs) fall down, because the provisions need to be applied in an effective way by developing countries, and they often cannot be. Therefore, UNEP is concerned to provide regional support measures to ensure that the objectives of the MEAs, such as the Cartagena Protocol, can be effectively applied in developing countries. I think we are right to seek the objectives, but we need to do more to ensure that it can be feasibly carried through.

185. It would have to be recognised that the Cartagena Protocol has not yet been ratified, and that to build capacity in the number of countries we are talking about is a vast project even with the large sums of money that you have just referred to, which are perhaps only drops in the ocean if you have to trace every producer's production.

Lord Walpole

186. Does the Government believe that the labelling of GM products and materials should be restricted to edible items, or perhaps other objects made from, for instance, cotton, which could be included? We have been told by people appearing before us that there are people in this world who object to GM on religious grounds. I am not sure you would want underwear made of GM cotton if you did believe that.

(*Mr Meacher*) It is the first time I have heard that they objected on religious grounds—certainly non-scientific grounds, or possibly ethical grounds, but I have not heard it suggested that it is contrary to some religious doctrine. However, be that as it may, I think our view would be that any product that contains viable GM material, either in the form of novel DNA or protein that has been subject to genetic modification, should be labelled. That applies, of course, to seed, to human food, to animal feed, vaccines, and raw material for textiles such as cotton, which you are referring to. That is of course labelling above the threshold for adventitious contamination by low levels of GM in conventional products. Of course, the Commission's proposals only affect food and feed, although controversially they would be extended to cover products derived from, but not actually containing, GM material, like highly refined oil. Our view would be that it is reasonable and desirable that that information should be given to consumers. The real concern is over edibles: there is no doubt about that, but there seems to be no reason

to forbid it, or preclude it, or discourage it in other cases.

Countess of Mar

187. You have just about touched on pharmaceuticals, because pharmaceuticals are obviously ingested. Is there any cross-referencing between the Medicines Control Agency, DEFRA and the Food Standards Agency?

(*Mr Meacher*) There certainly is. There have been many discussions which I have attended in Misc 6, as it was before the election and SCI(BIO) now, where this difference of attitude between the use of genetic modification for vaccines and that for food have been remarked upon. It certainly seems to me that people are prepared to take a risk with vaccines and pharmaceuticals, if they believe that it may save them from death, illness or pain; but there is a very different attitude in the case of food, where it is a necessity, and people as at this time are not yet persuaded that the consumer benefits are sufficient to take the risk. That does not mean to say that that could not change over time, but there has been over-emphasis on the producer benefits and not enough for the consumer. There has indeed been a suggestion that we should try to use the willingness of people to accept genetically modified material for pharmaceuticals in order to sell GM food, but there is the other view that there is such resistance to GM food in some quarters that it might actually undermine the confidence people have in pharmaceuticals which may have some GM material in them. There is an overlap of course, but there are widely different consumer attitudes.

188. It is not just vaccines in pharmaceuticals; there is insulin and the blood-clotting factor.
(*Mr Meacher*) Absolutely.

189. More than we probably know about.
(*Mr Meacher*) I do not think anyone, with the possible exception of Jehovah's Witnesses, believe that we should not take full advantage, and, even with new and innovative products, to be prepared to take some very carefully controlled and regulated risks. That attitude does not apply to food.

Lord Crickhowell

190. Your answer touches on what is quite a difficult issue—whether the primary object is health, safety or other impacts. Perhaps the question of cotton brings it up very strongly, because presumably the primary concern here is not the impact on health over here, but possibly on the environment where the cotton is produced. When you talk about the public reaction and how some of the public believe that only the producers benefit, that may well be because they do not understand that the primary object is to avoid use of fertilisers or some other consequences that are themselves damaging to the environment. We get into the question therefore of whether we can take a balanced view of the issues here. Food safety is very simple and straightforward, in a way. We can make judgments on that. However, I am not at all clear on how people

Lord Crickhowell *contd.*]

are expected to make judgments, or even get choice, when the argument about the environmental benefit is not presented at all. It is an issue that has come up in session after session here. I have produced examples where the use of GM products is producing enormous environmental benefits locally that are not being considered in the debate at all. How do you approach these issues?

(*Mr Meacher*) I think that is a good point. The Government's farm-scale evaluation trials are designed to try and give some quantification of environmental impacts, although that is limited to differential herbicide management techniques—the use of particular kinds of herbicides, as opposed to non-GM crops of the same kind. We will, I hope, get more environmental data from these trials, and it is a matter of argument. I am in favour of providing that environmental data for the consumer, if we can do so succinctly and accurately. You made another good point, too, about cotton because one of the arguments has been—and it is not for me to make a judgment, but it is certainly asserted—that the herbicides that are used can cause damage to the workers who are obliged to use sprays that can affect health. That, again, is an issue that many consumers would be interested in. There are campaigns to stop the purchase of products that are made with child labour, which we all understand. Equally, if people knew the conditions under which GM products can in some countries in certain conditions be applied, I think they perhaps would expect to have that information in order to take their own view.

Chairman

191. It is a difficulty. We are now setting up proposals on labelling to protect our own health, or to protect our own view about environmental damage primarily over here, which may be inflicting health risks and severe health risks on producers in producing countries.

(*Mr Meacher*) I think that is absolutely true.

Lord Fyfe of Fairfield

192. What risks do you think are associated with growing soya on the American continent, in terms of UK agronomy or environment?

(*Mr Meacher*) I think that is really a matter for each importing country to decide for itself. Indeed, there is provision for that under the Cartagena Protocol. If there is sufficient evidence of uncertainty about the risk, then it is for the importing country to use that as grounds, ultimately, not to import. Obviously, those grounds would have to be stated and justified. It needs to be said with regard to soya that it has only been imported into the EU for processing, not for cultivation. As far as I know, the only GM soya bean product that has been proposed for the EU market, was granted a consent. It is for importing countries to take their own view, so long as they justify it to international opinion; and it certainly cannot be used as a trade barrier.

Chairman

193. If we follow this by extension, it leads on to the evidence we heard from the United States last week. If we take, for example, maize oil, which we are told will not itself contain genetically modified material but is produced from a GM crop, the present draft regulation that we are looking at from the European Union suggests that this should be labelled. But the evidence from the Food Standards Authority suggests that as this is unenforceable, it is probably not a very sensible proposal. Would you confirm, therefore, that you would think that the route of trying to have a GM-free product is more logical, rather than trying to trace something that is ultimately unprovable as to whether it is accurate or not?

(*Mr Meacher*) Taking the advice of FSA, which we have, it is indeed the case that it is probably not practical, and it is certainly disproportionate. I think that is a fair point to make. On the question of GM-free, this increasingly becomes a term of art. As to how far it is actually possible to have GM-free is a moot point. One can have a country that is free of GM cultivation, if it makes that choice. Given that trace elements may be present, possibly even below the level of detection, in conventional seed coming in to the country, despite the best efforts that we or others make in order to detect it, I do not think one can make an assertion of an absolute kind that certain products are absolutely GM-free.

194. I think, Minister, that it is clear that absolutes are very difficult to achieve in this respect. Perhaps it is salutary to look at the experience of North America itself, where the concept of identity-preserved lines is well understood, and where there are some identity-preserved lines that are described as non-GM. I accept that that is a different terminology to "GM-free". If this is a concept that we wish to pursue—in other words, if the onus is on those who want to have food that is not GM to go for the identity-preserved line, as with organic products, just to be sure that it is produced by a certain agricultural system, and similarly with fair trade products from the third world— is this a route that is logical or sensible? We note, however, that the cost of IP food, like organic food, is inevitably higher because the onus is on the IP food to demonstrate its preserved status?

(*Mr Meacher*) I am in favour of providing as much detailed accurate information to consumers as possible. It is of course true with identity-preserved lines that you have paper-based trails in order to label GM, and that there is a price premium involved in that. GM bulk commodities do have a long and complex supply chain, which is very difficult to verify. All of that is true. My concern is that whatever label is put on a product, it is actually understood. Even if we do not use "GM-free", which I think is controversial because we cannot in any absolute sense guarantee it – if we use an alternative formulation such as "non-GM", I wonder how many consumers out there really understand what that means. What we mean by it is that it does not contain more than 1 per cent, or up to 1 per cent GM material. If you went into a supermarket and asked a random collection of shoppers what they understood

Chairman *contd.*]

by "non-GM", even if they saw it on the product, I do wonder how many would give the accurate answer. I suspect that most people would think that it did not contain GM, but that is not what we mean. We need to do a marketing exercise and explain to people why we cannot say "GM-free" and explain what we mean by "non-GM" so that the message is understood and everyone knows what they are doing. I think that that is not the case at the moment. There is a gap in the application of the regulatory framework, and I think it is one that we should try to close.

195. Would you favour an international standard for what is meant by "non-GM" and what is meant by "GM-free"?

(*Mr Meacher*) Yes, I would. I think if each country has its own different standards, it would be very confusing; and there is so much trading and importation that different products with different standards would completely confuse most consumers. I think that an international standard is exactly what is needed. At EU level certainly I think we can achieve that, but it would be much more helpful if this could be done internationally, involving particularly the North American continent.

Lord Crickhowell

196. Minister, the example of highly refined maize oil is a good illustration of the difficulty. I have the Food Standards Agency's evidence in front of me, in which they say that, although they are derived from GM sources, such products are identical in all respects to their non-GM counterparts; and they therefore present no different risk from those produced by conventional means. It is certainly clear that the sort of labelling that we are talking about at the moment is not going to tell the general public that, and there is a real difficulty about that.

(*Mr Meacher*) I entirely agree with that. The UK does take a different view from the Commission on this matter.

Chairman

197. I come back to this point: if the onus ultimately—however you term it, non-GM to an international standard, or GM-free—is on those who wish to buy such food to pay for the identity-preserved route, as opposed to the proposal that all GM food should be traceable from the point of production and then labelled accordingly, the onus in one case is put on the GM producer, and on the other the onus and the cost is put on the consumer. Do you follow what I am saying, and is it reasonable that the consumer should bear the cost, as opposed to the producer of GM foods?

(*Mr Meacher*) I understand the distinction you are making, but I am not sure how far in practice it will apply in the real world. If people are unwilling to buy GM products—and some are unwilling to buy it in principle—then that certainly has an impact on the agricultural chain. If people are unwilling to buy a GM product unless it is properly labelled, then that is going to impose a requirement on a GM producer, which they are going to have to bear. If, as a result

of that, there is a significant price differential, a price premium, the GM producer has to decide how far they are prepared to reduce their pricing, or to absorb the price of identity-preserved mechanisms, in order still to be competitive within the market. I certainly think it is for the GM industry to find a way of providing the information that the consumer wants, and to do so in a competitive manner.

Countess of Mar

198. We are back to the Precautionary Principle. We have had this in another context many times. Can you tell me how you define it when it comes to GM crops, please?

(*Mr Meacher*) I wish I could define it in an area where you and I have talked many times over chemicals. This is a principle that almost everyone agrees with but which is difficult to put into operation in an effective and comprehensive manner. With regard to imports, I have already answered this question. Where there are grounds that are internationally acceptable, then it is for importing countries to decide under the Cartagena Protocol whether or not they wish to import. There is a precautionary principle operating there in respect of trade. In regard to cultivation, the way to proceed is on the basis of caution, proceeding step by step, and checking all the way as you go. That is exactly what we have done in the UK. There are tests that are carried out in the laboratory; we then proceed to small test sites in the field; you then progress from small-scale to large-scale, as in the farm-scale valuations which are, as it says, field scale; and then the one thing beyond that, if we proceed in that direction, is mass cultivation, which is a step change, a quantified change. Every step along the way needs to be checked, including the last one. Indeed, there is provision for post-market monitoring under Directive 2001/18, which is extremely important. It is not a fire-and-forget missile, but absolutely the opposite. There may be unforeseen or unforeseeable effects that we should be checking all the time. We have to do that as a regulatory authority, in order to provide evidence to a sceptical public that this is safe, and that it is not having undesirable environmental impacts. Clearly, there is a great deal of scepticism about this—and that is understating it. We need to be seen to be thoroughly, rigorously, openly and transparently checking as we go along, at every stage, providing that information openly and fully to the public. That may still not be enough for some members of the public, but that is what I mean by the Precautionary Principles. There are also Precautionary Principles written into Directive 2001/18, compared to its predecessor Directive 90/220: for example, the requirement to assess the longer term as opposed to medium impacts, and the indirect effects, as opposed to direct, on wildlife and habitats in managing GM crops; and, as I say, close market monitoring at all stages and for a substantial period of time. That, I think, is the only way to proceed. I am on the side of caution. I am not saying that we should not proceed but that we should do so very cautiously and do everything we can to take opinion with us.

Countess of Mar *contd.*]

199. You mentioned the scepticism from the public; do you think this could have arisen from the awful muddle that there seemed to be at the beginning when GM crops were first being planted on farms, when the distance was first 200 metres? People know that bees, for example, fly more than 200 metres, and that the wind blows things more than 200 metres, and science tells us that pollen is found beyond the Arctic Circle, when nothing actually grows up there. It does make one wonder about how much precaution one can actually take.

(*Mr Meacher*) That is a very good point. There continues to be intense argument about this issue. Those who assert that current separation distances are entirely adequate, and those who assert that very substantially increased separation distances are necessary—basically, it is a SCIMAC (Supply Chain Initiative on Modified Agricultural Crops)) argument in the former, and a Soil Association argument in the latter. Of course, there are many points in between, between 100 metres and 6 miles, whatever it is, which is rather a big gap. The real problem, as we know, is that there is a bell curve for the dropping of pollen in most plants, and within 50 metres the vast majority will have fallen to ground; but then there is a kind of leptokurtic curve, which proceeds just above the baseline for a very long distance. If you take one mile, you will certainly exclude the vast majority—and we are getting into the 98 or 99 point something per cent; but you will still not be at 100 per cent. There probably is not a point where you can guarantee that in exceptional climatic, gusty heavy wind conditions, that some pollen will not go further. There is the other argument that it is not the presence of pollen as such but the presence of pollen that alights on a female flower, on the appropriate stigma, that will have an impact. It is not just the availability of pollen, although the more pollen there is, the more likely that that will happen. It is a very difficult issue. There has been talk about zoning as a way of trying to resolve the separation distance or the whole concept of co-existence, which is deciding what is the appropriate separation distance. Ultimately, because there is a functional relationship between the level of cross-pollination or contamination and the extent of the separation distances, it is almost a linear relationship. It is a question of deciding what is the threshold that you are prepared to put up with, as a consumer, and then reading it back into the separation distances. That, I think, is the right way to proceed. If we knew what consumers out there were prepared to accept, we can then, almost mathematically, work out the separation distances that will deliver it.

Chairman: Inevitably, we always tend to wander further than traceability and labelling regulation, but this is an inevitable part of the debate and, as Lady Mar said, creates the public interest and concern.

Baroness Miller of Chilthorne Domer

200. We have the Precautionary Principle in this country and, as you have said, now written into EU Directives, but these proposals would involve imports from third countries, and may encourage the growing of GM in those countries. Is there anything in the Cartagena Protocol that adopts the same Precautionary Principle approach, and how does that translate into the WTO's rules and regulations? Clearly, if they do not accept it, they will just see it as a trade barrier.

(*Mr Meacher*) Since I was present at Montreal, when the Cartagena Protocol (so named after a first attempt to settle a protocol at Cartagena in Colombia, which failed, but it was then settled in Montreal and, curiously, it is still called the Cartagena Protocol) the big issue, going right into the final night, until we settled it at about half past five in the morning, was exactly over this question of the compatibility of WTO rules and a multilateral environmental agreement like this biosafety protocol. The Americans insisted right up to the end that there should be priority or pre-eminence for the WTO rules; but if it came to a clash, then the fall-back was that the WTO rules would take priority. We were not prepared to accept that and the final decision was that there is parity between the two; neither overrides the other. That is not a wholly satisfactory conclusion, but by five in the morning almost anything is acceptable, and actually it is not a bad compromise I think it is just about workable. Of course, it has not been tested in the WTO, and it may well be that neither side wishes to press it that far. I hope that that is the case. Your other point is what provisions apply if GM crops are grown in developing countries. Again, in practice they will not apply in many developing countries. That is just simply a fact. It is a regrettable fact, but it is true. I do not think anyone is saying they should not be permitted to grow GM crops until all those provisions are in place—we are not saying that—but we are saying that the developed world ought to do more to assist the third world countries to be able to apply these provisions as rapidly and effectively as possible.

Lord Palmer

201. We were on the same train on Friday evening, and I found it terribly difficult to resist the temptation to tackle you about some of these problems. Why does the Government believe that the level of tolerance for organic produce of 5 per cent is appropriate, but that 1 per cent is correct for GM; and how does it balance scientific justification, consumer concern and commercial feasibility?

(*Mr Meacher*) I think your last point probably answers your first. We have to provide, as fully as we can, what the consumer wants to know, but we also have to balance that against what is commercially feasible to deliver, bearing in mind that absolutes are not possible in the messy world in which we live, and that a zero requirement is unrealisable. In the case of organic, there are various food products that are not yet obtainable in organic form, and the view is taken, which I think is a reasonable one, that for practical reasons the level should be up to 5 per cent of the total agricultural ingredients in organic processed foods. As you have several ingredients in a processed food, then it becomes more and more difficult to identify at a very low level a particular organic

Lord Palmer contd.]

ingredient. I think that is reasonable, although I have to say that the only inputs from outside organic farming forming an organic product that are permitted, are those listed in Regulation 2092/91. It is therefore not the case that you can add all sorts of other ingredients. They are specifically listed in this EU regulation, so it is still controlled. If you turn to the GM threshold, we are looking for the lowest that is practically enforceable. That can be done either through DNA-based testing, or protein-based testing. The former is mostly qualitative, although I am told—and I am not a scientist—that realtime PCR (Polymerase Chain Reaction) is an approach that can quantify down to a very low level, even though—and this is the problem the lower you get—you may get errors, and below 1 per cent there is the question of whether consistency and reliability can be secured. The figure of 1 per cent is generally agreed throughout the EU as a GM threshold that is enforceable. It is under review. The Commission's regulatory committee believes that it is possible to go as low as 0.1 per cent but that would only apply in the case of seeds under ideal seed production and conditions. There may well be situations where it might be problematic. We are saying that 5 per cent, bearing in mind processed food in the case of organic, is probably the best that we can achieve. It would be better if we could go lower, but we probably cannot. In the case of GM, 1 per cent is pretty reliable, but if it were possible to go lower, and that is what the consumer wanted, then we should seek to do so. There are new techniques. Again, I am not a scientist, but there are biosensors and polymer-binding technologies that may enable us to go lower. Once those have been tested, and if they are reliable, I think they should be used.

Chairman

202. Coming back to your central thesis, which I am sure everyone sympathises with, the objective of these EU regulations is to give the consumer the fullest information to provide consumer choice. Nevertheless, we have written evidence from FSA which says that the EU proposals go too far in the sense that they require GM labelling where it is impossible to enforce—in other words for food produced from GM crops but not containing GM material. That is the proposal at the moment, and as I understand it that is something that you are saying is not just impossible to enforce, but also somewhat illogical, as other products derived from GM processes such as cheese and wine—when the enzymes might be modified—would have to be labelled, so that is another inconsistency. I am saying that in the attempt to get greater full consumer choice, it is not realistic to go for the labelling options that have been promoted by the European Commission, and we need something based perhaps on maintaining the current labelling regime and introducing a scheme that differentiates for those who require it—non-GM, or GM-free food, as a separate line. Is that the Government's stance?

(Mr Meacher) It is not the case that we disagree with the Commission proposals across the board—not at all. We do believe that in the case you have mentioned, we have accepted FSA advice, and that it is impractical and disproportionate as it affects products that are derived from but do not actually contain GM material, such as highly refined maize oil. We do accept that FSA view, and that is the Government's position. In the case of foods in general, I think we are broadly accepting what the Commission has said, because it is designed to provide a realistic 1 per cent threshold that is meaningful to the consumer. However, we have made some detailed comments. This is an ongoing process within the Commission at the present time, but we are broadly in support of their proposals. As I say, there are some detailed further considerations that we would like to see.

Baroness Maddock

203. I was interested in what you were saying about the improvements in testing. There is a proposal that we build in to the protocol the ability to review the level as testing improves. Would that be something you would be putting?

(Mr Meacher) Yes, I very much agree with that. I think we should go as far as is technically feasible in order to provide the most detailed and refined information to consumers, so long as it is not significantly subject to error that you do not get false positive or false negative results, and also taking into account the application of whatever limit you choose is less accurate when you come to processed food. Subject to those complications, let us make it more accurate still if we can.

Countess of Mar

204. Who is going to pay for it?

(Mr Meacher) The consumer pays for food when he or she finds it in the marketplace, and there is competition between GM foods, conventional food and organic food. One of the problems with regard to our cheap food policy, so-called, is that organic products at the moment can often only be produced at a premium, unless, and perhaps partly as a result of the Commission reports, we could find ways of easing the position of organic farmers so that they can compete in the marketplace. The same is the case in regard to GM. I think the consumer is entitled to have the information, and it is for the GM production industry to find ways of doing that without imposing a price hike for the consumer, which will not be acceptable.

Chairman: That, as they say, is the $64,000 question. Minister, thank you very much for the patient way in which you have handled these very difficult subjects. We are most grateful to you and your colleagues.

Examination of Witnesses

PROFESSOR SIR JOHN KREBS, Chairman, and DR JON BELL, Deputy Chief Executive, Food Standards Agency, examined.

Chairman

205. Welcome, Sir John and Dr Bell, we are grateful to you for joining us. I know that you sat in on the last evidence so you will be familiar with some of the issues that we are grappling with. Sir John, would you like to say anything, by way of introduction, to introduce yourself and your colleague?

(*Professor Sir John Krebs*) Thank you very much, my Lord Chairman. Just very briefly, to remind Members of the Committee that the Food Standards Agency is the Government Department with responsibility for protecting consumer interests in relation to food. With regard to GM our responsibilities include safety assessment from the point of view of food safety and human health, labelling and choice, and the provision of consumer information. You will be aware, I am sure, of the fact that one of our principles is to operate in as open and transparent and honest a way as possible and all the policy issues relating to GM and indeed all the other areas of responsibility of the Agency are discussed and debated in public, indeed only in public. So the issues of GM labelling and GM safety have been discussed in our Board meetings over the last year and a half. In addition we have held public stakeholder debates on difficult areas, for example the 1 per cent threshold in relation to GM labelling. Also the expert advisory committee that helps us in assessing the safety of GM foods, namely the Advisory Committee on Novel Foods and Processors, meets from time to time in public and it has now adopted a practice of putting the dossiers on which its safety assessment will be based for novel foods, including GM, on its website to allow public comment. I think I will leave it there.

206. I do not know whether it will be helpful in the light of the discussion we have had if I try to summarise what we understand to be the options that the European Union looked at on labelling and indeed the extra option which I understand the Food Standards Authority looked at. Also if I try to summarise what I think has emerged from this transparent process you have just described. I think it will be helpful to get it on the record so that if I have got it wrong, I would be enormously grateful at this early stage in the deliberations and then you can put us right and we will start from a position where we all recognise where we stand. As I understand it, the Commission considered four options for GM food labelling. The first was to maintain the current labelling regime. The second was to maintain the current labelling regime and introduce a GM free scheme. The third was to introduce labelling of all foods derived from or produced with GM material, and that was the option proposed by the Commission. The fourth was to introduce labelling for all foods derived from or produced with GM material, including GM feed and GM enzymes. I understand also that the Food Standards Agency commissioned an evaluation of costs, benefits, risks and uncertainties of these along with a fifth option which was to introduce labelling for all foods derived

from GM material and introduce a GM free scheme. Am I correct in saying that the Food Standards Authority sees the option which maintains the current labelling regime and introduces the GM free scheme as representing the best balance between costs and benefits?

(*Professor Sir John Krebs*) You are right in the last point and you are right in the first four that you laid out as the Commission options. Essentially our position is that option two of the Commission proposals, which is to maintain the current regime but to extend it by the addition of a GM free option—and you might wish to discuss what we believe that means—is the most practical, enforceable and proportionate option. We believe, also, and this is very important, that this will be the most effective in providing honest information for consumers. I emphasise the reason we did not support the Commission proposal of extending the labelling requirement to derivatives, is that, as you discussed with Mr Meacher, it would not be testable chemically by any means because the derivatives are chemically identical. We believe that is potentially leading to a situation in which consumers will be deceived about the GM content of their food rather than providing them with better information. Our starting point was what will provide the best information for consumers that can actually be delivered? We did not consider the Commission proposals would do that.

207. That is the labelling proposal. Just to get on the record the other part of our inquiry which is traceability, perhaps you can just tell us whether you thought the traceability proposals were practical?

(*Professor Sir John Krebs*) That really links directly to the labelling proposal because the only way that you could enforce and check on the labelling of purified derivatives that had no trace of the protein or DNA would be through a traceability and IP system. It is our belief, based on the expert advice that we have had and our own judgment of the evidence, that to maintain an accurate traceability system and identity preservation system for commodities which are moved around the world in bulk, such as soya and maize, would be extremely difficult if not impossible at the moment. That is why if you were to buy a food that had a soya derivative in, which claimed not to be GM, there would be no way of us guaranteeing, as the regulator, that this indeed was the case. Because of the complexity of the route of transport and the processes involved we believe the traceability on that global scale is not practical at the moment as an option. We see the linkage between the labelling and traceability as being very intimate.

Chairman: I think that sets the scene very clearly. I think we need now perhaps to go back to some of the questions that we predicted we might wish to ask. Sir John, you have been before and you know that nothing is predictable in these matters.

Baroness Miller of Chilthorne Domer

208. Good morning, Sir John. Thank you for reminding us of what your remit is at the beginning. You heard our questions to the Minister just now.
(*Professor Sir John Krebs*) Yes.

209. It seemed to me, when I read what you had been asked to submit on behalf of the UK Government, that this really takes you beyond what I had imagined your remit was into areas, for instance in Section 8, of export obligations and in Section 9 into the environmental issues.
(*Professor Sir John Krebs*) Yes.

210. First of all, can I ask, do you feel comfortable with that?
(*Professor Sir John Krebs*) I would reiterate what the Minister said, that although we were the authors of the Government response which was submitted to the Committee, we did that as the Department within Government co-ordinating the response from across different parts of Government. The element to do with trade and to do with the environment and to do with international development reflect the input from DTI, DEFRA and DfID but we drew the whole thing together. I feel quite comfortable that we should sometimes play a role as the lead Government Department in drawing together a co-ordinated response, on other occasions we would feed our input in and it might be drawn together by DEFRA, for example. To reiterate what the Minister said, in terms of the co-ordination across Government, as well as the work at official level and the work in Ministerial correspondence, of which I am a part, there is also the SCI(BIO) which is the Cabinet Committee which deals with bio-technology and I attend SCI(BIO) to participate in the discussions and contribute an FSA perspective.

Chairman

211. Are we allowed to know who chairs that Committee?
(*Professor Sir John Krebs*) Yes, you are. It is chaired by Robin Cook.

Baroness Miller of Chilthorne Domer

212. The point I am trying to drive at, and I know you share this interest, is accountability.
(*Professor Sir John Krebs*) Yes.

213. My basic worry is where is the accountability for this issue? With which Minister does it rest, do you imagine, for the public?
(*Professor Sir John Krebs*) As far as the Food Standards Agency's role is concerned, the accountability lies through Health Ministers and that is true throughout the United Kingdom because we are a UK wide body and so Health Ministers in England, Wales, Scotland and Northern Ireland answer for us. In terms of the co-ordinated view, such as the submission that you received, I think different Ministers would hold accountability responsibility for different parts of it. In that sense I agree with what Michael Meacher said.

Lord Crickhowell

214. Just before we leave this responsibility area, clearly the situation as to who takes the lead may change. If we get into a major conflict about world trade other Ministers may come to the fore.
(*Professor Sir John Krebs*) Yes.

215. As I understand the position now, and you have effectively repeated what the Minister said, in presenting the evidence—your evidence—you are actually speaking for what is currently the collective agreed view of Government taken after proper decisions in an appropriate Cabinet Committee and therefore the charge made in advance of this meeting by Friends of the Earth that this was going to be a punch up between you and the Minister is simply not true. You have both confirmed this is the agreed position of the British Government?
(*Professor Sir John Krebs*) Absolutely.

Chairman

216. Can I move on to how within the Board—I am not talking now about your wider responsibility that you referred to but how you have, as you say, in a very transparent, open and protracted way discussed these issues over many months? To what extent in these deliberations do you feel that you have to reflect not just health and safety aspects and food safety aspects but also consumer concerns, which may not be based on what some would describe as sound science?
(*Professor Sir John Krebs*) We are an evidence based department. For the assessment of safety and public health we rely strictly on the scientific evidence as interpreted by our expert advisors: independents, academic and industrial and institute advisors. When it comes to issues of labelling and consumer choice, there is, of course, again an evidence base, an evidence base of what public opinion is which we ascertain through a combination of different techniques, MORI poll type opinion polls or focus groups or other kinds of social science research. There is also an evidence base to do with what is enforceable. In this area, of course, the scientific contribution to that is the evidence base about what can be detected with accuracy and reliability in terms of GM content. I would say that broadly we base all our policy on evidence, some of that is strictly scientific evidence in the sense of natural sciences, other times it may be perhaps more the softer end of the social sciences which includes ascertaining public opinion and taking into account perceptions. I do not think perceptions can be ignored but they cannot be the basis, for example, of safety assessment whilst they might contribute to a view about what kinds of information and choice people like to have.

217. I understand from that, therefore, that you do give due recognition to perceptions. I suppose, therefore, that leads one to ask, in so far as there still appears to be widespread concern—perhaps not so great as there was 18 months ago, but there is still widespread concern—about how one can identify food which might have been derived from GM crops and your recommendation, which you are presenting on behalf of Government, that this transparency, this identification is not achievable.
(*Professor Sir John Krebs*) Yes.

Chairman *contd.*]

218. To what extent therefore are you recognising that you are not able to meet the aspirations of a large minority or perhaps a majority of UK consumers?

(*Professor Sir John Krebs*) I think your last point, Chairman, is a very important one that there is no one category of consumer. There are some consumers who are very concerned about the use of GM technology in food, and there are many consumers who are not concerned about it. Indeed in our most recent national opinion poll where we asked people in an unprompted way what their food concerns were, GM came out very low, much less than 10 per cent. If you prompt people and say "Are you sure you are not concerned about GM" then of course it goes up a bit but you can say that about virtually any concern, if you ask people they will begin to wonder if they should be concerned. There is not just one category of consumer. Coming back to the main focus of your question, we do recognise that the view that the Board of the Food Standards Agency came to, whilst it was based on our opinion of what was the best option for consumers, was not popular with some consumer representative groups. We have had full and frank discussions with those groups since the Board decision as well as beforehand. It is not a difference in what one is trying to achieve: we are trying to achieve a labelling regime in which those who want to make choices and to avoid GM technology can do so. In that sense we are in complete agreement with the consumer representative groups. Where we differ is in how to get there. Our opinion is that the Commission proposals will not be enforceable and will not be deliverable. What I have said to various consumer groups who have come to see me about this is that if the Commission proposals were implemented then in a couple of years' time people would turn round to us and say "Well, how are you checking that actually these products that claim to contain no GM derived products, are in fact doing that?" I would have to say "Well, I am sorry, there is no way of guaranteeing it other than a paper trail which refers to a batch of soya grown perhaps in South America, shipped in a bulk transporter, processed in a bulk mill, then shipped in a large container arriving at the door of Europe when, under the European Commission proposals, the traceability starts." Because as you know the proposal is that traceability should start when the product arrives in Europe not on the farm where it is grown in another part of the world. I do feel, and the Board of the Agency feels, that the Commission proposal potentially offers what we call a Cheat's Charter, that it would not be possible to check whether people are cheating on the system.

219. Some of the organisations who have given evidence to us are prepared to put their confidence in this audit trail, this traceability. Would you say that they were misguided?

(*Professor Sir John Krebs*) To give you a "for instance". Last month we published a research study in which we had looked at the GM soya content of 200 odd examples of baked goods from the shelves of the shops in Britain. We found that about 15 per cent of those baked goods contained small traces of GM soya. Sometimes the soya was actually in wheat flour so it was an adventitious presence in a wheat product.

In three out of the 200 or so cases the presence of GM soya exceeded the 1 per cent threshold. Now all of those products were products which were produced through a traceability and IP system. One of the ones which had GM in was an organic product. This to me is a practical demonstration that traceability and IP does not give a guarantee. In these cases we were able to test for the presence of GM because we were testing for the DNA, the actual chemical signature. Had those been derivatives, a purified soya derivative or a purified starch or a purified oil we would have had no way of checking. I think the evidence speaks for itself, that however good IP and the traceability systems are they are certainly not a guarantee. In that sample there was a 15 per cent failure rate, roughly speaking.

Lord Crickhowell

220. On this question of practicability and traceability, we have had evidence from some large organisations who say "Yes we can do it". Do you think there is a difference between specific big purchasers with the capacity to organise and indeed to get things because of their big purchasing power and the wider range of smaller traders? It seems to me that if you are a Tesco or a Sainsbury or Unilever you may be in a position to establish a much more secure system than many others.

(*Professor Sir John Krebs*) Yes.

221. By the time we get down to buying from a number of shops or indeed in the restaurants it may well become much more difficult.

(*Professor Sir John Krebs*) Yes.

222. Am I wrong in making that distinction and simply basing it on the fact that some people say they can do it at the moment might be misleading?

(*Professor Sir John Krebs*) I think you are right to suppose that the big purchasers will have more clout and indeed have more resources to go back and check at the source. From my conversations with some of the major retailers they do, for some of their products, go back and check at source. It is still the case, from my conversations with some of the major supermarket chains, that they rely to a very large extent on paper trails. They have typically in many areas a one step back checking system. So they check the paper work from their immediate supplier and they place upon their immediate supplier the obligation to check his or her paper work, the further step back in the chain. Even for the major retailers, whilst certainly they have more capability to deploy resources right back through the chain and demand proper systems from their suppliers, even there, the evidence I have heard from the retailers themselves is that they cannot provide guarantees in many cases.

Countess of Mar

223. I will declare an interest as a cheese maker and a small producer. My concern is that the EU labelling requirements will be too onerous on small producers to be able to continue in business. Is this something that you have taken into consideration with your proposals?

Countess of Mar contd.]

(*Professor Sir John Krebs*) We started from the point of view of what will deliver the best for consumers because that is our basic remit. But it is also incumbent upon us to look at what is practical and proportionate. That is in the Act that set us up.

224. And to give them choice.

(*Professor Sir John Krebs*) And to provide choice to consumers. Certainly we are concerned about the overall question of practicality and enforceability and of the burden of regulation that is imposed on the food industry, particularly small producers because as in all sectors, as Lord Haskin said to me, large food industries love regulation because it puts their small competitors out of business. Certainly, it is the smaller producers who are more likely to be adversely affected by regulation and that has to be part of our thinking although we start from the position of what will provide the best information and choice to meet the needs of consumers.

Baroness Miller of Chilthorne Domer

225. You have talked about what the supermarkets have said to you, but in their evidence to us—for instance the British Retail Consortium were saying in their oral evidence they were very unhappy with your suggestion of GM free status. They prefer the term "non-GM".

(*Professor Sir John Krebs*) Yes.

226. It has been pointed out, also, that having a GM free status may raise the price of food in the way that organic prices have been high which would not be in the interests of consumers.

(*Professor Sir John Krebs*) I will just take two points there. I think non-GM, as we know, is used to mean it contains a bit of GM. I suspect that is quite confusing to a lot of people. Certainly when I ask my friends back at home whether they know the distinction between non-GM and GM free, they are completely unaware of it and they would assume that non-GM meant GM free so there is a confusion there.

227. Is that because you have not explained it to them as an Agency?

(*Professor Sir John Krebs*) I will come back to that in a moment. I think there is an important issue about explaining to the public what is going on with GM technology, and let me just return to that. The second point about GM free, it has been put to us that all the arguments that I have just mounted about the traceability and the difficulty of managing IP systems would apply in spades to a GM free option. If you are complaining about tracing derivatives how can you propose a GM free option? The answer to that is that we envisaged this GM free option as being initially at least a rather niche market. Again, to go back to the analogy drawn in the previous session between it and organic food, organic food at the moment is a niche market. It is something where people are willing to pay a premium for a specific production method because they perceive benefits in it. We would envisage that GM free, if it was introduced, would be very much of that kind. It would probably be based on local production systems with short supply chains where traceability could be guaranteed and where the sourcers could be identified as definitely not having a GM basis. That is the distinction. We would accept that probably in that case the GM free in the strict sense would carry a price premium. There is a debate, and certainly I do not claim to have the magic answer, as to whether the premium should be paid by those who want GM free or by the rest of the consumers. Because you can argue that the burden should be paid by those who want to have GM rather than by those who want to avoid it. We are where we are and the fact of the matter is that GM on a worldwide basis is being grown increasingly and therefore those who want to avoid it are likely to have to pay a premium. If I could just finish on the point about consumer information. I could not agree more that that is important, and although it is not widely advertised, when the Board of the Agency discussed the labelling options and came down in favour of the option that it did come down in favour of, it asked the Executive of the Agency also to devise methods of effectively communicating to consumers what actually is going on at the moment. I think most consumers are unaware of the fact that the bulk of hard cheese produced in Britain is manufactured with a GM processing aid, more than half the bread in Britain, I understand, is produced with a GM processing aid. In people's minds the difference between a processing aid, a derivative and GM material, is very vague. I guess if people were told these things they would say "For me most hard cheese is GM, it does not contain any trace of GM material but it was produced with a GM enzyme, therefore it is GM". We are now in the process of studying through focus groups what people want to know and how most effectively to put those messages across. I think it is an important part of empowering consumers, to complement whatever labelling regime is in place, to explain what actually is going on. Even if the Commission proposal were adopted, and derivatives were labelled, there would be no requirement to label processing aids, to label animals fed on GM feed and for people who have a profound objection to the technology, those issues are at least as important as derivatives.

228. In the light of the Royal Society report recently about infant feed and food for young children, surely people are likely, with very small children, to want to continue to buy non-GM food for them?

(*Professor Sir John Krebs*) Yes.

229. Do you think your comments would apply to those foods which contain novel proteins when it comes to small children?

(*Professor Sir John Krebs*) Well, of course, if GM were used in infant formula and they contained novel proteins then they would be labelled under the current requirements. As far as I know GM derivatives or indeed GM proteins are not used currently in infant formula. Certainly we always recognise that infants could be a vulnerable group in relation, for example, to allergenic effects and that, whether or not they are, parents may have particular concerns in wanting to make choices on behalf of their children or their infants. Certainly any discussion that we have about consumer information and what we should put out would recognise the

Baroness Miller of Chilthorne Domer *contd.*]

particular needs of groups such as parents of young children or those catering for young children as well as those with particular religious or other principles which might lead them to want to avoid GM technology.

Lord Crickhowell

230. I was going to come on to this question later on, it is the question of labelling and whether there are any alternatives. Obviously there is a severe limitation of labelling on almost any food product. Indeed very many food products such as bread usually do not have a label of any sort on them.
(*Professor Sir John Krebs*) Yes.

231. Are you looking for possible alternative means—the internet and other ways of getting this information across? Even then, do you not think that there is a real difficulty about getting consumer choice, because people have to be given a lot of information about why they do things and what other benefits are being achieved? We heard earlier about cotton and the fact that perhaps we are avoiding producers dying through the use of chemicals. In an earlier inquiry Friends of the Earth actually advanced the argument that it is perfectly acceptable to use DDT in areas that are heavily malaria-infested because you have got a choice of evils or a choice of benefits.
(*Professor Sir John Krebs*) Yes.

232. Certainly this is true of environmental benefits. How on earth are we to get the arguments out so that there is a choice? I have been struck by the fact that whatever labels we use in a simplistic way we are actually obscuring the issue rather than clarifying it for consumers. What view do you have of how we overcome these problems?
(*Professor Sir John Krebs*) Certainly I would agree with you that a label is only one source of information and a label cannot hope to contain all the information that some consumers want. I once heard the analogy that a label, to use the American term, is like prime real estate. So if you are going to develop it you have to develop it very carefully, you do not just put any old rubbish on it. There is a choice to be made about what is the priority for labelling. I think there is also to be a recognition that for many consumers these more detailed and sophisticated arguments are not part of their purchasing habit. One is catering for a different clientele with different kinds of information. The Agency's overall approach to labelling, and we have an overall action plan on labelling, encompasses overall clarity of labelling, issues like misleading claims, things like "country style" and "pure and fresh" which may actually not mean what they appear to mean. If we could get rid of some of the guff, as my Deputy called it, and get some more explicit, easily understandable real information on to labels, that would help but I acknowledge, as you say, that there have to be other approaches. These may be through the use of the internet, and one thing that I know some retailers have discussed is the concept of i-labelling, so the label on the package has part of the information, if you want to get more, like looking at these environmental benefits, you hold the package up

against a bar code reader and a computer screen then pops up with all the history of environmental and welfare and other benefits that might relate to that product. I think technology may eventually provide more options, of course none of them come cost free and the retailers will have to decide how many people want it and what the benefits are. I accept fully that the label is not the answer to everything, it is a limited resource and it has to be used very judiciously and carefully.

233. Lady Mar has just prompted a question in a note she has passed to me. We could put phone numbers or e-mail addresses on labels.
(*Professor Sir John Krebs*) Yes.

234. So if people want supplementary information they know where to go to.
(*Professor Sir John Krebs*) Yes.

Lord Fyfe of Fairfield

235. That happens to a great extent. I think most of the major retailers would have help line numbers which would encourage one to contact them for further information.
(*Professor Sir John Krebs*) I think my colleague, Dr Bell, would like to say something on this.
(*Dr Bell*) Yes. There are, as we have discussed, a wide variety of different ways of tackling this issue, and certainly labels is one possibility and the internet is another. We have talked about having some sort of address on labels for further information, that is another approach. Also, in the Agency, we recognise that we have an obligation to try and get information more generally out there so that people can understand against what background they are making these choices, if not information specifically relating to the product. As Sir John has said, that is why we are carrying out focus group work to try and understand better how we can put this information out in a way that people can understand and in a way they want. We will be taking action on that probably later this year and then we will get feedback hopefully from that and we will take it forward from there. We have an obligation as well as retailers I think.

236. I did ask the Minister when he was in earlier on, Sir John, about the risks posed from growing soya on the American continent and coming to Europe. He gave a response to that.
(*Professor Sir John Krebs*) Yes.

237. Going on from there, does your Agency believe that there is a foreseeable risk to the health of UK consumers from eating products known to be available from outside the European Union which may ultimately be made available in this country? Now, we have had a little press release this morning which is headed *Krebs versus Meacher* which I found quite interesting. It comes from Friends of the Earth. The FOE challenges FSA to stand up for consumers. It says that you and Mr Meacher are likely to clash.
(*Professor Sir John Krebs*) Yes.

238. There is no evidence of you clashing, in fact you seem to have a perfectly civilised and friendly relationship. Would you like to comment on these points?

Lord Fyfe of Fairfield *contd.*]

(*Professor Sir John Krebs*) Would you like me to comment on the question about food coming in from outside the EU?

239. Yes.

(*Professor Sir John Krebs*) The first point is that any GM food that is marketed in the European Union, whether it is produced within the EU, or whether it is coming in from outside would be subject to a rigorous scientific safety assessment as part of the approvals process and that will be done on a case-by-case basis. The same standards of rigour of safety assessment apply to food wherever it comes from, I think that is the first point. The second is that the international bodies which deal with food safety and standards, notably the obscurely named Codex Alimentarius, which is a WHO body, are working towards an internationally agreed standard of safety assessment that will be applied by all countries throughout the world. I do believe in an increasingly global world where GM will be increasingly grown, we need to have an internationally agreed standard of safety assessment is the right way.

Chairman

240. Can I interrupt you on that and just ask how long is it going to take before we have a meaningful output from WHO in this respect?

(*Professor Sir John Krebs*) The task force of Codex which is currently meeting in Yokohama has agreed, I think, a position now which it will put to Codex Alimentarius at its meeting in Rome in July 2003 for adoption. The task force statement—of which I have a copy here—says "The principles will provide a framework for evaluating the safety and nutritional aspects of GM foods. They define the need for a pre-market safety assessment of all such foods on a case-by-case basis." so that is a year and a half from now.

241. Perhaps I could ask if you could refer us to that statement. I am sorry, I interrupted, I think you were going on to point three.

(*Professor Sir John Krebs*) The third point really is one that the Minister touched on, and indeed came out of both the Edinburgh conference that I chaired and the Bangkok conference that you yourself chaired, and that is the issue of capacity building and access to scientific expertise in the developing world. I think if we have an international assessment framework, if we have increasing numbers of countries in the developing world growing GM, we have an obligation to help those countries in ways that we can to develop the rigour of scientific assessment of safety that we would want to have in our own countries. I would see those are the elements of the process for international trade but the starting point is that all foods marketed in the European Union, whether they are grown here or produced elsewhere, are subject to the same safety assessment in the case of GM.

242. I think the other point you have referred to already in an answer to Lady Miller. You do not want to add anything more about the speculation that the Government might be riven in these issues?

(*Professor Sir John Krebs*) I think both Mr Meacher and I have answered that very fully. I do not think there is really anything to add.

Lord Fyfe of Fairfield

243. I can understand your saying that, Sir John, and I appreciate the reasons for it. You did explain, as you have done previously, the objectives of the Agency and the reported relationship. I sometimes find it difficult to really follow your Agency's relationship with the politicians, the various ministers, and how independent you really are of the political process. You may not wish to comment . . .

(*Professor Sir John Krebs*) I am very happy to comment.

244. . . . but it would be interesting if you could.

(*Professor Sir John Krebs*) I am very happy to comment. The Act that set up the Food Standards Agency was quite clear about this. We are independent of ministerial influence. We operate at arm's length from ministers. As I explained in response to Lady Miller's question, our accountability route is through Health Ministers.

245. Sure.

(*Professor Sir John Krebs*) The key thing, the key plank of our independence is that by the Act that set us up, we are empowered to publish our opinions, our advice, our view, without seeking prior ministerial approval. There has been no case in the two year history of the Agency where there has been any ministerial intervention. We have simply published our opinions, as we did indeed on GM labelling and GM safety and the Government as a whole has, I think, always accepted our opinion and our advice. I think I can state with confidence that my Board feels very strongly that they operate at arm's length from ministers and they do not feel under political pressure.

Countess of Mar

246. Sir John, does the Food Standards Agency propose to introduce any scientific testing of possible risks to health prior to recommending the introduction of new products containing GM material?

(*Professor Sir John Krebs*) The science of safety assessment, as indeed was brought out in the Royal Society report two weeks ago, is, as with all areas of science, a developing field. Indeed, we are investing in a programme rising to about £3 million a year in the novel science of GM safety assessment. The novel science will be particularly using novel molecular techniques, as we understand more about how genes are expressed in the cell and how the chemical constituents of the cell are influenced by gene expression we will be able to devise new techniques of safety assessment. We do not think the current safety assessment techniques are inadequate, we think they are robust and rigorous but as new scientific knowledge develops, those techniques will be improved. I should emphasise that the safety assessment is not just for GM but for other novel foods as well so the benefits of new science are not

Countess of Mar *contd.*]

simply narrowly applied to GM. The other area in
which we are carrying out pilot work is to meet the
comment that is often made that we have not been
eating GM foods for very long. How do you know
that in a long time period—ten, 20, 30 years—
unexpected adverse effects might not crop up? Again
the same argument could be applied with equal force
to any novel food that we eat, probably most of the
stuff that we eat in our diets has elements in it which
are either novel varieties of produce or novel
processes in manufacturing. What we have done is to
set up a pilot study based at Imperial College to look
at the methodology to see whether there is a
methodology for monitoring over a long time-scale
the health of groups of people in relation to the kinds
of food they are eating. This is a very complex area
because as you can imagine my health and your
health is influenced by a huge number of things, of
which the dietary component is only one. So whether
indeed it will be possible to tease out ultimately the
effects of consumption of GM or other novel foods is
questionable but we have put in place a study to try
and ascertain whether it is possible to do it or not.
The answer to your question is that we will
continually introduce novel scientific information,
novel scientific techniques as they develop. The
current process is based on the best available science
but the envelope of available science is continually
expanding and we will bring that into play as it
develops.

247. You brought in my major concern, the fact
that we are steadily being exposed to more and more
new things, not just in food but a lot of it is in our
food, with chemicals, and just how would you tease
out these things? We had the impression from the
Americans last week that it is a *fait accompli*, you
take it or leave it. You have no option but to accept
GM is here and, too bad, if there are any adverse
effects they will be very small, and so what?
(*Professor Sir John Krebs*) Well, certainly it is the
case that in the States, and indeed in other parts of
the world where GM is widely grown and consumed,
a large amount has been consumed in the last five to
ten years with as yet no detected adverse effects.
When I chaired the first of the two OECD
conferences in Edinburgh two years ago on GM food
safety in human health I asked the assembled 450
people from around the world whether anybody
could point to a scientifically established adverse
effect of consuming GM food. There was silence,
nobody could point to any piece of evidence that
demonstrated an adverse effect. That does not mean
to say that we should not continually strive to look
for new methods to ascertain whether there could be
long-term side effects. I share with you the view that
if there are such effects there is no reason to
particularly isolate GM from all the other novel
foods that we are exposed to in looking for potential
long-term effects.

248. There has been a lot of concern about obesity
in recent years and that could be put down to any
number of things—lack of exercise, diet.
(*Professor Sir John Krebs*) Absolutely. Multi-
factorial and very complicated to tease out
individual things.

Lord Walpole

249. I was going to ask whether you were confident
in the enforcement of the current legislation
regarding the labelling of products containing GM
material. I felt in fact you had covered this fairly well,
is there anything else you wish to add?
(*Professor Sir John Krebs*) I think I have covered it.

250. I felt you had.
(*Professor Sir John Krebs*) Yes. Given that one can
test chemically for the presence of GM DNA or
protein then there is a rigorous basis for backing it
up. Yes, we are confident about that. What we would
not be confident about—to reiterate—is the
enforcement of a system based purely on traceability
and identity preservation.

Lord Palmer

251. Could I just ask Dr Bell, does the FSA believe
the proposed extension to labelling legislation to
animal feed really can be enforced? Has it made an
estimate of the cost of enforcement? Who do you
really believe is going to support this cost? It is a
tricky one.
(*Dr Bell*) It is undoubtedly a difficult area as many
are that involve GM. As far as enforcing labelling in
the animal feed area is concerned it very much, I
think, parallels the situation in the human food area.
Where we can do tests in the way that Sir John has
described, looking for DNA or protein, then animal
feed labelling is very much enforceable and we very
much welcome that. We think an extension to the
animal feed area is right in that it gives farmers that
choice and ultimately they can pass that information
on if that is required. When we come down again to
derivatives, we are in much the same position as we
are with human food. It is not going to be possible to
do those tests and therefore we think it would be
extremely difficult to enforce effectively. We have
those difficulties and I think that very much parallels
the situation on the food side. As far as cost is
concerned, we have not ourselves made an estimate
of what the increased costs would be but we are
making £7 million available to local authorities over
the next three years to increase generally their ability
to do checks on animal feed. It is an area we think
that more effort needs to be put into and we are
making some resource available for that and clearly
that would also embrace any new rules on GM
labelling. Ultimately though it is a question of
whether the industry can absorb any costs themselves
in terms of what it costs to do checks and inevitably
some of these will probably be passed on. As far as
local authorities are concerned, as I say, we are going
to make some more money available to them for
animal feed checking generally which is an area
where we think more resource is needed.

Baroness Maddock

252. I think you touched on this issue about
information to people. It may be that legislation has
improved and maybe not. Whatever is the case, who
does the FSA feel should bear responsibility for

Baroness Maddock contd.]

explaining to the electorate the reasoning behind the decision?

(*Professor Sir John Krebs*) I think the Food Standards Agency has an important role as the lead Government Department in this area in explaining to the public the basis of the decisions and what that implies to the public. I think, as Dr Bell said, one of the challenges for us is to devise effective ways of getting information across to the many different publics, because it is not a one size fits all. You might produce a very nice piece on your website which helps a certain sector of the population. There may be others who either do not have access to the internet or do not want to use the websites. I think we have to think creatively about different ways of getting the message across. I think, also, in this area, as in many others, an important element of communicating with the public is to have a continuing dialogue which is why, to reiterate where I started from, in all of the debate about GM that we have been involved in, whether it is safety or labelling and choice, we have taken a very public approach. We bring people in to talk about it so that people are aware already, or those who are interested are aware, of the basis of the arguments and they do not suddenly pop up as a complete surprise. I think the past record shows that when Government keeps quiet about something and then suddenly starts explaining in the last minute what is going on, that leads to more difficulty in public acceptance than if there has been a continuing dialogue where issues have been debated back and forth over a time period. It is an area where there is no single right answer, I do not claim the Food Standards Agency has got a magic solution. It is a complicated area and different points of view are bound to be around for a long time to come.

253. I find that quite interesting because I consider myself to be actually quite interested in this topic and particularly since I have been in the Committee nothing has come my way in the course of ordinary life.

(*Professor Sir John Krebs*) That is a useful piece of feedback.

Baroness Miller of Chilthorne Domer

254. Yes, going on from that, I would say that for an ordinary person to whom the price of food is very important who has a full-time job and perhaps two small children, the last thing they need to do is to go to an open forum in London or Exeter. Actually they will get their information through the media because that is the one thing they do every day.

(*Professor Sir John Krebs*) Yes.

255. I think it is a difficult circle for you to break into now because of the fact that the media have taken one position and you are not, as my colleague said, getting through to what I would term most of us.

(*Professor Sir John Krebs*) Yes. First of all, I agree with you that our main channel of communication with the public at large is through the media. We put a lot of effort into working with the media to try to ensure that our words and our way of expressing things is represented. Also, we do quite a lot of social science research to find out how many people are

aware of our messages through the media. After a story has appeared in the press, we will then carry out an opinion survey the following day or the following week to try and ascertain how many people around the country have heard what we have said and understand what we have said. In some areas we have had quite a high hit rate, well over half the population have heard what we have said and have understood what we have said. In the GM area, as Dr Bell said, this is an area where currently we are doing some preliminary focus group research to try and see what is the best way of getting the message across. I fully accept that in the GM area we have got more to do to get the messages across about what is going on, what the labelling regime means and what any changes in the future might mean. I fully accept we have got a job ahead of us and I agree with you that where the media has already taken a stance we may have to fight our way in to get a different perspective presented. I believe that is one of the challenges that we have got to face and we all do our best.

Countess of Mar

256. A thought has just gone through my mind— I did not mean Lord Crickhowell to ask my question by the way, I was just passing him a note – most of us go into supermarkets, or rather we all go into food outlets of some sort or another, and that would be an ideal source of information. Have you thought about compiling a fairly simple leaflet which explains GM which can be there to hand and then ask manufacturers to put something quite clearly on a tin? Sometimes you have a job finding an address and phone number on the containers.

(*Professor Sir John Krebs*) In our experience sometimes the retailers are keen to co-operate in that kind of venture but they have to look at their own interests as well. They may in other areas see that it is not to their advantage to put across the kind of information that we want to put across. Yes, I agree with you about leaflets in supermarkets, that is a route and one that certainly we would consider. I do not know whether, Jon, you want to add anything?

(*Dr Bell*) Yes. We will be looking at all these possibilities and trying to judge which is likely to be the most effective. We will do that by talking to people about what they would most like to see and how they would like to receive the information. Clearly we will talk to supermarkets and others as well to see to what extent they will be prepared to co-operate.

257. When you talk about a paper trail, I think about the huge quantities of paper that we produce already and who on earth looks at it? One gets through things about once every two years and in the meantime the paper is piling up. The only time that it is looked at is when there is a problem. Then you put ticks in boxes very rapidly in the hope that nobody noticed that you did not do it before.

(*Professor Sir John Krebs*) We know—nothing to do with GM—from the case that came up last year of recycled unfit poultry meat that not all the traceability systems that one might wish to be in

Countess of Mar contd.]

place are in place even for quite major food producers and retailers.

Countess of Mar: You have mentioned the possibility before.

Chairman: I must try and bring us back to traceability and labelling of GM crops. Can I ask Lord Walpole to ask his question?

Lord Walpole

258. We have not actually spoken to anyone about the implications for the catering trade. We have had one or two submissions from the restaurant and pub trade and indeed the whisky trade. How would you expect restaurants to make things clearer? Would you expect people to put on the menu "This course may contain . . .", "this course does not contain . . .", "our suppliers suggest that it does not contain . . . or does contain . . ." and so on?

(*Professor Sir John Krebs*) There is currently a regulatory requirement for catering establishments to indicate the presence of GM ingredients. Our consumer research gives a fairly mixed picture about this. I think on the whole consumers are less concerned about what is in their food when they eat out than they are when they are at home. We are where we are with that. There is a regulation in place. I think at this stage we are not intending to propose changing that. We keep track of consumer concern about it and certainly would want to review that in due course. We did ask also the representatives of the catering industry whether this requirement was found to be unduly burdensome and we got back, on the whole, a response that it is not considered to be unduly burdensome, although I would have thought for some caterers it might be. I guess what they do is go back in the usual way to their source of supply and they ask their suppliers "Are you supplying me with non-GM" and if they say yes then they feel there is no need to put anything on the menu. Since most of the retailers now are sourcing non-GM then I guess the situation has worked its way through so the suppliers for the caterers are providing non-GM and the caterers are not finding it an issue.

Chairman

259. Could I bring you back to the issue, Sir John, of the WHO who, it has to be welcomed, are striving towards a consensus on the safety assessments for GM foods. This is an attempt to get a uniform approach to the principle of substantial equivalence. Is the concept of substantial equivalence a valid one?

(*Professor Sir John Krebs*) As the Royal Society report which came out two weeks ago affirmed, it is the best option available. Substantial equivalence is sometimes misunderstood and misrepresented—I am sure not in this Committee—as being a criterion for approval. It is not that it is a framework for thinking. It is a framework for analysis and the framework is that every GM food has a conventional counterpart. If it is a GM soya, a GM maize, the conventional counterpart has a history of human consumption and therefore in scrutinising the novel variety the key thing to look at is how the novel variety differs from its conventional counterpart because that may give you the clues as to where the GM variety could potentially give rise to harm. It is no more than a framework for thinking and it has been endorsed by the WHO, it has been endorsed by the Board of the Food Standards Agency when it looked at this issue and by the Royal Society and all the other independent bodies that looked at it as the best option available at the moment for scrutiny of the safety of GM foods. As I said earlier in response to Lady Mar's question, the science which will contribute to the assessment of GM safety through substantial equivalence is expanding and will continue to develop both as a result of our research and that of others. I believe it is a robust framework for safety assessment and the best we have got.

Baroness Miller of Chilthorne Domer

260. The Chairman of Unilever said recently in the annual City Food Lecture that given the choice between a plate of fish and chips and the precautionary principle, he believed the public would prefer the plate of fish and chips. How are you going to balance that view, because Unilever clearly are taking the view that it really wants to go with the new science and the public actually, from what we have heard in evidence through the Consumer Association and so on, do not?

(*Professor Sir John Krebs*) The consumer concern about GM is falling off. That may be because most people believe there is no GM technology used in food production in Britain at the moment, which is not actually the situation because a lot of GM technology is used. I prefer to call it the precautionary approach rather than the precautionary principle. The precautionary approach implies that when there is uncertainty in the scientific assessment of risk, which is more often the case than not, because rarely does the science come up with a crisp definitive answer, when there is uncertainty you come to a judgment, and it is a judgment, an informed judgment, about how much regulatory or other restriction you want to place on, in this case, the marketing or development of a new food. I do not think there is a formula you can look up in a book which tells you how precautionary you should be, it is a judgment. In my view the judgment should be informed by wide public debate taking into account the views not just of the particular representative stakeholder groups that may have a particular agenda but also of the wider public. I think we do try to take account of those who would prefer a plate of fish and chips to the precautionary principle as well as those who feel that a very extreme precautionary approach is required. There is, as I say, no formula, the trick is to make a balanced judgment in each situation.

Chairman

261. I think we are running out of time. There is one last question I would like to put to you. I think you will agree that over ten or 15 years, particularly in the United Kingdom and in Europe there has been a constant attempt to lean over backwards with the

Chairman *contd.*]

precautionary approach and give consumers as much information as is realistic and feasible, for instance in any number of statements from the Royal Commission on Environmental Pollution, Select Committees of this House, and others. Would you agree it is the principle that consumers should have the right of informed choice regarding what they want to consume and there should be this traceability? We have now this situation where the European Commission is putting forward one set of proposals on traceability and labelling and you, the Food Standards Authority, are saying this is a step too far, it is unenforceable, it is unrealistic. Do you feel, therefore, that you are reneging on these assurances which have been given to consumers over the years?

(*Professor Sir John Krebs*) I think that our position is the one that delivers real consumer choice as opposed to a veil which covers the possibility of consumers being misled because there will be no way of checking. I am all in favour of consumers having the right to choose, the right to know what is in their food but I am not in favour of introducing regulations that will subsequently prove to be unenforceable, will not be checkable and therefore will be possibly providing misinformation to consumers.

Chairman: Thank you very much. I think that brings our session to a conclusion. Thank you, Sir John and Dr Bell, for a very helpful morning.

WRITTEN EVIDENCE

Memorandum by the American Soybean Association

SUMMARY AND PRELIMINARY OBSERVATIONS

The American Soybean Association (ASA) represents North American soybean producers beyond that covered by individual state soybean farmer associations. In the international marketplace, ASA represents the interests of the 600,000 US soybean growers. Approximately half of the US crop goes to export markets, either for crushing in those markets, or as soymeals for animal feed and other uses.

At the outset we would like to state that ASA fully supports enforceable, science-based regulation of agricultural biotechnology, to provide assurance of the safety of food supplies and to allow industries to operate and plan according to a clear, legal framework.

In 1996 the first transgenic (Roundup Ready) soybeans, which enable plants to survive post emergence applications of the glyphosate-containing herbicides, were placed on the market.

The responses that follow reflect the on-farm experience of the agronomic and environmental benefits of the technology and the fact that farmer adoption continues to extend (in 2001, 70 per cent of the total US acreage and 95 per cent in Argentina were biotech soybeans. Brazilian authorities estimate at least 30 per cent of its soybean acreage is planted to biotech varieties not yet commercially legalized).

It is clear that given the way world trade in animal feed materials has developed, the main impact of the Commission's proposals would fall on the soybean sector, on whole soybeans and on soymeals entering the EU from not only North America but also South America.

This interest on the ASA's part should not obscure the fact that the United States is in third position, and has been for some years, behind Brazil and Argentina, in supplying the EU market in soy products. This has to do with the recent enormous acreage increases in those two countries, and the investments in transport infrastructure and processing capacity, geared towards the export market together with South American changes in currency exchange rates and export tax credits.

RESPONSES TO THE SUB-COMMITTEE'S QUESTIONS

1. Do these proposals adequately address the requirements of European consumers for regulation, traceability and labelling of GM food and feed and of food and feed products derived from GMOs?

In the ASA's view, they do not.

The traceability and labelling proposals calls for all operators to record and pass on information regarding the GMOs, including the unique codes of all events in their shipments and to keep such records for five years. No clear explanation has been provided in the proposal as to what purpose this excessive documentation would serve for end users or consumers. Such a requirement would be extremely difficult (if possible at all) to implement and verify, and would greatly disrupt the importation of soybeans to Europe to meet the 70 per cent deficit in vegetable protein needed for the EU's livestock and poultry industries.

The EU currently imports in excess of 26 million metric tons of soybeans or soybean equivalent, predominantly from the US and South America. Of this, nearly eight million tonnes comes from the United States.

A single boatload of commodity soybeans can contain 50,000 metric tons (note: one metric ton of soybeans contains more than seven million individual soybeans). The soybeans, which make up such a shipment from the US, for example, will have been collected and commingled (mixed together) at every point of a ten-stage handling system from several thousand different farms. Each farm would typically have grown between six and ten different varieties of soybeans—biotech and non-biotech according to on-farm practices—from the several thousand soybean varieties commercially available to farmers.

Even were a list of the biotech events, import tonnages and individual growers to be collected and supplied to an end user, the result would be an extremely long document that would be meaningless as there is no way of tracing any single batch to its source.

As we understand these requirements, they seem to us to reflect a lifestyle choice, akin to a preference for organic food. An identity preserved system, based on maintaining the integrity of a specific crop eg non-GM, is the only practical method of meeting (and tracing) demands for non-GM and assuring consumers that they are not being duped by marketing ploys. The ASA's own considerable organic farmer membership is well used to applying identity preservations techniques to meeting demands for specific products. We take pleasure in noting that they have be become very sophisticated practitioners of their chosen method.

We note that the novel foods and feeds proposal promotes process-based labelling so that products produced from biotechnology are to be labeled irrespective of whether or not any genetic modification can be found in the end product. For example, soybean oil derived from a biotech soybean would have to be labeled even though no DNA protein from the modification appears in the oil.

To label such a product as recommended in the proposals as "produced from genetically modified [name of organism] but not containing a genetically modified organism" is confusing, misleading and unnecessary. It is clearly unenforceable, discriminatory and open to fraud. The proposals do not cover labelling requirements for other biotech food products/derivatives such as enzymes and vitamins (used in the making of cheese and beer for example).

There is no clear scientific basis for making such a distinction. We question whether consumers will be helped (or indeed interested) by knowing about biotech content of vegetable oil and not cheese. We would argue that products, which have been derived, but do not contain GMOs (such as soybean oil), should similarly be excluded from the labelling requirements.

Finally, the EU has yet to develop technical guidelines on the sampling and testing methods necessary to operate the traceability requirements. There are many questions from within the EU industry on the viability of any such system and on the liability issues raised by making declarations.

2. Do they make sensible distinctions between the requirements of animal feed and those of food for human consumption?

Any measure which distinguishes between the conditions under which products can be marketed for feed and those applying to food is likely to give rise to problems as products often cross unintentionally between the two sectors. The events surrounding StarLink maize in the United States are an object lesson in this regard.

Overall, the needs of both sectors, should it be desired that transgenic product be excluded, can only seriously be met by a tight identity-preserved system.

3. How effective are the proposals likely to be in ensuring full traceability of GM material at all stages of the chain from producer to consumer?

The Commission proposal implies that "traceability" means the ability to trace GMOs and products produced from GMOs at all stages of their placing on the market through the production and distribution chains.

If we consider only glyphosate-tolerant soybeans, the requirement would mean that if a soybean has, at any point in its pedigree, perhaps over as many as 30 generations, an inheritance relationship with the single soybean plant, designated 40-3-2, in which the recombinant DNA event giving glyphosate tolerance was carried out, then that soybean must be traceable at least until the point of emergence from the ground of the plant that bore it.

The proposal's intention for traceability implies knowing where a genetically-modified organism was produced, on what farm, and in effect in what field, and being able to show that this can be verified: as such failure to be able to demonstrate this "traceability" will be tantamount to breaking the law when any attempt is made to put a single transgenic soybean into circulation in the EU.

Since the situation outlined in the preceding paragraphs is not one which can be envisaged in the real world, the only answer that the ASA can offer to the Sub-Committee's question is that the proposals cannot remotely meet the end stated.

4. Are the proposals likely to be enforceable in practice, particularly where no novel genetic material is contained in the food or feed?

Only in the context of a strict identity preservation system, and then not entirely.

5. A threshold level of one per cent or lower for the accidental presence of GM material in food and feed has been proposed, below which there would be an exemption. Is a threshold of this level, common to both food and feed, appropriate?

An accurate description of any soybean or soymeal bulk consignment which satisfies existing or proposed EU labelling rules would have to include the GM declaration. The odds of finding a commercial bulk cargo from any of the three main exporting countries without transgenic beans are microscopically, not to say impossibly, small.

The idea of requiring the GM label only for material from cargos in which fewer than 99 per cent of the beans do not have the original single Roundup Ready plant as an ancestor does not really open the window any wider in practical terms: the numbers are such that only a breeders seed level of varietal purity would give some grounds for confidence, and that would require bagging directly off the field.

Operational IP systems sometimes function with products which can be visually distinguished in some degree from the general run of the crop. For example, a handful of clear-hilem food grade beans (used for tofu) and a handful of commodity beans can, with explanation from an expert, be seen to be different on visual inspection.

Distinguishing cultivars from one another is a different matter. Even the smallest of co-operative country elevators is likely to have about 50 distinct soybean cultivars being taken in at harvest, all intermixed, in any one of its storage silos. While attempts can be made to see that only non-GM beans go into certain bins, they depend on the driver of the truck knowing clearly what he has taken from the combine operator, something which leaves wide windows for error, and which compromises at a very early stage the overall description of a batch based on that bin.

This of course presupposes that the farmer has grown and harvested his GM and non-GM separately.

In any one year, it can be expected that about 2,500 cultivars of soybean are on sale in the US over the 15 maturity zones, very few of which will have a commercial life-cycle exceeding three or four years before being supplanted with new improved crosses: the genetic base of the cultivated soybean is both mobile and innovative. In 2002 nearly 2,000 of those cultivars will incorporate the Roundup Ready trait.

6. Is the role proposed for (a) the European Food Authority and its scientific committees and (b) Member States in the authorisation process for GM food and feed appropriate?

The ASA has no observations to offer on this question.

7. Are the proposals likely to be compatible with the requirements of the Cartagena Protocol on Biosafety and with other international commitments, including OECD programs?

The ASA does not wish to comment on the Cartagena Protocol, but it feels that the contents of the various consensus documents on biotechnology traits developed within the OECD should be noted in its report.

8. Are the proposals compatible with obligations towards non-Member States seeking to export food and feed to the EU?

The EU's own overview agencies have expressly declared these products to be safe, both for human health and for the environment. Since no issue of health, safety or environmental concerns have been demonstrated to be present, it will not, in the ASA's view, come as a surprise if the EU's trading partners make an issue of these proposals in international trade fora, and that any dispute settlement will be costly in terms of compensation.

9. Should the present EU-wide moratorium on approving GM food and crop product applications be maintained until the issues concerning traceability and labelling of GMOs have been resolved?

The ASA understands that the moratorium, founded on the arbitrary refusal of a blocking minority of Member States to complete due process in respect of consent applications, is, in the view of the European Commission, illegal. To that extent, the moratorium should never have been tolerated in the first place.

That said, the ASA has had to negotiate with a provider of a promising biotech soybean trait, approved in the US and comparable to the Roundup Ready soybean product, in order to postpone its marketing until an EU release consent is obtained. Currently, the moratorium is the only effective obstacle to the marketing and use of this product. Indeed, the moratorium is prohibiting US and EU farmers access to and benefit from up to 12 products which have been cleared by the EU's scientific experts.

10. What other aspects of the proposals require further consideration before the UK Government can sign up to them?

The ASA believes that the UK Government would be better placed than most to raise the implications for the world food system of any statutory obligations on grain producers and traders which reduce the worldwide efficiencies in transport, storage, handling, price discovery and standardization which have developed over the last century and a half.

The modern bulk commodity handling system has adapted over this period to a fivefold increase in world population, in which, in more recent decades, there has been enormous concentration of population in cities of unprecedented size, especially in the developing world. (London has dropped out of the top 30 cities by population in the world.)

The risks of additional compliance burdens on the system, unmotivated by health or environmental concerns, but intended to frustrate in a roundabout way innovation and ease of supply because of theories about the exercise of economic power, will call for a price to be paid in the overall quality of basic human nutrition in those parts of the world which can least afford it.

St Louis
Missouri

13 February 2002

Annex 1

EUROPEAN COMMISSION PROPOSALS FOR A REGULATION OF THE EUROPEAN PARLIAMENT AND THE COUNCIL CONCERNING TRACEABILITY & LABELLING OF GMOS AND TRACEABILITY OF FOOD AND FEED PRODUCTS PRODUCED FROM GMOS AND AMENDING DIRECTIVE 2001/81-COM (2001) 182

PROPOSAL FOR A REGULATION OF THE EUROPEAN PARLIAMENT AND THE COUNCIL ON GENETICALLY MODIFIED FOOD AND FEED COM (2001)425

COMMENTS FROM THE AMERICAN SOYBEAN ASSOCIATION AND THE UNITED SOYBEAN BOARD, JANUARY 2002

INTRODUCTION

US farmers have always supported science-based laws and regulations to assure consumers that their food supply is properly regulated. But any law or regulation must be based on sound science, workable, and enforceable.

As such, we view with considerable concern the above two proposals published in July 2001 and have concluded that in their present form they would not be workable nor enforceable and would not contribute to their stated objective of improving transparency for consumers. In addition, in the absence of any scientific basis, the traceability and labelling proposal covering imports into the EU could be viewed as a technical barrier to trade.

Given that commercialized biotech products are approved as safe under the EU's own authorization system and that there is no record of any human safety issues from approved biotech product, a process-based system as proposed in novel foods and feeds would only serve to undermine the regulatory, science-based system that the Commission is anxious to project as the consumers' safeguard.

TRACEABILITY

We fully understand that the climate of food scares in Europe. BSE, *E.coli,* and dioxin in poultry have focused consumer and regulatory attention on food safety. As such, a traceabilty system for public health and food safety reasons is perfectly understandable.

However, the assertion that the traceability and labelling proposal will allow biotech crops and products to be traced back in the event of a human health or environmental issue is meaningless given the very nature of bulk production and distribution of commodity crops. Requiring traceability for biotech products that have received full health, environmental, and safety clearances by EU regulatory authorities not only is not scientifically justified, but also is trade restrictive.

The traceability and labelling proposal calls for all operators to record and pass on information regarding the GMOs, including the unique codes of all events in their shipments and to keep such records for five years.

We note that no clear explanation has been provided in the proposal as to what purpose this excessive documentation would serve for end users or consumers. Such a requirement would be extremely difficult (if possible at all) to implement and verify and would greatly disrupt the importation of soybeans to Europe to meet the 70 per cent deficit in vegetable protein needed for the EU's livestock and poultry industries.

The EU currently imports in excess of 26 million metric tons of soybeans or soybean equivalent, predominantly from the US and South America. Of this, nearly eight million tonnes comes from the United States. A single boatload of commodity soybeans can contain 50,000 metric tons (note: one metric ton of soybeans contains in excess of seven million individual soybeans).

The soybeans which make up such a shipment from the US for example, will have been collected and commingled at every point of a ten-stage handling system from several thousand different farms. Each would typically have grown between six and ten different varieties of soybeans—biotech and non biotech according to on farm practices—from the several thousand soybean varieties commercially available to farmers. A similar distribution system exists in other soybean exporting countries.

Even were a list of the biotech events, import tonnages and individual growers, to be collected and supplied to an user, the result would be an extremely long document that would be meaningless as there is no way of tracing any single consignment to its source.

Proposing a traceability system through this process is incomprehensible, if not impossible.

As you may be aware, EU feed and farm groups have already indicated their concern with this prospect, particularly in the light of concerns of further protein shortages following the EU ban on the use of meat and bone meal in animal feed.

These unclear and unenforceable restrictions would not only adversely affect the smooth and efficient flow of bulk commodity crops, but would also raise considerable liability issues for EU and US suppliers and customers.

LABELING

We note that the novel foods and feeds proposal promotes process based labeling so that products produced from biotechnology are to be labeled irrespective of whether or not any genetic modification can be found in the end product. For example, soybean oil derived from a biotech soybean would have to be labeled even though no DNA protein from the modification appears in the oil.

To label such a product as recommended in the proposals as "produced from genetically modified [name of organism] but not containing a genetically modified organism" is confusing, misleading and unnecessary. It is also clearly unenforceable, discriminatory and open to fraud. We note that the proposals do not cover labeling requirements for biotech products/derivatives such as enzymes and vitamins (used in the making of cheese and beer for example). There is no clear scientific basis for making such a distinction and we question whether consumers will be helped (or indeed interested) by knowing about biotech content of vegetable oil and not cheese. We would argue that products, which have been derived, but do not contain GMOs (such as soybean oil), should similarly be excluded from the labeling requirements.

We note that the EU has yet to develop technical guidelines on the sampling and testing methods necessary to operate the traceability requirements. There are many questions from within the EU industry on the viability of any such system and on the liability issues raised by making declarations.

WAYS FORWARD

US soybean growers have long defended the right of consumer choice, and for those consumers who want non-biotech products that they should have the right of choice, in a similar manner to organic foods for example.

For many years, US soybean growers have offered identity-preserved crops for customers (such as Japanese tofu makers) who want a specific drop type. This Identify Preserved (IP) system provides assurances to the customer that they will get what they want and for which they are prepared to meet the market price. However, IP supplies are typically substantially smaller than bulk supplies and given their specific handling needs would be more expensive.

We believe that this system could be used to underpin meaningful, more appropriate and effective traceability and labeling legislation for biotech products. Under such a system, those making a non-GM claim would be required to substantiate this claim and the IP system would enable that person to do so. In our view, strict compliance with such a system would offer consumers the true choice that the Commission's proposals in their present form would deny.

CONSUMER GUARANTEES

A system such as described above would remove any potential for misrepresentation or fraud on consumers.

Such a system would require that operators shall make no claims implying that genetically modified ingredients are not present in the food or feed unless such ingredients have been produced, harvested, transported, stored, processed in accordance with a specification designed to substantiate that claim and adopted by the Commission. The procedures that would need to be addressed under such a scheme would be:

(a) the level of varietal purity required for seed planted for the production of the crop in question:

(b) the standard distances to be respected between varieties planted;

(c) the methods to be applied to cleaning harvesting equipment to eliminate traces of GMO prior to harvesting a crop in respect of which it is to be claimed that it is GM-free;

(d) the measures to be taken to avoid the presence of DNA segments of GM origin in the GM-free product, in particular insofar as such segments are present in dust;

(e) the level to which transport equipment must be cleaned to ensure the absence of GMO traces in the GM-free product;

(f) the arrangements to be made at the point of first delivery to ensure the absence of comminglement of the GM-free product, including cleaning of bins and tanks, and of transfer equipment (augers, conveyor belts, etc);

(g) the arrangements to be made for certifying by independent surveyors, for sealing onward shipments by road, whether bagged, by container, by bulk in trucks, by rail wagon, or by barge, to the point of further loading, including the preservation of the integrity and identity of the shipment at each point of transfer before an ocean terminal or transfer point is reached;

(h) the arrangements for sampling and testing at each stage of the transport, having regard to the need to deliver the GM-free product to the final user in a form which respects the level of absence of GM material required by this regulation for the GM-free claim to feature on the labeling of the food or feed product in question.

The above verifiable system would provide consumers with a true choice and a guarantee that they will get what they are prepared to pay for when they want non-biotech. It also would serve to resolve the trade, discrimination, WTO compliance, fraud, and misrepresentation issues surrounding the entire traceability and labeling proposal by simply replacing the Commission's proposal with such a system based on positive labeling.

Dr Hans Hoyer
Regional Director West Europe and Maghreb
American Soybean Association
Brussels

Annex 2

THE AMERICAN SOYBEAN INDUSTRY
A BACKGROUND NOTE FOR UK PARLIAMENTARIANS

THE AMERICAN SOYBEAN ASSOCIATION (ASA):

The ASA is an 80-year old voluntary association representing the interests of soybean growers from the 29 soybean growing states. In the international marketplace it partners with the producer funded and run United Soybean Board to develop markets and represent the interests of American's 500,000 plus soybean growers. The ASA is headquartered in St Louis, Missouri and has offices in 14 countries throughout the world. Its European headquarters are in Brussels, Belgium.

MEETING THE EUROPEAN DEMAND:

Europe's demand for soybeans as a vegetable protein source cannot be met by local production. Almost all soybeans, whether in the United States, Brazil or Argentina, are grown and harvested as a bulk commodity. Bulk commodity production and distribution keeps costs down—a crucial factor for the UK and Europe's livestock industry—the main users of imported soybeans. There is no practical and efficient system that would allow easy separation of bulk handling of soybeans either on farm or when they flow through up to 10 different handling points before they reach end customers.

BIOTECHNOLOGY:

In 1996, American soybean growers began growing biotechnology derived soybeans modified to be resistant to the glyphosate herbicide. These soybeans allow growers to control weeds—a critical concern in soybean production—with reduced use of chemicals and operational inputs. These biotech soybeans have been approved as safe and as the substantial equivalent of their conventional counterparts in the United States, Europe and all our overseas markets.

In the past five years, production of biotech soybeans has risen to nearly 70 per cent of the total production in the US of some 75 million acres. US Department of Agriculture estimates for this year's planting of biotech soybeans show a 15 per cent increase on 2000 plantings. By growing biotech soybeans growers are able to reduce both the use of chemicals and operational costs. This has resulted in the production of a better quality and, because of the considerable reduction in weed seed (much of which can be toxic) an even safer end product.

SEGREGATION:

Soybean growers are concerned that in the debate over the use of agriculture biotechnology, information can often be misunderstood. For example, demands for segregation of bulk commodity crops are often made without a full appreciation of the logistical difficulties and economic inefficiencies that would add costs for UK and European customers as well as American growers. The Identity Preservation system is, and always has been, available for those seeking non-biotech supplies.

IDENTITY PRESERVED CROPS:

US soybean growers can meet the needs of customers with specific requirements through a supply system called Identity Preservation (IP). This system is based on an agreed contract reached between buyer and seller for the production and shipping of specified varieties at an agreed premium price and purity threshold. The IP system has been used for many years to supply the Japanese tofu soybean market. The system is governed by three main criteria: small shipments (to ensure the integrity of supply); a price premium (to allow for the extra handling requirements) and no 100 per cent guarantee on purity (to allow for accidental commingling of product).

July 2001

Memorandum by the Biotechnology and Biological Sciences Research Council (BBSRC)

BACKGROUND

1. The BBSRC was established by Royal Charter in 1994 as one of six national research councils funded principally through the science budget of the Office of Science and Technology. BBSRC is the leading funding agency in the UK for academic research and training in the non-medical biosciences (agriculture, food and healthcare). We are also a source of impartial scientific advice for Government and civil society. Our mission statement is at Annex 1.

2. BBSRC recognises that the public debate on genetic modification (GM) goes wider (and must do so) than science alone. However, we wish to stress the importance of a strong science base to inform the debate and to support the development of a sound regulatory framework. The last four years have seen a significant reduction in the market for GM foodstuffs in Europe and an accompanying disinvestment in the UK agricultural biotechnology industry. Despite the situation in Europe we believe that agricultural biotechnology, of which GM is only a part, will in the longer-term have a place alongside other approaches in helping to provide a safe and nutritious food supply that is produced in a more sustainable way. BBSRC aims to support high quality science, in partnership with other public sector funders such as DEFRA, so that UK know-how in this area is not lost and future opportunities for investment can be realised.

3. In this submission we draw attention to some key science based issues pertinent to the labelling and traceability of GMOs in the food and feed chain. In raising these issues we have been guided, but not constrained, by the questions posed by the Committee in its call for evidence.

THRESHOLDS

4. In OCED countries to date there have been more than 10,000 experimental field trials (1,600 in the European Community) with over 30 different groups of GM plants (1,2). The global area of commercial cultivation GM crops in 2001 was in the order of 52.6 million hectares (130 million acres) in 13 countries (3). The USA, Argentina, Canada and China accounted for 99 per cent of this area. The principal GM crops grown were Soybean (33.3 million hectares), maize (9.8 mha), cotton (6.8 mha) and oilseed rape (2.1mha).

5. Faced with the scale of commercial cultivation and field testing of GM crops it is increasingly likely that non-GM food and feed products, whether imported or produced in the European Community, will contain unavoidable trace amounts of GM material. This is particularly so for grain and grain products from out-crossing crops such as maize and oilseed rape and for commodity crops (soybean, maize and oilseed rape) from some of the major exporting nations. Similarly, the adventitious presence of GM seeds in conventional certified seed stocks is to be expected if the seeds are produced in regions where GM crops are grown commercially or trialed. Separation distances between sexually compatible GM and non-GM crops, such as those employed for many years to preserve varietal purity in convention plant breeding, can do much to limit the level of cross-pollination but can not guarantee to eliminate it entirely (4). BBSRC and the Natural Environment Research Council are funding basic research via a joint initiative aimed at increasing our understanding geneflow from GMOs in the environment. Some of the work is directed towards technologies, eg plastid transformation, that promise to reduce greatly the transfer of transgenes from GM crops via pollen. The Advisory Committee on Releases to the Environment has recently explored a range of such technologies to reduce the spread of transgenes from plant to plant (5).

6. A zero level of GM material in food or feed is now impractical in many cases. The Commission is proposing a threshold of 1 per cent unavoidable GM material below which it would not be labelled. It is not clear scientifically why the same threshold should be applied as strictly to feed as it is to food. Most DNA and proteins derived from GM material in an animal's diet will be broken down quickly in the gut. There is evidence that small amounts of "gene-sized" DNA from food can be taken up by cells of the gastrointestinal tract (see ref 6 and citations therein). This probably a natural process and there is no reason to believe that if "GM DNA or proteins" were to be present in meat, milk or eggs then they would be there in anything other than trace amounts. It follows therefore that the threshold for GM material in feed could be higher without the animal products approaching the 1 per cent threshold that is permitted for a food ingredient.

7. Alternatively, application of the 1 per cent threshold for feed as well as for food might simply reflect the practical consideration that 1 per cent is about the current minimum limit of reliable routine quantification of transgenic sequences in complex samples.

ENFORCEMENT

8. Enforcement of the proposed labelling regime will depend on the scientific and technical capability to detect, identify and, where necessary, quantify unknown GM material in samples. The analytical methods employed must be robust, sensitive and able to cope with mixed transformation events from a variety of background sources eg commodity shipments, processed foods and refined sugars and oils. It is not possible at present to analyse highly refined products that contain no DNA or protein to establish whether they are from GM or non-GM sources.

9. Various methods can be used for detecting transgenic DNA sequences or their protein products in samples. These tend to be based on the polymerase chain reaction (PCR) for DNA detection and immunological methods for protein. Diagnostic technologies are advancing, for example DNA micro arrays offer the promise of simultaneously identifying more than one transformation in a single sample.

10. In our view it is within current technical capabilities (where protein or DNA is present) to deliver the 1 per cent threshold diagnostic requirements implicit in the proposed traceability and labelling regime. However, accurate identification of transformation events requires detailed information about the transgene cassette and site(s) of insertion in the recipient plant genome. Such information is often the preserve of the technology provider and lacking from the public domain. The situation is likely to get more complicated as the number and range of transformation events approved outside the EU grows. It is therefore essential that the provisions enshrined in Directive 20001/18/EC and the Cartagena Protocol for the provision and dissemination of such information are enforced.

REFERENCES

1. http://biotech.jrc.it/dbplants.asp

2. http://www1.oecd.org/ehs/summary/htm

3. James, C 2001. *Global review of commercialised transgenic crops: 2001.* ISAAA briefs No.24: Preview. ISAAA, Ithica NY.

4. *Gene flow from genetically modified crops.* Background paper by the Advisory Committee on Releases to the Environment (ACRE).
http://www.defra.gov.uk/environment/acre/annrep7/pdf/annexf.pdf

5. *Guidance on principles of best practice in the design of genetically modified plants.* The Advisory Committee on Releases to the Environment (ACRE).
http:/www.defra/gov.uk/environment/acre/bestprac/guidance/index.htm

6. *Genetically modified plants for food use and human health—an update.* The Royal Society, 6-9 Carlton House Terrace, London SW1Y 5AG.

13 February 2002

Annex 1

BBSRC Mission

To promote and support high-quality basic, strategic and applied research and related postgraduate training relating to the understanding and exploitation of biological systems.

To advance knowledge and technology, and provide trained scientists and engineers, which meet the needs of users and beneficiaries (including the agriculture, bioprocessing, chemical, food, healthcare, pharmaceutical and other biotechnological related industries), thereby contributing to the economic competitiveness of the United Kingdom and the quality of life.

To provide advice, disseminate knowledge, and promote public understanding in the fields of biotechnology and the biological sciences.

Memorandum by European Modern Restaurant Association (EMRA), European Federation of Contract Catering Organisations (FERCO), and Hotels, Restaurants & Cafés in Europe (HOTREC)

SUBMITTED BY THE BRITISH BEER AND PUB ASSOCIATION

RE: PROPOSAL FOR A REGULATION OF THE EUROPEAN PARLIAMENT AND THE COUNCIL ON GENETICALLY MODIFIED FOOD AND FEED (COM(2001) 425 FINAL)

Comprehensive legislation on food safety is essential for consumers as well as for the food businesses. For this reason EMRA, FERCO and HOTREC welcome the efforts of all of the European Institutions to secure food safety. However, this goal can only be achieved if legislation is drafted to take full account of the interests of all of the stakeholders concerned. This requires a full analysis of the impact of the proposed legislation on each sector involved in the food chain and the different dimensions of those businesses. It also requires clear justification for the type of legal instruments to be used, and for simple, clear, concise and readily understandable guidance rules to be available to help food businesses comply in a uniform manner.

Article 14.1(d) of this proposal requires specific information to be displayed on the GMO content, including any of its ingredients containing GMOs, of any non-packaged food offered to the ultimate consumer. The restaurant sector (traditional restaurant, quick service, including take-away and delivery, and contract catering) is very concerned about this requirement and would urge that Article 14.1 (d) be amended as follows:

> "Where foodstuffs are offered for sale to the ultimate consumer or to mass caterers without pre-packaging, or where foodstuffs are packaged on the sales premises at the consumer's request or pre-packaged for direct sale, the Member States shall adopt detailed rules concerning the manner in which the particulars specified under this Article are to be shown.
>
> They may decide not to require the provision of all or some of these particulars, provided that the purchaser still receives sufficient information."

The wording of this amendment is taken directly from Article 14 of Directive 2000/13/EC of the European Parliament and of the Council of 20 March 2000 on the approximation of the laws of the Member States relating to the labelling, presentation and advertising of foodstuffs.

EMRA, FERCO and HOTREC believe that it is vital that there is the flexibility to allow Member States the competence to introduce their own different legal requirements for pre-packaged food (sold by retailers through their shops) and non pre-packaged food (sold in traditional restaurants, quick service including take-away and delivery services, and contract catering units). And in order to reflect differing national sensitivities, national cultures and national traditions.

The restaurant/catering businesses operate very differently to food retail/shops and food manufacturers/processors and have more direct contact with their customers and suppliers.

Customers or guests perceive restaurant/catering businesses to be totally different from retail/shopping businesses. This was clearly demonstrated by a recent study of consumer behaviour by the UK's Food Standard Agency. The objective of a restaurant customer is for leisure experience and goes far beyond simply buying food. They want to enjoy tasty food, presented in an attractive way and in an appealing atmosphere as part of an enjoyable social experience.

This distinction is clearly recognised by the NACE classification and related statistics.[1] According to NACE (Nomenclature générale des activités économiques dan les Communautés européenes), processing of food and drinks is covered by Division 1.15; retail trade by Division 1.52.2; restaurants by Division 1.55.3 and canteens and catering by Division 1.55.5.

In the vast majority of EU countries, the distinction is so evident that it is not even reflected in their national laws. The legislation of three European countries (Austria, Sweden and the UK) clearly distinguishes between the retail trade and the restaurant/catering sectors.

RE: PROPOSAL FOR A REGULATION OF THE EUROPEAN PARLIAMENT AND THE COUNCIL CONCERNING TRACEABILITY AND LABELLING OF GENETICALLY MODIFIED ORGANISMS AND TRACEABILITY OF FOOD AND FEED PRODUCTS PRODUCED FROM GENETICALLY MODIFIED ORGANISMS AND AMENDING DIRECTIVE 2001/18/EC (COM(2001)182 FINAL).

Comprehensive legislation on food safety is essential for consumers as well as for the food businesses. For this reason EMRA, FERCO and HOTREC welcome the efforts of all of the European Institutions to secure food safety. However, this goal can only be achieved if legislation is drafted to take full account of the interests of all of the stakeholders concerned. This requires a full analysis of the impact of the proposed legislation on each sector involved in the food chain, and the different dimensions of those businesses. It also requires clear justification for the type of legal instruments to be used, and for simple, clear, concise and readily understandable guidance rules to be available to help food businesses comply in a uniform manner.

---

[1] Panorama of European Business 1999, data 1998–99; Eurostat, Office for Official Publications of the European Communities, Theme 4: Industry, trade and services, Luxembourg 2000.

Article 4.4 and Article 5.2 of the proposal mentioned above require "operators" to keep records of their suppliers and of the products concerned for a period of five years from the date of each transaction. EMRA, FERCO and HOTREC are concerned that this requirement will create additional record keeping burdens for their enterprises and propose instead that both articles should be completed with the following provision:

"Existing documentation eg that for tax purposes, should be deemed to fulfil this requirement."

12 February 2002

Memorandum by the British Society of Plant Breeders and the British Sugar Beet Seed Producers Association

INTRODUCTION

The British Society of Plant Breeders (BSPB) and the British Sugar Beet Seed Producers Association (BSBSPA) together represent all the major private and public sector plant breeding organisations with interests in arable and edible horticultural crops in the UK. The Society and the Association (hereafter referred to as BSPB) have jointly around 50 members including large multinational companies with strong commercial interests in the development of biotechnology and smaller breeding companies with no current involvement in the commercial development of GM crops.

BSPB fully supports effective, science-based regulation of GM crop technology, both to underpin public safety, confidence and choice, and to provide a framework of legal certainty in which industry can operate and plan for the future. The need for clear, consistent and predictable regulation is of particular significance in the plant breeding industry, given the long-term nature of developing a new crop variety (an introductory booklet entitled "Plant Breeding—the business and science of crop improvement" is enclosed with this submission for Committee Members' background information (*Not printed*)).

The UK plant breeding industry considers that regulatory controls surrounding the development and commercial application of GM technology should be governed by a number of guiding principles:

(I)   The primary objective of regulations must be to deliver safety in terms of human health, animal health and the environment;

(ii) Regulatory controls must be consistent, proportionate and enforceable;

(iii) Regulations should enable, not stifle, technological progress and innovation;

(iv) EU regulation should be compatible with equivalent third country regulatory processes, and should not present unnecessary barriers to international trade;

(v)   Regulations must be sufficiently flexible to respond to future change—both technological and commercial;

(vi) Regulation has a role to play in promoting the provision of choice and meaningful information to consumers. It is not, however, the responsibility of regulators to attempt to gauge or reflect prevailing public attitudes or consumer preferences.

The following responses to the specific questions posed in the Committee's call for evidence reflect an assessment of the Commission's proposals against these key criteria.

1. *Do these proposals adequately address the requirements of European consumers for regulation, traceability and labelling of GM food and feed and of food and feed products derived from GMOs?*

This question is difficult to answer in the absence of an authoritative understanding of "the requirements of European consumers". European surveys of consumer attitudes towards GM foods have been shown to vary considerably over time, and may change in the future.

However, it is reasonable to suppose that European consumers will continue to require reliable and affordable supplies of safe, wholesome food, produced in sympathy with the environment. GM crops and foods currently undergo more stringent safety assessment than equivalent conventional products. Indeed the European Commission recently stated that GM crops, because they are developed using more precise technology and are subjected to greater regulatory scrutiny, are "probably even safer than conventional plants and foods".

Once safety has been established, therefore, the key objective of the proposed legislation should be to provide a framework in which consumers can exercise an informed choice. BSPB is fully committed to providing such choice, as evidenced through members' involvement in producing certified seed of different crop varieties to high levels of genetic purity and integrity, and through the Society's central involvement in SCIMAC, a cross-industry initiative established in the UK to support best practice in the on-farm management and identity preservation of GM crops.

However, two issues give particular cause for concern. Firstly the practicalities and enforceability of requiring traceability and labelling for highly refined ingredients and additives whose provenance or composition cannot be detected or verified in the end-product (see response to question 4). Secondly, the need to ensure consistency in approach between EU proposals relating to traceability and labelling in food and feed and those addressing the presence of GM material in seed (see response to question 10).

2. Do they make sensible distinctions between the requirements of animal feed and those of food for human consumption?

Industry urgently needs a framework of certainty in which to operate, and BSPB therefore welcomes the proposed establishment of GM labelling thresholds for both food and feed.

Other organisations may be better placed to comment on the practicalities and cost implications of the respective threshold levels proposed. Clearly there are differences in provenance, volume and trading practice in relation to ingredients destined for animal feed in the UK as distinct from those used in food manufacturing. Such differences should be reflected in the final legislation to ensure traceability is workable and enforceable in practice, serves to inform rather than confuse consumers, and does not present unnecessary barriers to international trade or to the competitiveness of the UK livestock industry.

3. How effective are the proposals likely to be in ensuring full traceability of GM material at all stages of the chain from producer to consumer?

BSPB notes that certain details of the traceability regime are left flexible within the Commission's proposals and will to some extent depend on how individual Member States implement them. Implementation should not seek to re-invent the wheel, but to build upon proven systems of traceability and identity preservation already established within the food supply chain.

Such systems have operated effectively for many years within the UK farming and food production sectors, for example in producing seed crops to guaranteed levels of purity and varietal identity, or in segregating harvested crops destined for different end uses, eg breadmaking vs. biscuit wheat, or malting vs. feed barley.

In addition, the SCIMAC Code of Practice and On-Farm Guidelines were specially developed to deliver identity preservation for GM crops grown in the UK, based on the proven experience of existing traceability systems. As such this initiative offers a framework for safeguarding the integrity of both GM crops and neighbouring non-GM crops within a practical farming situation, up to and including the ex-farm delivery of harvested produce.

It is important to note, however, that the effectiveness of current traceability and identity preservation systems can be verified through sampling and testing regimes at appropriate points in the chain. As detailed in our response to question four, there is currently no reliable detection method to verify the full traceability and therefore the accuracy of labelling claims made in relation to certain highly processed ingredients, additives and derivatives. In BSPB's view this gives cause for concern on issues such as enforceability, the scope for fraudulent claims, and the potential to mislead rather than inform consumers.

4. Are the proposals likely to be enforceable in practice, particularly where no novel genetic material is contained in the food or feed?

BSPB considers that regulations in this area can only be meaningful and enforceable by focusing on the end-product rather than the production process.

Meaningful because a clear distinction can be drawn between products containing detectable GM material and the almost limitless range of products which could at some stage involve the use of modern biotechnology.

Examples of such products range from those currently within the scope of the Commission's proposals, such as highly refined ingredients or additives, to those outside, such as foods produced using GM processing aids or livestock products reared with the use of GM medicines.

Enforceable because the presence of detectable GM protein or DNA can be verified through testing. The practical implications of developing a traceability system around claims which cannot be substantiated through end-product testing—in terms of compliance and enforcement, as well as the considerable scope for fraud—are more likely to confuse than inform consumers, and weaken rather than strengthen public confidence.

The safe and legitimate application of GM technology should not be subjected to measures which simply add cost and bureaucracy while achieving little (if anything) in terms of informed consumer choice. The role of labelling should be to promote choice, not to provide a route for denial of access and choice.

Once GM products have been assessed as safe in terms of human health and the environment, regulations governing their use should not be determined by arbitrary (and potentially transitory) commercial conditions specified by those seeking to make claims about freedom from GM for marketing purposes. The primary responsibility for meeting such additional conditions must lie with those seeking to exploit any marketing or commercial advantage from such claims, and should remain the preserve of market forces rather than regulation.

5. *A threshold level of 1 per cent or lower for the accidental presence of GM material in food and feed has been proposed, below which there would be an exemption. Is a threshold of this level, common to both food and feed, appropriate?*

BSPB has consistently supported a benchmark labelling threshold of 1 per cent for presence of GM material, in terms of its practicality, enforceability and clarity to consumers.

The Commission's proposals also establish a legal basis for the technically unavoidable presence of GM material which has been subject to a risk assessment in the EU, but which has not been fully cleared for marketing. This has the Society's strongest possible support, but appears to be at odds with the Commission's current proposals to address GM thresholds in seed (see response to question 10).

6. *Is the role proposed for (a) the European Food Authority and its scientific committees and (b) Member States in the authorisation process for GM food and feed appropriate?*

BSPB supports measures which will improve the transparency and accountability of the risk assessment and authorisation process. The proposed role of the EFA as a "one-stop shop" represents a welcome step in this direction. A major weakness in the current approvals process has been the ability of individual Member States to delay authorisation on political rather than scientific or safety grounds. This uncertainty must be addressed to ensure that regulation fulfils its intended role to enable, rather than disable, technological progress and innovation.

7. *Are the proposals likely to be compatible with the requirements of the Cartagena Protocol on Biosafety and with other international commitments, including OECD programmes?*

With major crops traded globally, there is an urgent need to establish harmonised international regulation in this area, or to introduce the concept of reciprocal recognition for third country GM approvals within the EU regulatory process. Failure to establish such arrangements at an international level represents an unnecessary and unacceptable barrier to the technology, and may have the effect of denying access and choice rather than promoting it.

8. *Are the proposals compatible with obligations towards non-Member States seeking to export food and feed to the EU?*

In the absence of harmonised international regulation, or reciprocal recognition of third country authorisation procedures (for example under OECD or FAO guidelines), the EU authorisation process and proposed traceability requirements look set to impose additional obligations on importers of food and feed materials to the EU. This will not only penalise importers through increased segregation, sampling and testing requirements, it will also affect cost and availability to customers within the EU, including livestock farmers who rely on imported feed material such as soya.

9. *Should the present EU-wide moratorium on approving GM food and crop product applications be maintained until the issues concerning traceability and labelling of GMOs have been resolved?*

The *de facto* EU-wide moratorium on new GMO authorisations has no basis in safety or science. Continuing to block new approvals risks serious damage to future European research in both industrial and academic sectors.

The moratorium has no effect on those GM products already approved for marketing within the EU. For these products, the supply chain is already addressing traceability requirements in response to the demands of customers.

The market is seeking clarity, consistency and direction. The current moratorium offers none of these, but threatens instead to drive investment and innovation out of the EU, and deny choice and access to the technology's potential benefits for consumers, farmers and the environment.

10. *What other aspects of the proposals require further consideration before the UK Government can sign up to them?*

In crop-based agriculture, seed is the starting point for any traceability system for food and feed. It is therefore imperative that conditions applied to seed are consistent with those required further along the traceability chain. BSPB is extremely concerned that this is not the case with current EU proposals.

The European Commission is proposing to establish legally enforceable thresholds for GM presence in seed via amendments to EU seed marketing legislation. Progress is expected to take place in parallel with the proposals for a new EU regulation on traceability and labelling of GM food. At the same time, the revised and strengthened Deliberate Release Directive EC2001/18 has now been ratified for implementation by Member State authorities in October 2002.

This may sound like joined-up thinking to address consumer concerns and allow the *de facto* EU block on new GMO approvals to be lifted. In practice, however, the Commission's proposals on GM thresholds in seed could seriously disrupt conventional plant breeding and seed production. They may also prove a disincentive to EU-based research and development into GM crops. This would disadvantage future progress and competitiveness within European agriculture while other regions of the world forge ahead with the technology (2001 saw a 19 per cent in global GM plantings to 52.6 million ha).

Central to BSPB's concerns with the Commission's current proposals is an inherent conflict between the different legislative approaches. While the revised Deliberate Release Directive provides a framework for experimental (Part B) GM crop trials to take place safely, the Commission's seed proposals set a zero threshold for the presence of Part B material in seed. Not only is a zero threshold biologically impossible to achieve (or verify), such a requirement would inevitably impose an "either/or" decision between GM trials and seed production. Furthermore, the Commission's traceability and labelling proposals explicitly recognise the need to establish thresholds for adventitious, or unavoidable, presence of GM material which has been subject to a risk assessment within the EU system.

BSPB therefore highlights the need to remove this potential conflict by establishing workable thresholds for the presence in seed of GM material cleared as safe for deliberate release into the environment. The Society is also calling for a system of international equivalence to recognise and establish tolerance levels for GMOs approved by non-EU authorities.

For EU-approved GM material, the Commission has proposed different threshold levels for GM presence in seed according to crop type. These range from 0.3 per cent for oilseed rape and 0.5 per cent for maize through to 0.7 per cent for soya. The purpose of these thresholds, as recognised in the Commission's proposals, is to support consumer choice in relation to food and feed labelling. Yet the current threshold for food labelling is 1 per cent—a similar tolerance is proposed for animal feed. Once again, there is incompatibility between the different legislative approaches and no practical or biological justification for the threshold levels proposed.

In practice, the Commission's seed threshold proposals would simply add cost and bureaucracy to commercial seed production, with no tangible benefit to consumer choice or information.

On a more technical point, BSPB also questions the ability of current testing methods to detect GM presence in seed accurately to the levels proposed by the Commission. Legal thresholds cannot be enforced without reliable and standardised methods of detection. It is therefore of serious concern that the most widely used testing method, known as PCR, is not reproducible or consistent between laboratories. Furthermore, the potential for false positives and margins of error at levels of below 1 per cent introduces an unacceptable degree of uncertainty which cannot, and should not, be borne by seed producers.

The Society is therefore pressing for parity in GM thresholds between seed, food and feed, with a 1 per cent tolerance level identified as the limit realistically achievable within practical agriculture and seed production.

Furthermore, BSPB is concerned that controls applied to GM presence in certified seed will not apply to crops grown from farm-saved seed. Standards and protocols for the production and independent verification of certified seed are set out in detailed regulations. No such controls apply to the use of farm-saved seed, and BSPB considers that this is a potential weakness in the traceability chain which must be addressed.

February 2002

Memorandum by GeneWatch UK

GeneWatch UK is a policy research group which takes a public interest, environmental protection and animal welfare perspective in its analysis of developments in genetic technologies.

Overall, GeneWatch UK welcomes the European Commission's proposals for labelling and tracing of GM, food and feed, particularly because they are based on the means of production (GM) rather than on the basis of the presence of foreign DNA or protein in the final product. All the evidence on public opinion supports this position as it demonstrates that people wish to make choices from a variety of perspectives, including environmental and ethical, not the chemical composition of the final product. A copy of our submission to the Food Standards Agency (FSA) on this subject is enclosed with this submission *(Not Printed)*.

In our new evidence, we would like to draw the Committee's attention to fundamental flaws in the Food Standards Agency's analysis of the Commission's proposals which have led them to favour a retention of the *status quo* in terms of only labelling when foreign DNA or protein is present in the final product at a level of greater than 1 per cent supplemented by a "GM-free" label[1].

---

[1] Minutes of the Food Standards Agency board meeting, 19 September 2001, The Spires Centre, Belfast http://www.food.gov.uk/multimedia/pdfs/fsa010601.

The Food Standards Agency appear to have based their commendations on two grounds:

1. That a GM label would be subject to fraud and consumers would be misled because "paper trails" would not be reliable.

2. A multi-criteria analysis of labelling options prepared by National Economic Research Associates (the NERA Report) which favoured the FSA's chosen approach [2].

Both of these grounds are flawed and because the FSA's position is one which the Committee seems likely to consider, GeneWatch wishes to draw the uncertainties and shortcomings in their analysis to the Committee's attention.

A GM-Free Label is the Fraudulent Approach

The FSA conclude that the Commission's proposals would result in a system that would be subject to fraud and consumers misled as a consequence. However, all schemes may be subject to fraud and it is the responsibility of the authorities to ensure that systems are as robust as possible and policed properly. What is so illogical in the FSA's position is that they recommend a GM-free labelling system which would be subject to exactly the same pressures as a GM label. Because an outcome of their recommendations would be that "GM-free" would become a high-cost, niche market, fraud may be even more likely as potential profits would be greater.

More importantly, by introducing the FSA's system, consumers would be faced with:

A GM label where products contained over 1 per cent GM protein or DNA

No label if products contained less than 1 per cent GM protein or DNA

No label if products contained 0.1-100 per cent of a GM crop derivative eg oil

A label "GM free" if no GM protein, DNA or derivatives were present

GeneWatch believes that such a system would be confusing and misleading for consumers and advocating it is to defraud consumers by not providing a label where foods containing ingredients from GMOs are labelled (including derivatives as the European Commission propose) and those that do not have a label. This is the most simple system for all concerned.

The National Economic Research Associates (NERA) Report—Biased to the Biotechnology Industry

The NERA report uses a methodology, multi-criteria analysis, which GeneWatch believes shows considerable potential for evaluating policy options. In collaborative research with the Science Policy Research Unit at Sussex University, GeneWatch UK has used a similar approach to evaluate GM and non-GM options for growing oilseed rape in a study funded by Unilever[3]. Therefore, we are extremely disappointed that such a promising methodology should have been misapplied by the consultants employed by the FSA. The problems with the report include:

A lack of validation of the criteria, scoring and weighting—whilst the report acknowledges stakeholder view points it then goes on to ignore them in the choice of criteria, scoring and weighting. There appears to have been no process of peer review to establish how robust the criteria, scores or weights are. Because the choice of criteria (the framing) has been shown to drive the final outcome of a multi-criteria analysis.[4], ensuring that all relevant criteria have been included and have wide acceptance is crucial if there is to be confidence in the outcome.

The criteria representing the range of benefits from labelling being ridiculously restricted. Only two criteria consider benefits of labelling—"standardisation of GM-free claims" and "restoring public confidence in GM foods". Extraordinarily, a criterion relating to labelling being a source of research information on the impacts of GM foods was rejected on the advice of the FSA that labels would not be specific or reliable enough and cause-effect linkages too distant to be of any value. Not only did NERA go no further than the FSA in seeking advice, but the FSA's attitude in this case appears to contradict wider efforts to put in place identity preservation schemes and promote the generic benefits of traceability in food safety, animal welfare and environmental protection.

---

[2] Economic Appraisal of Options for Extension of Legislation on GM Labelling. A Final Report for the Food Standards Agency. Prepared by NERA May 2001.

[3] Stirling, A & Mayer, S (2000) Precautionary risk appraisal of a genetically modified crop.
International Journal of Occupational Health and Environmental Medicine 6(4): 296-311; Stirling, A & Mayer, S (2000) A precautionary approach to technology appraisal?—A multi-criteria mapping of genetic modification in UK agriculture. TA-Datenbank-Nachrichten 3: 39-51; Stirling, A & Mayer, S (2001) Multi-criteria mapping the genetically modified crop debate: A pilot study of a genetically modified crop in the UK. Environment and Planning C: Environment and Planning C 19: 529-555; Mayer, S & Stirling, A. (2002) Finding a precautionary approach to technological developments—lessons for the evaluation of GM crops. Journal of Agricultural and Environmental Ethics. In press.

[4] Stirling, A & Mayer, S (2001) Multi-criteria mapping the genetically modified crop debate: A pilot study of a genetically modified crop in the UK. Environment and Planning C: Environment and Planning C: 19: 529-555.

The exclusion of many important criteria. Criteria that GeneWatch consider should have been part of the multi-criteria analysis have been excluded:

— Clarity/simplicity for the consumer

— Respect for rights of low-income consumers to choose non-GM food

— Information benefits of traceability

— Meeting majority wishes

— Proportion of foods using GM ingredients labelled

Other stakeholders are likely to add to this list. By restricting criteria according to NERA's preferences, the FSA have not gained a robust insight into the relative performance of the options.

The range of uncertainties expressed in scores is rather small and should have been subjected to peer review.

The bias of the researchers towards GM foods is seen in their emphasis on how to increase public confidence in GM foods and their suggestion that future research should focus on this.

CONCLUSIONS

The Committee should therefore ignore the findings of the NERA report in coming to its conclusions and also question why the FSA have placed such great emphasis on the potential for fraud with one option and discounted its importance in their preferred option. GeneWatch believes that the FSA should be advised to conduct another multi-criteria analysis which involves a range of stakeholders in establishing the criteria, scoring and weighting to provide a more robust picture of the relative costs and benefits of the different policy options.

8 February 2002

Memorandum by the Genetic Engineering Alliance (Five Year Freeze Campaign)

The Genetic Engineering Alliance is a coalition of over 120 national organisations (see Appendix 1) and 200 local groups, calling for a moratorium on the growing, patenting and importing of genetically modified food and crops. In addition over 60,000 members of the UK public have signed our petition.

One of the core objectives in the calling of a moratorium is to provide the time necessary to ensure that the regulatory processes concerned with the introduction of GM in food and agriculture safeguards the right of the public to choose to eat foods derived from GM technology or not. In a recent Eurobarometer survey of European citizens, over 94 per cent said that they wanted this right to choose. We therefore welcome the current proposals from the European Commission as they strengthen existing legislation and recognise that consumers wish to know if a product is derived from GM technology even if DNA is not present in the final product. We would like to stress that people have many differing reasons for wanting to exercise this choice— a look at the diversity of organisations which comprise our membership will demonstrate this—trade unions, religious bodies, consumer groups, organic gardeners, development agencies, allergy organisations, environmental groups.

We are aware that many of our supporting organisations, with expertise in particular areas, have submitted evidence to the Committee, so as a result will keep our submission short. However, we feel particularly concerned that the position that the UK Food Standards Agency has taken on this issue does not fully represent the interests of UK consumers, and would therefore like to address this issue more comprehensively.

POSITION OF THE UK'S FOOD STANDARDS AGENCY (FSA)

The Food Standards Agency has taken the position of not supporting the proposals and of maintaining the current regulations with the addition of a GM-free labelling system. While on the surface the latter proposal may seem attractive and advantageous for consumers wishing to avoid GM, in reality it is not. The FSA have rejected the EU proposals on the grounds that they are unenforceable, unaffordable and open to fraud. They argue that a GM free label system will be easier to implement as there will be fewer foods involved and therefore less vulnerability to the above. The FSA is proposing to create a niche market of "GM-free" projects the extra cost of which will be borne by the consumer. As the majority of consumers consistently indicate that they wish to avoid eating GM derived products it is unacceptable that they should pay more for such products. Indeed, given that currently the market for GM products is far smaller, then it would be logical for GM to become the niche market, for it to be labelled as such and for the costs of this to fall on consumers wishing to exercise that choice. The producers of the product, and the owners of the technology, would be responsible for costs incurred. In the case of a "GM free" label the costs and the onus of proof would fall on the final producer of the GM free product to ensure that the product is GM-free—hardly an equitable situation.

The "GM-free" proposal also denies low-income consumers the right to purchase such products, as they will be priced too high. In recent research carried out by the National Consumer Council with low-income consumers they indicated that they wanted a full labelling system in order to choose not to buy GM products.

Low-income consumers are already denied the choice to eat organic foods because of excessive costs and it is unacceptable that they should be denied further choice.

The new EU Deliberative Release Directive 2001/18/EC requires Member States to ensure the traceability of GMOs and if this is not agreed at Community level then Member States will have to develop their own traceability scheme anyway.

We are very concerned that the FSA's position will become the official position of the UK in negotiations on this issue and we feel that it is not in the best interests of UK citizens that this line is taken. We hope that the Committee will reflect these views to the UK Government.

ADDITIONAL POINTS

The Commission proposals whilst including labelling for animal feed do not include proposals to label the produce from animals fed on GM animal feed ie milk, eggs, meat. This is contrary to the wishes of consumers who have indicated that they would like this information.

Several Member States, although not the UK, have indicated that they wish the current *de facto* moratorium to continue until the current Commission proposals have been put in place. We feel similarly that the moratorium should hold until the regulatory process is adequate to protect consumer choice, and until the omission of a liability regime is in place.

The current threshold of 1 per cent for adventitious contamination should be reviewed. Consumers want a threshold at the lowest level of detection, ie 0.1 per cent. Given advances in testing technology this should be achievable. No contamination from GMOs, which have not been subjected to the full EU approval process, should be permitted.

February 2002

APPENDIX 1

SUPPORTERS OF THE FIVE YEAR FREEZE ARE:

Action Aid
Action Against Allergy
Agricultural Christian Fellowship
Baby Milk Action
British Association of Nature Conservationists
Biodynamic Agriculture Association
Black Environmental Network
Body Shop International PLC
British Allergy Foundation
British Association of Fair Trade Shops
British Naturopathic Association
Caduceus
Centre for Alternative Technology
Chartered Institute of Environmental Health
Christian Aid
Christian Ecology Link
Catholic Institute for International Relations
Compassion in World Farming
Communities Against Toxics
Council for the Protection of Rural England
Ecologist
Ecology Building Society
Elm Farm Research Centre
Farm-A-Round
Farming and Livestock Concern
Federation of City Farms and Community
  Gardens
Find Your Feet
Food Commission
Food for Health Network
Fresh Food Company
Freshlands UK
Friends of the Earth
Friends of the Earth Scotland
Gaia Foundation
Gardeners GMO Group

Islamic Foundation of Ecology and Environment
Institute for Science in Society
Intermediate Technology Development Group
International Society for Ecology and Culture
Islamic Concern
Living Lightly
Local Government Association
Longhouse
Maternity Alliance
Medact
National Federation of Women's Institutes
National Society of Allotment and Leisure
  Gardeners
Natural Law Party
Neal's Yard Bakery
Neal's Yard Remedies
New Economics Foundation
New Internationalist
Noah Project
Organic Farm Foods Wales
Organic Gardening
Organic Shop
Organics Direct
Oxfam
People & Planet
Permaculture Association UK
Permanent Publications
Pesticides Trust
Plamil Foods Ltd
Planet Organic
Positive News
Pret A Manger
Resurgence
Scientists for Global Responsibility
Scottish Consumer's Association for Natural Food
Small Farmers Association

GE Free Forests
Genetic Food Alert
Genetics Forum
GenetiX Snowball
GeneWatch UK
GMO Campaign
Good Gardeners Association
Green & Blacks
Green Books
Green Network
Green Party
Greenpeace
Guild of Fine Food Retailers
Guild of Food Writers
Henry Doubleday Research Association
Health Food Manufacturer's Association
Help International Plant Protein Organisation
Hyperactive Children's Support Group
Iceland Frozen Foods

Soil Association
Splice (Genetics Forum)
Student Environment Network
Trade and General Workers Union
The Harbour
Townswomen's Guilds
Triodos Bank
Unison
Vegan Society
Vegetarian Society
Vetwork UK
Vinceremos Wines & Spirits Ltd
World Development Movement
Whole Earth Foods Ltd
Wildlife Trusts
Womankind Worldwide
Women's Environmental Network
World Development Movement
World Wide Fund for Nature

Memorandum by the Grain and Feed Trade Association (GAFTA)

GAFTA POSITION ON THE EU PROPOSALS FOR NOVEL FOOD/FEED AND GM TRACEABILITY

NOVEL FOOD/FEED

This proposal is essentially a single harmonised system to scientifically assess and approve GM food and feed products and sets down the labelling requirements to the final consumer.

Single Approval

GAFTA considers a single approval system for both food and feed usage as sensible. The system would avoid the market disruption recently experienced by the USA with the Starlink corn.

TEN YEAR REVIEW

The system does propose a ten-year renewal requirement for approved GM foods and feed. GAFTA would seek assurances that the review is expedient and that products undergoing such a review may continue to be freely circulated within the EU. The review system does not however set out the official control authorities' actions where a GM product does not gain re-approval. It is clear that a transitional time period would be necessary for this product to be progressively removed from the EU supply chain. GAFTA would take the prudent view that the EU rules governing the unapproval process of novel food/feed needs to be addressed well in advance of the ten year review system actually being initiated. In essence, both traders and the control authorities will therefore be informed and market disruption is minimised.

Novel Food and Feed Labelling

The labelling relates to the final consumer, ie the person who eats the food or the farmer who purchases the feed. The information is delivered at the end of the respective supply chains. The labelling of products derived from GM ingredients but containing no GM material appears to be unenforceable. With no detection method the legislation cannot actually be applied. GAFTA can only view this provision as being poorly thought out legislation, ie can not be checked on whether compliance has been achieved or not.

Adventitious Thresholds

The commercial market has been operating with thresholds for several years now, having recognised the fact that unavoidable traces of GM material can be present in bulk commodity consignments. The sheer quantity and scale of bulk commodity movements has finally been recognised in the EU Commission's proposals which GAFTA has repeatedly pointed out. This provision clearly provides realism as absolute zero limits have or never will be achievable.

This provision is equally applicable to GAFTA's position on the GM Traceability proposal.

GM Traceability

The EU Commission has sought to define traceability in its proposed horizontal legislation on the principles of food law. It can be defined as knowing who you bought from and subsequently sold to. On the basis of that definition the requirements of traceability have been operated for many decades by the grain and feed materials trade through the use of standards contract terms. However, the GM traceability proposal comes beyond this simplistic definition and seeks extensively greater amounts of information.

The burden of information gathering initiated by the first supplier within or to the EU falls on the last buyer in the EU to inform the farmer or consumer.

Bulk Commodity and Unique Event Codes

As it currently stands today in the commercial market place an EU feed compounder or food manufacturer will only wish to seek information from their EU supplier on whether the product contains GM material or not within agreed thresholds. They have no requirement for any additional information such as the proposed listing of unique event codes that may be within a bulk consignment.

In relation to the proposed EU legislation, of course GAFTA members will be making the declaration on import into the EU that the product is for food or feed use, or for processing. The problems centre on the listing of unique event codes. There are currently no internationally standardised codes. This is demonstrated by Canada and USA who have different event codes for the same genetic modification. The actual need for such codes can only be equated to environmental damage assessment. The import declaration made shows the imported products are not destined for EU cultivation, the only place where environmental damage could occur. The assertion that the codes would help human health monitoring is also foundless since the traceability stops at the food retailer. Therefore the unique codes listing on bulk imports which may be contained within the consignment has no actual function. Human health monitoring can't be achieved, whilst environmental damage can only equate to seed imports that will be cultivated in the EU. The furthest that the EU Commission could require would be that for imported food and feed materials a simple requirement to label as "does contain genetically modified organisms" when above a threshold level.

Testing

The EU legislation can only be applied with the European Community. Therefore the EU importer has to bear the information burden. There will be no legal requirement for third country exporters to provide information on a consignment's GM status. Therefore, the importer must either seek the information via commercial negotiations or test on arrival for non-EU approved GM products (ie adventitious threshold).

Conflict with WTO Rules

GAFTA would assert that the GM traceability covering imports into the EU can only be viewed as a technical barrier, since its scientific basis is removed as it is not able to address environmental damage or human health (as identified in earlier sections). The GM traceability proposal with regard to imports therefore only offers consumer choice which has no scientific validity as a barrier to trade under WTO rules and would therefore be open to a challenge under the WTO dispute procedures.

5 February 2002

Memorandum by Greenpeace

PROPOSED REGULATION ON GM FOOD IN FEED

1. *Do these proposals adequately address the requirements of European consumers for regulation, traceability and labelling of GM food and feed and of food and feed products derived from GMOs?*

Consumers have a right, enshrined in Article 153 of the Amsterdam Treaty, to know what is in their food. They should have access to clear information about whether food products have been produced using GMOs. This is what consumers want. Opinion polls have repeatedly shown that the vast majority of UK consumers want labelling of GM foods and products derived from GMOs. Consumers are not simply concerned whether foods contain DNA or protein of GM origin but want to know in more detail how their food has been produced and whether GMOs have been used in their production (Consumers' Association opinion poll—February 1999). Consumer decisions about purchasing GM foods are not solely about whether they are going to ingest GM DNA or protein but are also about environmental, religious and socio-economic issues as well. Labelling of all foods that have been produced using GMOs is needed to ensure full consumer choice.

The proposed extension of labelling to cover foods produced from GMOs, irrespective of whether there is DNA or protein of GM origin in the final product, is a welcome extension of the labelling regulations, giving consumers additional choice.

2. *Do they make sensible distinctions between the requirements of animal feed and those of food for human consumption?*

Inclusion of a requirement for labelling of GM animal feed is also welcomed and will assist farmers in making choices about the feed they buy. This will make it easier for farmers to produce the non-GM fed animal products, which consumers want and which the major food retailers are demanding from producers (cf press releases from Asda, 26 January 2001 and Tesco, 19 January 2001).

However, the proposed regulation does not go far enough as it does not require labelling of products derived from animals fed on GM feed. In an NOP poll for Greenpeace, in September 2000, 66 per cent of consumers said they wanted to buy products derived from animals fed on non-GM feed. In the same poll, 90 per cent of consumers thought that eggs, meat, milk etc from animals fed on a diet containing GM crops should be labelled as such. The proposed legislation will not go far enough in meeting consumer concerns. Food products from animals fed on GM crops should be labelled.

— The proposed regulation should include a requirement that food products derived from animals fed on GMOs be labelled.

3. *How effective are the proposals likely to be in ensuring full traceability of GM material at all stages of the chain from producer to consumer?*

Traceability

According to the EU Commission's explanatory memorandum to the regulation, the aim of the traceability legislation is to facilitate:

"withdrawal of products should an unforeseen risk to human health or the environment be established; targeted monitoring of potential effects on human health or the environment; control and verification of labelling claims."

The Commission also says that an effective traceability system will prevent economic loss and brand damage and refers to:

"The recent case in the US, where a genetically modified maize variety approved only for use in animal feed entered the food chain, demonstrates that the lack of mandatory traceability requirements imposed on all operators in the production and distribution chain can result in huge costs".

"It will require traceability of GMO's throughout the chain from farm to table", EU Commission press release 25 July 2001.

However the proposed legislation does not fulfil the Commission's requirement of traceability "throughout the chain from farm to table". Nor will it facilitate withdrawal from the market of accidentally contaminated products.

Traceability is denied in the memorandum as "the ability to trace GMO's and products derived from GMO's at all stages of the placing on the market throughout the production and distribution chains. . . ." and goes on to say that "It is not necessary to establish the detailed history and origin of individual GMO's, through a traceability system, to provide for comprehensive labelling."

The traceability system proposed in the regulation is then limited to the identification of the GMO's present in a product at each stage within the production and distribution chain. Whilst this level of labelling through the supply chain may be effective to back up labelling claims, this is not an effective traceability system. It would not for example permit the identification of the source of the GMO, right back to the farm or elevator. Without full traceability the withdrawal of products and the investigation of contamination at source will remain as difficult and expensive as it was in the Starlink case. But this is something which the Commission appears to want the traceability legislation to achieve.

The food and feed industries have already spent a considerable amount of time and energy setting up traceability systems to ensure the supply of identity preserved non-GM soya and other bulk commodities into the UK and other parts of Europe in response to consumer demand for non-GM food and feed. These traceability systems are of varying quality but the best of them track the movement of product right from the farm. So that it is possible to say which farms supplied each elevator and which elevators supplied each shipment from which the bulk soya delivered to the UK has come. Unlike the system proposed by the regulations these traceability systems are effective at locating the source of GMO contamination. In addition these types of traceability systems do not add significantly to the cost of the product as they only add paperwork, which can be incorporated into the invoicing process.

The Regulation requires that information that a product contains GMOs is transmitted to the recipient of the product "at the first stage of placing on the market", this is defined as the initial transaction. However the memorandum clarifies this with respect to imports from third countries and the requirement is for the importer into the EU to provide the information, not the first person in the chain of transactions in the third country.

Yet much of the GM derived material currently (and likely in the future) imported and consumed in Europe is in the form of bulk commodities and also food products imported from third countries such as the USA and Canada. With a system that stops at Europe's borders it will be impossible to trace the movement of a product within the third country before it reaches Europe. For example, if there was an elevator level contamination in a third country, there would be no full paper chain through from the contaminated elevator to the product in Europe. Similarly if a product is found to be contaminated after import into Europe there is no paper chain required back to the third country to permit location of the source of the contamination.

The system proposed in the legislation relies on testing by the importer which is expensive and unreliable (false positives are common, for example the prevalence of the naturally occurring cauliflower mosaic virus means that many samples are producing false positives when tested for the presence of promoters). Whereas a paper trail back to the farm permits less testing to be done, except to check that the system in place is operating correctly, thus keeping costs down.

The proposed legislation also seems to set up an advantage to third countries exporting to the EU, as there is a requirement to have traceability and labelling GM produce back to the producer for products produced within the EU but not those imported from third countries.

— The regulation should require a traceability system that tracks the movement of the produce through the supply chain and can identify the source of the GMO, in addition to the limited testing and traceability regime proposed, which simply tells you what GMOs are present in a product.

4. *Are the proposals likely to be enforceable in practice, particularly where no novel genetic material is contained in food and feed?*

See answer to question 3.

5. *A threshold level of 1 per cent or lower for the accidental presence of GM material in food and feed has been proposed, below which there would be an exemption. Is a threshold of this level, common to both food and feed, appropriate?*

Thresholds

The current threshold of 1 per cent (for the accidental presence of approved GMOs in food is based on political and commercial assumptions not scientific ones. The threshold should have been set at zero, ie the limit of detection using best available technology for sampling and detection (the detection methods currently in routine use (ELISA and PCR testing) are capable of detecting at levels of 0.1 per cent. Tight restrictions will encourage better practices among producers with better segregation at all stages from cultivation, through harvesting and transport to processing the final food/feed products and prevent the slippery slope to ever higher contamination levels Legislation should be reducing contamination not accommodating it. The balance of economic burden on producers versus safety and choice of consumers has swung too far towards the producers.

The 1 per cent threshold for accidental presence of approved GM material in feed brings the feed industry in line with the current legislation of the food and industry. However, parts of the animal feed industry have already shown that it is possible to work to a 0.1 per cent level of contamination (essentially at the limit of detection of the current methods), for example exports of bulk non-GM soya from Brazil to the UK are frequently certified to this level of contamination. Again the threshold should be set at zero.

The proposal in the regulations that 1 per cent "adventitious" or "technically unavoidable" contamination of unauthorised GMOs be permitted in food feed is unacceptable. This is commercialisation by the back door for the unauthorised GMOs. The contamination of food products with unauthorised GMOs will undermine consumer confidence in the safety of food.

Unauthorised GMOs should not be permitted as food contaminants when there is the possibility that they may never be approved. In authorising a GMO the Commission can take other factors (eg socio-economic factors) into account so there is the possibility that a GMO may be accepted as safe by the Scientific Committee but not authorised by the Commission.

— The threshold for contamination by authorised and unauthorised GMOs should be zero or at the limit of detection.

6. Is the role proposed for (a) the European Food Authority and its scientific committees and (b) Member States in the authorisation process for GM food and feed appropriate?

Authorisation Procedure

That the proposed regulation specifically includes rules for the approval and labelling of GMOs for use in animal feed is welcomed. The requirement that products likely to be used both as food and feed should only be authorised after they have fulfilled the authorisation criteria for both food and feed is also weclomed.

The "One door-one key" principle leads to highly centralised decision making at EU level rather than by Member States on food safety issues. National authorities should play a bigger role in the initial evaluation of new GMOs, for example they should receive the application for authorisation with all the relevant, information and be able to give advice to the European Food Authority before the Authority gives its opinion.

The procedure for public comment on authorisations is inadequate. Informed public comments will be on the fine detail of applications and the public should be allowed to see as much information as possible. All non-confidential information in the application for authorisation should be made available to the public, not just a summary. The period of 30 days for public consultation is inadequate, a period of 60 days would allow greater public participation in the consultation process.

The recognition in the proposed legislation that scientific risk assessment alone cannot provide all the information on which a risk management decision should be based and that other legitimate factors may be taken into account is a welcome step. Although it would have been useful to include within the proposed legislation a non-exclusive list of the types of factors which might be relevant eg socio-economic factors.

The abandonment of the simplified procedure for notification of GM foods which are "substantially equivalent" to existing foods is welcome as is the 10 year limit on authorisation of licences which will allow the active reconsideration of the application and any new information accumulated during that period.

— National authorities should play a bigger role in the initial evaluation of new GMO's.

— All non-confidential information in the application for authorisation should be made available to the public.

— The period for public consultation should be extended to 60 days.

7. Are the proposals likely to be compatible with the requirements of the Cartegena Protocol on Biosafety and with other international commitments, including OECD programmes?

We do not see any reasons why the proposals should be incompatible with the Cartegena Protocol, or with any other international commitment, including OECD programmes.

8. Are the proposals compatible with obligations towards non-Member States seeking to export food and feed to the EU?

9. Should the present EU-wide moratorium on approving GM food and crop product applications be maintained until the issues concerning traceability and labelling of GMO's has been resolved?

Greenpeace supports the EU-wide moratorium and believes it should be extended for reasons other than traceability and labelling provisions, as described elsewhere in our response.

10. What other aspects of the proposals require further consideration before the UK can sign up to them?

Emergency Measures

The replacement of Article 16 in EC 90/220 by Article 35 in the present Regulation is unacceptable. Member States should retain the right to restrict or prohibit the use and/or sale of a GMO on their own territory.

— Article 35 should be deleted and replaced with wording similar to that in Article 16 of EC 90/220.

Liability for damage caused by GMO's

We note that there are provisions in the Regulations that require Member States to lay down penalties for infringement of the provisions on labelling, thresholds and traceability. However there is still no legislation in place that imposes liability on producers for damage caused by GMO's on human health or the environment. A statutory GM liability regime with strict liability on consent holders should be put in place immediately.

Conflict with non-GM and GM-free claims

There has been a considerable delay in the production of EU labelling legislation for animal feed. In the meanwhile the market has acted in response to consumer demand and many retailers have put in place non-GM or GM-free policies. There is now the likelihood of some difficulty and confusion both for farmers and consumers because of differences in these two approaches. The traceability and labelling regulations require positive labelling of all GMO's including all feed additives, but the non-GM and GM-free policies which have been put in place by the food/feed industry have concentrated mainly on sourcing GM-free or non-GM macro ingredients such as soya and maize and have not generally been concerned with the sourcing of non-GM feed additives.

Detection of unknown GMO's

In addition to potential contamination by approved and unapproved varieties which have been assessed as safe by the EU Scientific Committee there is also the possibility of contamination of food and feed products by GMO's which have not been approved at all in the EU but have received some level of regulatory approval elsewhere in the world or have never been through any regulatory process. How do you detect contamination by these GMO's? How do you avoid Starlink again, this was not approved in the EU and so would not be required to be labelled or subject to the traceability legislation? How will it be possible to distinguish between unknown GMO's and known and approved ones, if the details of the sequences which will allow their detection are not available? There is currently no requirement on companies to provide reference samples/ provide details of tests for detection of GMO's except those that are going through the authorisation process. There needs to be established a database of DNA sequences and analytical procedures to detect all unauthorised GMO's.

Detection Methods

As set out in the Regulation, the onus must be on the applicant to supply details of the detection methods for the gene sequence in the GMO for which authorisation is being sought. There will of course be no possibility of sampling refined food products that have been derived from GMOs and no longer contain GM DNA or protein. The truthfulness of claims will need to reply on traceability through the supply chain back to the raw materials producer rather than on analytical methods. We do not agree however with those in the food industry who say that the proposed labelling of products derived from GMO's, such as oils, is unenforceable and will lead to increased fraud. Provided that effective traceability systems are in place (see below for more on effective traceability systems) these will provide the means to inspect and control labelling claims, via a paper trail back to the producer.

CONCLUSIONS

Proposed regulation on GM food and feed:

— The proposed regulation should include a requirement that food products derived from animals fed on GMO's be labelled.

— The threshold for contamination by authorised and unauthorised GMO's should be zero or at the limit of detection.

— National authorities should play a bigger role in the initial evaluation of new GMO's.

— All non-confidential information in the application for authorisation should be made available to the public.

— The period for public consultation should be extended to 60 days.

— Article 35 should be deleted and replaced with wording similar to that in Article 16 of EC 90/220.

Proposed regulation on GM traceability and labelling:

— The regulation should require a traceability system which tracks the movement of the produce through the supply chain and can identify the source of the GMO.

February 2002

Memorandum and Press Release by the Institute of Food Research

Thank you for your letter of 22 January inviting submissions of evidence to this Inquiry.

I attach a recent Press Release relating to the work of IFR on the safety assessment of genetically modified foods, in particular concerning the potential risk of novel allergens and investigation of the mechanisms by which unintended effects of genetic modification may arise, and in regard to the findings of the Royal Society Working Panel.

In the context of the present Inquiry, we would draw especial attention to p 6, para. 2 of the EC document COM(2001)182 Final, viz: "Further information, in particular precise information as to the genetic modifications of GMOs, may be necessary for post-market control and monitoring, including verification of the identity of GMO's contained within a product".

Whilst the "authorised transformation event" is the rational point of departure (COM(2001)182 Final, p 4 para. 6), it may not by itself provide a sufficient description of a GMO and of its properties. We support the view that continued research effort is necessary to develop the analytical and interpretative tools needed to characterise sufficiently the relationships between the "authorised transformation event" and the properties of a resultant GMO. We believe this is necessary to underpin the initiatives on labelling and traceability that are the objectives of the European Commission's proposals, and to provide an increasingly rigorous basis for assuring the safety of GMO's.

We shall be glad to expand further upon this short summary of our position.

Dr Nick Walton
Senior Scientist—Communications

13 February 2002

IFR SCIENTIST ON ROYAL SOCIETY WORKING PANEL BELIEVES NEW METHODS WILL IMPROVE MONITORING OF GM FOODS

A Royal Society report, published today, warns that safety assessments should be improved before a greater variety of foods made from genetically modified plants are declared fit for human consumption.

It concludes that there is no reason to doubt the safety of foods made from GM ingredients that are currently available, nor to believe that genetic modification makes foods inherently less safe than their conventional counterparts. However, the report calls for the tightening of regulations for all novel foods, particularly with respect to allergy testing and the nutritional content of infant formula.

The report also recommends that the methods for comparing GM foods with their conventional counterparts, by applying the principle of "substantial equivalence", should be made more explicit and objective during safety assessments, and harmonised between Member States of the European Union.

Dr Clare Mills, Head of Physical Biochemistry at the Institute of Food Research, was appointed to the working party because of her expertise in plant food allergens. Dr Mills's current research interests include investigating the way in which plant protein structure and food processing affect food protein allergenicity. Such research will pave the way for developing improved processing procedures to reduce allergen loads in foods.

Talking of the advances in analytical techniques, Dr Mills said, "Substantial equivalence has been the best method available, and it has worked well with the crops considered to date. Now we have the techniques to define the differences (if any) between GM and non-GM crops objectively, which will allow a transparent assessment of the new generation of crops now in development".

Other researchers at the institute of Food Research are working on the development of methods for the detection of possible "unintended effects" of genetic modification. The chances of this happening are no greater (indeed are less) than will conventional plant breeding, but the methods being developed will give early warning of any problems long before the products are approaching the commercial stage. The research is part of an EU-funded project involving 11 laboratories across Europe. The UK-based research is also supported by the Food Standards Agency.

4 February 2002

Memorandum by Monsanto S.A.

Monsanto welcomes the opportunity to provide evidence as regards the European Commission's proposals for the assessment, authorisation, labelling and traceability of genetically modified food and animal feed (COM(01)182 and COM(01)425).

Monsanto therefore wishes to submit the following evidence on this issue in line with the questions laid out in the call for evidence of 2 January 2002.

1. *Do these proposals adequately address the requirements of European consumers for regulation, traceability and labelling of GM food and feed and of food and feed products derived from GMO's?*

This question primarily addresses two separate issues, viz. (a) food and feed safety and (b) choice.

Safety: This is the focus of the GM food and feed proposal which, with the involvement of the European Food Safety Authority, is positive and will ensure consistently rigorous safety assessments for all GM products throughout the EU. Harmonisation of the EU's rules for the assessment of safety could be expected to improve public confidence in safety assessments in the single market. A rigorous safety assessment prior to permission to market is further intended to assure safety, however by way of insurance, another purpose of the Traceability and Labelling proposal is to facilitate the withdrawal of specific GM products when it is shown that an unlikely subsequent adverse effect might warrant this. Existing traceability systems in the food/ feed chains, combined with a GMO traceability system, should be complementary and not duplicative, of existing systems.

Choice: Currently, for the most part, citizens do not have a choice as regards purchasing GM foods or otherwise. This is due in part we think, to the overcomplicated nature of the existing regulations. As many have suggested, creation of a specific "non-GM" class of foodstuffs would help ease the confusion.

2. *Do they make sensible distinctions between the requirements of animal feed and those of food for human consumption?*

The requirements for the safety assessment and authorisation are very similar for GM foods and feeds in the Commission proposals, and the possibility exists to combine the procedures for products that have both food and feed uses. This is a sensible approach since the uses of most products are expected to include both food and feed uses. Furthermore the safety assessments for foods and feeds are based on similar information.

The Traceability and Labelling proposal makes no distinction between foods and feeds. The question of choice appears to be less relevant in the case of animal feeds, unless an operator wishes to offer "non-GM animal-based foodstuffs". This can be achieved by an operator designing his or her individual specifications such that the intended supply is obtained. However, in that respect, it is essential to implement a scheme to validate and ensure such claims.

3. *How effective are the proposals likely to be in ensuring full traceability of GM material at all stages of the chain from producer to consumer?*

Assuming that the phrase "GM material" means all material originating from GM sources, then the proposals are likely to fail in their objective. Many of the materials derived from GM sources such as grains, are highly purified products that are chemically identical to their "conventional" sources. Therefore, attempts to assure traceability based on GM-origin, without the possibility of analytical verification, will not be totally reliable. This is expected to be particularly true for products originating in third countries.

Existing traceability systems are mainly document-based and provide for Government Administrations and operators throughout the chain to assure traceability by following the document chain through the previous suppliers back to where it originated. Manufacturers use similar systems combined with specifications and analytical verification to assure product quality.

In a departure from this principle and faced with the practical reality, the question of traceability of bulk commodity mixtures has been addressed in the Commission proposal through the use of a listing of GMO's that the product "may" contain.

4. *Are the proposals likely to be enforceable in practice, particularly where no novel genetic material is contained in the food or feed?*

Many GM food and feed products derived from plants contain no novel genetic material that can be used to analytically verify the use of genetic modification techniques. Therefore, if there is no method for detecting differences, administration and enforcement of the proposals will be particularly difficult in practice, as there will be no factual or scientific basis for final decision-making or arbitration. Apart from the question of enforceability, the GMO-specific labelling of such chemically identical products risks confusing consumers and would likely further undermine consumer confidence.

5. *A threshold level of 1 per cent or lower for the accidental presence of GM material in food and feed has been proposed, below which there would be an exemption. Is a threshold of this level, common to both food and feed, appropriate?*

The proposal for a 1 per cent threshold for adventitious presence in food and feed has arisen in order to be consistent with the current food labelling laws as they pertain to the adventitious presence of GM ingredients in non-GM products. The current food labelling rules provide that, at a presence of above 1 per cent labelling for the presence of GM ingredients is required. The threshold was established to allow consumer choice, while recognising that absolute purity is unattainable. The selection of the threshold has no connection to safety.

An allowance for adventitious presence is necessary because in all production processes, and especially those that take place in the natural environment, small amounts of technically unavoidable traces of other components will be present. Nearly all product legislation recognises this fact and sets the maximum limits for such adventitious presence. In the case of seeds, the EU's Scientific Committee for plants has issued an opinion in which it is stated that "in ideal conditions levels of 0.3 to 0.5 per cent can be attained" and therefore the proposal for a 1 per cent threshold is reasonable from a practical perspective.

Thus, the threshold level for adventitious presence in GM foods and feeds in the proposal regulation must take into consideration the levels of purity that are achievable under normal agricultural crop production, transport and processing practices, as well as previous opinions on product safety issued by the authorities of countries which have allowed commercialisation of these products.

6. *Is the role proposed for (a) the European Food Authority and its scientific committees and (b) Member States in the authorisation process for GM food and feed appropriate?*

The creation of a European Food Safety Authority should allow equal high standards of food safety to prevail across the EU. In the past, many of the EU's problems concerning food and feed safety have arisen because of disparate decision-making. Ideally, the European Safety Authority should be allowed to issue opinions on product safety without political intervention and based solely on the results of careful scientific evaluation of dossiers submitted to them.

However, the GM Food and Feed proposal also provides for decisions to be taken on the basis not only of the European Food Safety Authority opinion, but also consideration of "other legitimate factors" without definition of what these might be. This opens the opportunity for Community decisions based on subjective, non-specific criteria and thus are a possible hindrance to a market-based economy.

7. *Are the proposals likely to be compatible with the requirements of the Cartagena Protocol on Biosafety and with other international commitments, including the OECD programmes?*

Due to the fundamental differences in the way the EU has organised its regulatory structures for biotechnology products (all biotechnology products are presumed to be risky and therefore require evaluation in contrast to non-biotechnology products which are often assumed to be safe) specific problems arise in the area of attempting to achieve compatibility with international rules. In addition, the Cartagena protocol has no binding national or international legal force and therefore it is difficult to match the legal requirements of a regulatory structure with those of an international protocol. It is inevitable therefore, that there will be differences around the world in interpreting and implementing the protocol.

8. *Are the proposals compatible with obligations towards non-Member States seeking to export food and feed to the EU?*

Currently there is a large disparity between the number of GM products authorised for use in the EU and the rest of the world due to the fact that the current regulations covering the approval of genetically modified products are not functioning in practice. This lack of (EU) approvals for products approved for consumption elsewhere is already causing disruption to third countries trade with the EU. Adoption of further complicated and un-administrable rules is likely to further complicate the situation. In addition, rules which are costly to administer and apply without discrimination to all food and feed imports will fall hardest on those countries least likely to be able to afford them, namely developing countries.

9. *Should the present EU-wide moratorium on approving GM food and crop product applications be maintained until the issues concerning traceability and labelling of GMO's have been resolved?*

There is no justification for ignoring current EU law in anticipation of future EU legislation and therefore no reason to maintain the current moratorium.

The EU Directive 2001/18 which will administer the approvals of foods and feeds after October of this year already contains traceability and labelling requirements consistent with those in the proposed regulation on Traceability and Labelling. The GM Food and Feed regulation may not be adopted for several years, and in any event, the regulation will be retroactive on all products, including those products currently on the market, without GMO-specific traceability and labelling requirements.

10. *What other aspects of the proposals require further consideration before the UK Government can sign up to them?*

Other aspects that the UK Government should consider are:
— The nature of the technical barrier to trade which the proposals might constitute.

—   Alternative schemes and proposals that would provide for consumer choice in a more effective and efficient manner.

—   The additional measures which would need to be agreed and implemented prior to the proposals coming into force and in order to make them operable from an administrative point of view, eg analytical methodology and validation, sampling and storage measures for administrative purposes and the consequent level of resources needed and the cost of administering the proposals within the UK or the institutions of the EU.

—   Scientific guidelines which must be provided to assist notifiers in the preparation of GM food and feed applications before the regulation comes into force.

—   The proportionality of the proposed measures for GM-derived foods in comparison with those generally in force for other food and feed products.

—   Supervision arrangements which must recognise that products will be handled by multiple operators in the food and feed chains and that all operators must have responsibility for legal compliance, not only authorisation holders.

—   Clarification of the relationship with other Community legislation, where there is a risk of duplication or inconsistency (eg additives legislation, EU Directive 2001/18/EEC).

February 2002

Memorandum by the National Consumer Council

SUMMARY

The National Consumer Council (NCC) welcomes the European Commission's package of legislative proposals that aim to establish a sound system to trace and label genetically modified organisms (GMO's)[1] and regulate the market introduction and labelling of food and feed products derived from GMO's[2].

We particularly welcome the proposals to strengthen the authorisation and safety assessment procedure for GM food and animal feed to help restore consumer confidence in GM regulation. However, we are concerned that the Commission proposes to allow small levels of adventitious contamination of food by GM crops and ingredients that are not yet fully approved for use in EU countries.

The Commission proposes to maintain a maximum threshold of 1 per cent adventitious contamination of crops by GM varieties. The NCC's recent research[3] shows that zero contamination is the ideal: 42 per cent of those who had a view expressed this preference. The NCC recognises that zero contamination may not be technically possible but believes that, as detection methods and monitoring systems improve, the 1 per cent threshold should be reviewed and preferably lowered.

We welcome the intention to introduce an integrated system to trace GMO's through the whole food chain. This will facilitate labelling and its enforcement, reduce the need for, and reliance on, testing of products, enable fast and efficient withdrawal of products in the event of unforeseen problems, and will facilitate post-market monitoring for effects on human health or the environment.

NCC's survey shows that consumers want more information about GM foods and ingredients. The proposals on traceability and labelling to extend labelling requirements to include GM derivatives (for example, oil and glucose syrup) and animal feed are therefore positive. However, we are concerned that these proposals do not extend to the labelling of meat and other products from animals fed GM feed. Our survey found strong consumer demand (eight out of 10 people) for the labelling of meat and other products from animals fed GM feed.

We welcome the requirement on companies submitting applications to supply standard reference materials and validated methods for detecting GM material. We also welcome the Commission's intentions to facilitate a co-ordinated approach to inspection and control across the EU prior to the legislation coming into force.

We are pleased that the simplified notification procedure for GM foods that are deemed substantially equivalent to existing foods has been abandoned, and that a more thorough analysis will be required.

The NCC's purpose is to make all consumers matter by putting forward the consumer interest, particularly that of disadvantaged groups. We research, campaign and work with those who can make a difference to achieve beneficial changes for consumers. One of our key objectives is ensuring that markets and public services work for everyone. We have been campaigning for measures to strengthen the authorisation and safety assessment procedure for genetically modified (GM) food and animal feed and to provide consumer

---

[1] Proposal of the European Parliament and of the Council for a Regulation concerning the Traceability and Labelling of Genetically Modified Organisms and Traceability of Food and Feed Produced from Genetically Modified Organisms (COM(2001)182).

[2] Proposal for a Regulation of the European Parliament and of the Council on Genetically Modified Food and Feed (COM(2001)425).

[3] *Genetically Modified Food Labelling* Omnibus Survey of 2000 representative UK adults conducted in August 2001 by RSGB for the National Consumer Council.

choice by improving labelling and traceability requirements for both food and feed products derived from GMO's.

Consumers want full information about the food they are purchasing and eating and therefore place great importance on the labelling of GM food and ingredients. The NCC's own research shows clear consumer support for the right to know whether food is from GM crops or is the produce of animals fed GM feed.

We welcome the opportunity to make a submission to this Select Committee inquiry. Our submission follows the order of the specific questions listed in the Committee's call for evidence and concentrates on those areas where we have carried out research.

THE QUESTIONS

1. *Do these proposals adequately address the requirements of European consumers for regulation, traceability and labelling of GM food and feed and of food and feed products derived from GMO's?*

1.1 The NCC welcomes the European Commission's package of legislative proposals that aim to establish a sound system to trace and label GMO's and regulate the market introduction and labelling of food and feed products derived from GMO's.

Traceability and labelling

1.2 The NCC particularly welcomes the proposals on GM labelling and the extension of the current labelling requirements to cover products derived from GMO's (where there is none of the original GM DNA or protein present) and animal feed for the first time.

1.3 The proposed extension of the labelling requirements will offer additional information and choice to that currently available about the foods consumers are purchasing and eating. This will better meet consumer expectations. We are pleased that in putting forward these proposals the Commission recognises that it is a basic right of consumers to decide if they wish to buy food produced from GMO's or not. We also consider that the extension of labelling requirements will help build public confidence in the EU regulatory framework for GMO's.

1.4 Recent consumer research by the NCC[4] shows there is strong consumer demand in Britain for GM labelling. A summary of the research results is provided in the appendix to this report.

1.5 Our survey found:

— Two-thirds (64 per cent) of consumers say it is important that foods made from genetically modified plants is labelled with this information.

— A third (33 per cent) say information on GM ingredients is among the three most important pieces of information provided on food labels, compared with full ingredient listing (67 per cent), nutritional information (59 per cent) and allergy labelling (47 per cent).

— Over half (56 per cent) support labelling of GM derivatives (for example, refined oils and glucose starch).

— Three-quarters (73 per cent) say it is important to know, in general, what has been fed to food producing animals, and 44 per cent of that group say it is very important.

— Eight out of 10 (79 per cent) say they think meat and other products from animals fed GM should carry this information on the label.

— The "right to know" is given as the most important reason for wanting GM food labelling (55 per cent), with important for health reasons (36 per cent), environmental concerns (8 per cent), ethical reasons (8 per cent) also cited.

1.6 Our survey found high levels of demand (eight out of 10) for the labelling of meat and other animal products derived from animals fed GM feed. We strongly support the labelling of GM animal feed as a pre-requirement for this demand, although we note that the mandatory requirement to positively label products produced from such animals is not currently proposed. We urge that this should be reviewed within two years of the labelling of GM animal feed.

1.7 We also note that the current proposals do not extend labelling requirements to food or feed produced with a GMO—such as food or ingredients produced using GM processing aids such as enzymes—nor to products obtained from animals treated with GM medicinal products. We note that the Commission intends to deal with enzymes separately and we urge the Commission to bring forward consistent proposals at an early date. We note also that the Commission proposes that the labelling rules for food and feed should be reviewed after two years of operation. We welcome this and would support the inclusion of a review of these current exemptions from labelling at that time.

---

[4] See footnote 3.

1.8 We do not consider that the proposal for a "GM-free" label as proposed by the Food Standards Agency is helpful in meeting consumers' expectations for labelling of GM foods. There are currently no legal definitions of GM-free. However the Food Standards Agency's (FSA) proposals envisage "GM-free" applying to a small niche market of products—probably equating with the current "organic" products, which are usually more expensive. As our research has shown, the majority of consumers wish to see labelling of GM ingredients extended beyond the current arrangements. Thus their needs would not be met by a "GM-free" label. Furthermore, low-income consumers would be disadvantaged as choice would be restricted to those able to afford the more expensive products.

1.9 A "GM-free" label would also introduce greater confusion for consumers, as it would be likely to result in three tiers of GM labelling:

1. labelled GM products over the 1 per cent threshold;

2. no labelling because products are under the 1 per cent threshold;

3. "GM-free" labels.

1.10 The FSA has raised doubts about the practicalities of a traceability system. However, because it would include derivatives, a "GM-free" label would still necessitate a traceability system to be in place. The NCC considers that traceability systems can work, and that governments and enforcement agencies need to work with the European Commission to put in place the kind of measures necessary to overcome the challenges, rather than ruling out traceability systems.

1.11 The NCC does not have direct experience on the impact of traceability requirements on small businesses and catering establishments. However we are aware that the FSA's recent review of food regulations on small businesses[5] considered the subject of existing GM labelling and concluded that this "does not constitute an unreasonable burden on small businesses". We therefore do not consider that the additional requirements made in this proposal will be unreasonably burdensome. Once a traceability system has been established, on-going costs should be minimal for the majority of small businesses.

Regulation

1.12 We particularly welcome the proposals to strengthen the authorisation and safety assessment procedure for GM food and animal feed to help restore consumer confidence in GM regulation.

1.13 We are pleased that the simplified notification procedure for GM foods that are deemed substantially equivalent to existing foods has been abandoned. The concept of substantial equivalence has been criticised and its use of this regulatory short cut has been extremely controversial.

1.14 We recommend that the GM food-feed proposal needs to set out a comprehensive list of criteria on which the risk assessment for GM food and feed should be based (as is now the case for the amended Deliberate Release Directive, 2001/18). We therefore urge the speedy development of these criteria. It is unclear from the current proposals how these will be developed. The NCC supports an open consultative process.

1.15 We welcome the clauses that would allow for the public to gain access to information on applications for GM food and feed. However, it is our strong conviction that in addition to a summary document, the full dossier should be made available for public scrutiny as is currently the case in the UK. This is not only an important point of principle, but a very practical one too, in that many of the consumer and public interest issues that have arisen over the applications have been based on issues of detail for which a summary document would not be adequate. Where a company requests that specific data is commercially confidential, this must be assessed for each piece of information against clear criteria. Any such material can then be placed in a separate annex not available to the public.

1.16 We support the principle that applications should be renewed every 10 years in the light of post-market monitoring and any new information relevant to risks to human or animal health or the environment. We welcome the proposal that existing approvals must provide additional information on risk assessment within six months of operation of the regulation. This will provide a means of regulatory catch up for existing products on the market.

2. Do they make sensible distinctions between the requirements of animal feed and those of food for human consumption?

2.1 The NCC welcomes the intention of the proposal to strengthen the authorisation procedure for GM food and feed. We support the proposal to set up a "one stop shop" procedure with a single approval process, covering both the environmental risk and risks to human and animal health.

---

[5] Task Force on the burdens of food regulations on small food businesses, Food Standards Agency, June 2001.

2.2 We welcome the improved scope of the regulation of GM food and feed to include for the first time, the authorisation of animal feed and its widening to include food (and feed) additives, flavourings and highly processed derivatives.

2.3 We support the proposal to ensure that authorisation should not be granted for a single use, when a product is likely to be used for both food and feed purposes.

3. *How effective are the proposals likely to be in ensuring full traceability of GM material at all stages of the chain from producer to consumer?*

3.1 The NCC welcomes the intention to introduce an integrated system to trace GMOs throughout the whole chain from farm to table, which would make it obligatory for businesses to transmit and retain information at every stage of production, process and supply. We believe there are a number of strong consumer benefits from such a system:

— Traceability is essential to facilitate the proposed labelling system and its enforcement.

— It will facilitate the introduction and enforcement of more extensive non-statutory labelling including negative claims.

— It will reduce the need for, and reliance on, testing and sampling of products.

— It will enable fast and efficient withdrawal of products from the market in the event of unforeseen problems.

— It will facilitate monitoring for effects on human health or the environment.

3.2 The NCC therefore considers that a workable system which has the confidence of consumers, industry and enforcement agencies can be developed, based on the Commission's current proposals.

4. *Are the proposals likely to be enforceable in practice, particularly where no novel genetic material is contained in the feed or food?*

4.1 To ensure consumer and industry confidence in labelling and its enforcement, it is essential that labelling is underpinned by full traceability. Where food or feed contains GM material—and testing is therefore feasible—this provides an additional backup enforcement tool.

4.2 Where food or feed contains ingredients from GM derivatives—such as refined oils, that do not contain GM material—enforcement will need to be based on traceability, together with the further development of segregation and identity preservation systems for non-GM supplies.

4.3 The NCC considers that enforcement will be facilitated by:

— the requirements for traceability;

— the development by the Commission of a more co-ordinated EU-wide approach to enforcement;

— the further development, standardisation and validation of testing methodologies;

— availability of standard reference materials and validated methods for use by public analyst laboratories and requirements on the biotech industry to supply these;

— sufficient resources being made available to enforcement agencies.

4.4 We welcome the Commission's intentions to facilitate a co-ordinated approach to inspection and control in each Member State by developing technical guidance on sampling and testing methods prior to this proposed legislation coming into force.

4.5 We also welcome the Commission's approach to working at an international level to achieve a common approach to sampling and testing. We would also like to encourage the work of the Organisation for Economic Co-operation and Development (OECD) working group on developing a system of unique codes to enable traceability of GM products worldwide. This will facilitate the enforcement of zero tolerance for non-EU-approved varieties.

5. *A threshold level of 1 per cent or lower for the accidental presence of GM material in food and feed has been proposed, below which there would be an exemption. Is a threshold of this level, common to both food and feed, appropriate?*

5.1 The NCC's research has sought the views of consumers on what they consider to be acceptable threshold levels. 55 per cent believe that this should be less than 1 per cent, with the greatest preference for zero GM in food (34 per cent). Only 17 per cent considered that 1 per cent is acceptable with a small percentage (9 per cent) finding more than 1 per cent acceptable. In total 89 per cent of those with a view considered either 1 per cent or less (or zero) acceptable. From this research it is therefore clear that the current threshold of 1 per cent is at the upper end of the scale of acceptability for the majority of consumers.

5.2 While there is strong consumer preference for zero contamination, the NCC accepts that in some instances a low level of adventitious contamination is technically unavoidable, though we do not accept that adventitious contamination is always inevitable. We note that the existing 1 per cent maximum threshold is not scientifically based.

It reflects both the sensitivity of current detection tests and the ability of the supply chain to deliver. We also note that many UK food producers and retailers are already operating to tighter specifications than the current legislation—for example, 0.1 per cent.

5.3 As detection methods improve and more extensive traceability and identity preservation systems are put in place we consider that lower thresholds will become more practical. The NCC therefore supports speedy moves to improve and validate detection methods and to introduce more extensive traceability and identity preservation systems of supply to facilitate the move towards a lower threshold than the current 1 per cent. We note that the Commission's proposal (preamble paragraph 25) allows for the possibility of lowering the threshold level of accidental contamination. The NCC welcomes this statement and we recommend the inclusion of a specific timeframe for review of current threshold levels—preferably no more than two years. We consider the threshold level should be common to both food and feed.

5.4 The NCC has a number of serious reservations about the proposal to set a threshold for non-EU-approved GM material in foods or feed. The NCC recommends that all GM varieties, whether seeking full authorisation or acceptance within thresholds for adventitious contamination, should receive the same degree of assessment and approval. We do not accept the proposal to set a threshold for non-approved GM material as it seeks to bypass a key stage (risk management) in the safety authorisation process. Until full authorisation is complete under the more rigorous and extensive risk assessment process of the revised 2001/18 Directive, a zero tolerance threshold for non-approved varieties should remain in place. The proposal to set a threshold for non-approved varieties should therefore be omitted.

5.5 The assertion by the Commission that the 14 non-EU-approved GM products, to which a proposed threshold is intended to apply, have had a risk assessment (a positive opinion from the Scientific Committee for Plants) and that this is sufficient to resolve any safety concerns regarding their presence through adventitious contamination is, in the NCC's view, not tenable. We do not consider it scientifically justifiable to disengage the risk assessment and risk management stages of the approval process in the way that is being proposed. This has not existed in practice to date and would set an unacceptable precedent. Furthermore we note that three of the 14 applications subsequently considered by the Commission's (risk management) regulatory committee in March 2000 failed to get approval. This further raises questions about the value of only considering a positive risk assessment by the Scientific Committee for Plants as basis for permitting a threshold for unapproved varieties.

5.6 The proposal that such exemptions would occur in future subsequent to a ruling from the EFA only on the risk assessment, would similarly short cut the full approval process, and would therefore be unacceptable to the NCC.

6. *Is the role proposed for (a) the European Food Authority (EFA) and its scientific committees and (b) Member States in the authorisation process for GM food and feed appropriate?*

6.1 In general, we welcome the intention to centralise the approval process and the risk assessment process under the EFA. We note, however that the EFA, as is currently proposed, is a "risk assessment" body and that "risk management" will remain within the remit of the Commission. Currently the Commission's regulatory committee (comprised of Member State competent authorities) plays a risk management role. However, we consider that one of the past failings of the GM approval process at an EU level was the way in which risk assessment and risk management was blurred and, at times, merged. We recommend that there is a need to clarify more fully the roles and responsibilities of, and liaison between the EFA, risk management bodies, and Member States competent authorities in order to facilitate greater consumer and scientific confidence in the whole risk analysis process.

6.2 Furthermore, we are unsure whether the consumer interest is strengthened by the intended role of the EFA. To date, it has largely been Member States that have proved the drivers of the current improvements in the regulation of GMOs and have been more responsive to consumer concerns. We remain concerned that the current proposals for the EFA do not include adequate consumer involvement and access to the proposed EFA risk assessment process. We advocate consumer representation on any risk assessment bodies and scientific panels responsible for conducting risk assessments under the approval process. Assessments should be conducted in an open, transparent and inclusive way.

7. Are the proposals likely to be compatible with the requirements of the Cartagena Protocol on Biosafety and with other international commitments, including OECD programmes?

The NCC does not take a view on this particular question.

8. Are the proposals compatible with obligations towards non-Member States seeking to export food and feed to the EU?

8.1 We cannot comment directly on how importers would apply the requirements in practice other than our comments above. However, this is an important question for consumer confidence, given that most GM material is produced outside the EU. We recommend greater co-ordination of enforcement EU-wide to ensure that standards of enforcement are equally high across all Member States and points of entry into the EU. We do not consider that non-Member States seeking to export food and feed to the UK are disadvantaged, as the rules would apply equally to EU and non-EU countries.

9. Should the present EU-wide moratorium on approving GM food and crop product applications be maintained until the issues concerning traceability and labelling of GMOs have been resolved?

9.1 Consumer confidence in the regulation of GM foods is unlikely to be enhanced until the issues of traceability and labelling have been resolved. Therefore, we consider it unwise to lift the current moratorium until issues of regulation, traceability and labelling have been resolved and agreed at a European level.

9.2 The NCC also remains concerned that the issue of liability remains unsolved and we question the advisability of lifting the *de facto* moratorium on new authorisations until this has been resolved. While the proposal on traceability allied to the labelling requirements will aid the detection of GM material throughout the food chain, we believe there needs to be clear liability legislation in the event of damage to the environment, health or trade.

10. What other aspects of the proposals require further consideration before the UK Government can sign up to them?

In our replies to the previous questions, we have noted those aspects of the proposals that the NCC considers are of concern to consumers and therefore require further consideration.

RECOMMENDATIONS

Our survey found strong consumer demand (eight out of 10 people) for the labelling of meat and other products from animals fed GM feed. While the Commission has not currently brought forward proposals, we recommend this should be reviewed within two years.

We recognise that zero contamination by GM crops may not be technically possible but believe that, as detection methods and monitoring systems improve, the 1 per cent threshold should be reviewed and preferably lowered.

A zero tolerance threshold for non-EU-approved varieties should remain in place until full authorisation is complete under the more rigorous and extensive risk assessment process.

The risk assessment process should include greater consumer involvement and access to the risk assessment process than is currently being proposed for the European Food Authority. In addition, we strongly recommend that the full application dossier for new approvals should be publicly available, as is currently the case in the UK, and not just the company's summary, as is being proposed.

We remain concerned that the issue of liability is unresolved. There needs to be clear liability legislation in the event of damage to the environment, health or trade.

A common approach to GM sampling and testing at an international level should be developed to enable traceability of GM products worldwide.

APPENDIX

SUMMARY TABLES FROM RSGB OMNIBUS SURVEY ON GM LABELLING FOR THE NCC
(AUGUST 2001)

SAMPLE: 2000 ADULTS (wtd BASE)

Q1. (a–c) *What in your view is first/second/third most important information on food labels?*

Ranked importance	First	Second	Third	Anywhere in first three
Full list of ingredients	717 (36 per cent)	373 (19 per cent)	248 (12 per cent)	1,338 (67 per cent)
Nutritional information	431 (22 per cent)	424 (21 per cent)	327 (16 per cent)	1,182 (59 per cent)
Information on allergic reactions	356 (18 per cent)	310 (15 per cent)	268 (13 per cent)	934 (47 per cent)
Information on GM ingredients	108 (5 per cent)	264 (13 per cent)	279 (14 per cent)	651 (33 per cent)
Country of origin	87 (4 per cent)	176 (9 per cent)	184 (9 per cent)	447 (22 per cent)
Organic	41 (2 per cent)	62 (3 per cent)	98 (5 per cent)	201 (10 per cent)

Q2. *How important is it to you that food ingredients made from GM plants is labelled with this information?*

	Very important	Fairly important	Not very important	Unimportant
Total	735 (37 per cent)	536 (27 per cent)	361 (18 per cent)	310 (16 per cent)

Q3. *Sometimes all traces of GM raw materials are destroyed during food processing. If this happens, would you still want to know that an ingredient (for example, oils or glucose syrup) had originally come from a GM plant or not?*

	Yes	No	Don't know
Total	1,121 (56 per cent)	796 (40 per cent)	84 (4 per cent)

Q5. *Foods containing GM ingredients do not have to be labelled if the GM material is present at a low level and is there accidentally. At the moment the permitted amount is up to 1 per cent—ie less than one part in 100. What level or amount of GM material in food would you find acceptable?*

	None at all, zero	Under 0.5 per cent	0.5 per cent to 1 per cent	1 per cent
All questioned (2,000 wtd base)	673 (34 per cent)	159 (8 per cent)	264 (13 per cent)	333 (17 per cent)
Of those who had a view (1,606)	673 (42 per cent)	159 (10 per cent)	264 (16 per cent)	333 (21 per cent)

Q6. *How important is it for you to know, in general, about what has been fed to the animals that produce meat, milk, eggs and cheese, including milk and cheese from sheep, cows and goats?*

	Very important	Fairly important	Not very important	Unimportant
Total	875 (44 per cent)	576 (29 per cent)	285 (14 per cent)	190 (9 per cent)

Q8. *Do you think meat and other products from animals fed with GM feed should carry this information on the label?*

	Yes	No	Don't know
Total	1,578 (79 per cent)	327 (16 per cent)	95 (5 per cent)

Q9. *You said that GM labelling is important. Why do you think food containing GM ingredients should be labelled?*

	Have a right to know	Important for: Health reasons	Ethical reasons	Environmental concerns
Of those who think labelling important (1,663)	917 (55 per cent)	606 (36 per cent)	135 (8 per cent)	131 (8 per cent)

Q10. *An effective labelling scheme for all GM materials in food will cost extra to put in place. Somebody will have to pay for these additional costs. Who do you think should pay for a full labelling scheme for food?*

	Manufacturers	Government	Shops/ supermarkets	Consumers
Total	958 (48 per cent)	789 (39 per cent)	412 (21 per cent)	196 (10 per cent)

Q11. *If the additional costs of a full labelling scheme for food were passed on to consumers, how willing would you be to pay extra for food that is labelled?*

	Any willing	Any not willing	Don't know	Other
Total	751 (38 per cent)	1,070 (53 per cent)	97 (5 per cent)	41 (2 per cent)

Hazel Phillips
Head of Public Affairs

13 February 2002

Memorandum by the National Farmers' Union of England and Wales (NFU)

1. *Do these proposals adequately address the requirements of European consumers for regulation, traceability and labelling of GM food and feed and food and feed products derived from GMOs?*

1.1 Yes. In principle, if effectively implemented and enforced, the regulations on traceability and labelling should provide consumers with sufficient information to make purchasing decisions based on content of GMOs or GM-derived ingredients. In particular, the NFU welcomes specific rules for the approval and labelling of GM animal feed. However, we are concerned that some aspects of the proposals are difficult to enforce.

1.2 In principle, we welcome the proposals for traceability throughout the food chain and the requirement for transmission of information on GM status between businesses. Farmers and growers have now developed farm assurance schemes for all major production areas, involving customers and consumers, and linked to food safety requirements and the need for traceability throughout the food chain.

1.3 Through the Supply Chain Initiative on Modified Agricultural Crops (SCIMAC) the NFU has worked with industry to provide acceptable codes of practice for on-farm management and segregation of GMOs. Other food industry initiatives for identity preservation are welcomed as a means of ensuring meaningful labelling. We believe these provide a sound starting point for industry-led traceability and segregation (for accurate labelling), should the UK Government decide commercial cultivation is appropriate.

2. *Do they make sensible distinctions between the requirements of animal feed and those of food for human consumption?*

2.1 The NFU welcomes specific rules for the approval and labelling of GM animal feed, and the setting of a threshold for adventitious contamination, above which labelling requirements are triggered. This will assist farmers supplying produce from animals fed on a non-GM diet to meet their customers' requirements. We welcome the proposal only to permit GM varieties to be marketed if they are authorised as safe for use in both food and feed products.

3. *How effective are these proposals likely to be in ensuring full traceability of GM material at all stages of the chain from producer to consumer?*

3.1 Despite the proposal taking the form of a Regulation, and therefore directly applicable to Member States, specifics of the traceability regime are left flexible and will depend to a certain degree on how Member States implement it.

3.2 Transmission of information on GMOs could possibly be integrated with other on-farm traceability systems, such as the UK's Assured Combinable Crops Scheme (ACCS). The requirement for a unique identifier relating to each specific GMO may assist in transmission of information and assist in providing traceability.

3.3 However, to allow labelling to be meaningful, traceability proposals should facilitate segregation of GM and non-GM products. The current proposals place emphasis on traceability systems, and suggest minimal sampling and testing will be required, for verification of imports and for control and inspection purposes. However, for the identity of a GM or non-GM material to be preserved, it must be traceable throughout a chain that is segregated from contamination, and the GM status verified by testing at appropriate points in the chain. We suggest the proposals underestimate the testing required to ensure accurate labelling.

4. *Are the proposals likely to be enforceable in practice, particularly where no novel genetic material is contained in the food or feed?*

4.1 Under these proposals, products containing GM material will be required to be labelled as such. In addition, products derived from GM ingredients but containing no GM material will have to be labelled to refer to the fact that the product was produced from a GMO but that no GMOs are present in the final product. The NFU is concerned that the proposal is based on processing methods, rather than the final composition of the product.

4.2 In cases of refined or highly processed material derived from GMOs where there is very little DNA or protein present, current detection methods are difficult to apply. As the labelling cannot be verified by testing the final product, we are concerned that this labelling requirement is unenforceable and potentially open to abuse, effectively penalising those who do comply, and potentially eroding consumer trust in labelling accuracy.

4.3 We suggest provision of such information on processing or production methods should not be a legal requirement if the composition of the product is unchanged. However, it could be encouraged through voluntary industry-led schemes, on the basis that this is marketing information on which some consumers may wish to make a purchasing decision.

5. *A threshold level of 1 per cent or lower for the accidental presence of GM material in food and feed has been proposed, below which there would be an exemption. Is a threshold of this level, common to both food and feed, appropriate?*

5.1 A threshold level of 1 per cent is already in place for adventitious presence of GM material in a food ingredient, above which labelling requirements are triggered.

5.2 We understand that the limit of quantitative detection of a specific GM variety is thought to be approximately 0.1 per cent, due to sampling constraints, so it would seem reasonable to set a threshold of an order of magnitude higher than this. For complex products, enforcement of the threshold level would require detection of 1 per cent GM material in a particular ingredient, which may itself be present in the finished product at a low level.

5.3 A lower threshold level should only be introduced after consideration of:

— the ability of industry to realistically deliver a lower threshold;

— the availability of low cost methods of sufficient sensitivity and accuracy to detect to a lower level in all products it is likely to be applied to; and

— a clear consumer demand for a lower threshold level.

5.4 The financial impact on the industry of introducing lower threshold levels should also be considered, in the context of what (if any) additional consumer benefit or protection would be delivered.

6. *Is the role proposed for (a) the European Food Authority and its scientific committees and (b) Member States in the authorisation process for GM food and feed appropriate?*

6.1 The European Food Authority (EFA), once established, will be responsible for undertaking a risk assessment covering both environmental risk and the risk to human and animal health when assessing a GM food or feed ingredient. The NFU welcomes a central system of assessment through the EFA with Member States taking the final decision on applications. The proposal that authorisations will be recommended for either both food and feed or neither should help to prevent crops, which may only be approved for one purpose, being widely cultivated and accidentally contaminating material intended for another purpose.

8. *Are the proposals compatible with obligations towards non-Member States seeking to export food and feed to the EU?*

8.1 It is difficult to see how obligations on importers will operate in practice. Testing of every batch would seem to be a costly proposition, and it is impossible to test for unapproved GMO varieties if there is no approved detection method or reference material available.

8.2 We are particularly concerned that those farmers who rely on feed material such as soya, imported from countries outside the EU, will be penalised by additional testing costs where documentation is not available.

9. *Should the present EU-wide moratorium on approving GM food and crop product applications be maintained until the issues concerning traceability and labelling of GMOs have been resolved?*

9.1 We do not believe that restarting the approvals process would adversely affect food or feed safety or the environment, provided the procedures laid out in Directive 2001/18/EC are implemented. The assessment process should determine on a case-by-case basis whether a food product is safe to release into the environment, or use as a food or feed material. The current moratorium prevents applications from being either accepted or rejected, and deters the submission of applications for improved varieties, which potentially offer benefits to farmers, the environment and consumers.

9.2 European labelling rules are already in force for GM food ingredients. GM feed is already being used, but is not currently required to be labelled. GM feed is mainly in the form of imported GM soya and maize varieties, which already have EU approval.

9.3 Proposed improvements in traceability and labelling must be balanced with the consequences of maintaining the moratorium.

10. *What other aspects of the proposals require further consideration before the UK Government can sign up to them?*

10.1 Detection methods: We consider that the Commission must be certain that credible and consistent testing for the presence of GM material is available before introducing a system which relies on testing for effective enforcement. The costs of testing for the presence of all GM varieties will be extremely high and appropriate reference material would need to be lodged with the EU when an application for approval is submitted, so that laboratories carrying out quantitative tests would have verification material available to them. There is a need for an accredited detection method, recognised across Europe, which can deliver quantitative results to an acceptable degree of certainty, especially where the level of detection approaches the threshold value set.

10.2 Public comments: The proposals require applications for approval to be submitted for public comment. A summary document may provide an adequate basis for public comment, but full details should be made publicly available where possible. Procedures could be put in place for editing of each dossier with respect to commercially sensitive material on a case-by-case basis.

10.3 GM-free labelling: It is disappointing that clear guidelines on the use of terms such as "GM-Free" have not been addressed in the current proposals. This term is being used increasingly on food labels, without a clear legal definition. We believe that the most logical definition of the term "GM-free" should relate to total freedom of any linkage with any GMO whether directly incorporated into the final product or used in its production. Those wishing to label a product as "GM-free" must be able to justify the claim. Where a "GM-free" claim is made, any GM content would be unacceptable.

10.4 We acknowledge that in practice it would be difficult to justify a "GM-free" claim under such a definition, particularly for processed food products and commodities. In order to ensure consumers are not misled, it may be more appropriate to make labelling claims in the form of a simple description, rather than a single-word definition. One commonly used example is the labelling of animal products for human consumption as "from animals not fed on a GM diet".

Elizabeth Hogben
Food Science Adviser

12 February 2001

Memorandum by the National Farmers' Union of Scotland (NFUS)

Thank you for the opportunity to comment on European Commission proposals concerning the labelling and tracing of GM food and feed.

SUMMARY

1. The following is a summary of our comments:

   (a) The EU Commission proposals are welcomed. There is a pressing need to provide choice to buyers of food and feed that could contain GM material.

   (b) The UK crop industry has developed protocols that should be adaptable to comply with the proposals. Government should establish a regulatory structure based on auditing of records and stocks.

   (c) The 1 per cent threshold on accidental presence of GM material is appropriate, but will not satisfy some consumers.

   (d) The proposals should apply equally to EU produced food and feed and to third country imports.

   (e) The present EU-wide moratorium of approving GM food and crop product applications is illogical.

NFU SCOTLAND POSITION ON LABELLING AND TRACING OF GM FOOD AND FEED

2. Our position on labelling and tracing of GM foods and feed:

   (a) Authorisation to use GM technology should be based on scientific advice on safety—for people and for the environment. Testing must take place to establish this advice.

   (b) Consumer views are very important and the right to choose should be protected. GM organisms and foods containing or derived from GM organisms should be clearly labelled.

   (c) Animal feeds containing or derived from GM organisms should also be clearly labelled.

3. NFU Scotland endorses the work of the Supply Chain Initiative on Modified Agricultural Crops (SCIMAC), whose protocols are aimed at delivering traceability from field to end consumer.

Question 1—Consumer Requirements

4. The true level of consumer interest is very hard to access due to the discrepancy between consumer views expressed in surveys and their buying, as measured by sales. The most obvious example are surveys of consumer attitudes to animal welfare issues, the results of which are contradicted by data on actual purchases. The virtual elimination of GM foods from retail shelves has effectively removed choice and the ability to accurately assess consumer views.

5. Within the minority of consumers with real concerns on GM technology there is an element that will never be satisfied. This group has no understanding of science and expects absolute assurances. This same group is unable to sensibly compare the relative risks of different types of food production.

6. We welcome the proposed labelling and believe that it should meet the needs of most consumers. It is relatively complex however and many consumers are likely to find the difference between a product containing GM organisms and one that was produced from a GM organism hard to understand. The suspicion is likely to be that the food may still have traces of the organism in them.

7. The size and prominence of the message is important. A message that is too small could cause angry reactions by consumers, directed towards retailers, if they do not see the notice until after having made their purchase.

Question 2—Distinctions between requirements for human food and animal feed

8. The proposals for food and feed have many common elements. This is sensible as retailers are increasingly requiring the same level of assurances on the use of GM feed in livestock production as they are in food products.

Question 3—Likely effectiveness of traceability proposals

9. The effectiveness of traceability will be largely dependent on what measures are put into place by the regulatory authority. The current SCIMAC protocols should be easily adaptable to meet the requirements of the EU proposals and ensure traceability of GM raw materials from UK farms to processors. Government monitored systems, if not already available, will have to be put into place to regulate the onward movement of food and feed to the end consumer, and to regulate imported food and feed.

Question 4—Are the proposals enforceable?

10. Enforcement based on analysis of products that do not include GM DNA will be problematic. The enforcement route should be based on auditing of records and stock inspections during spot checks. The SCIMAC scheme includes a penalty system for infractions.

Question 5—Is a 1 per cent threshold limit for accidental presence of GM material appropriate?

11. Given that the threshold only applies to GM material that has been assessed for safety 1 per cent would seem to strike a reasonable balance between consumer choice and the compliance cost to industry. As stated at paragraph 5 above it will not satisfy consumers who desire a zero tolerance, impossible to achieve without 100 per cent testing.

Question 8—Compatibility with obligations towards exporters to the EU

12. Businesses within the EU should not be put at a disadvantage to third country competitors. The obligations of the proposals on the EU food industry will have a real cost. To prevent the undercutting of EU products by third country imports, requirements for traceability and labelling should apply equally to both. Similarly, consumers should be offered the same assurances on imports (the current source of all GM food and feed) as from EU-produced food and feed.

Question 9—Maintenance of the EU moratorium on approvals of GM food and crop product applications

13. The moratorium is illogical, given that some GM-containing foods and feed products are already on the market. Approvals should be based on science.

February 2002

Memorandum by the Provision Trade Federation (PTF)

1. INTRODUCTION

1.1 The Provision Trade Federation represents the interests of all parts of the food chain involved in trading in dairy ingredients and products; and meat products, especially bacon, ham and chilled and processed meats. PTF's members are importers and exporters as well as companies involved in trading in nationally produced products in the UK. Our main service to members is to monitor and advise upon the effect of current and future issues and events on the markets for these products both here and abroad, and to represent members' views on these matters.

1.2 The products which fall within the scope of PTF's interests generally do not contain genetically modified ingredients. Furthermore, where soya or maize or other GM derivatives could be included in further processed foods produced by our members, they have actively tried to avoid them in order to guarantee GM-free status, rather than make declarations on the label. In this respect, they have an interest in the traceability requirements of the proposals.

1.3 Our main concerns are in relation to the enforcement of the proposals and their scope.

2. ENFORCEMENT

2.1 We do not believe that the proposals as they stand are enforceable for foodstuffs or ingredients imported from third countries which may be derived from GM ingredients but do not contain novel protein or DNA. The Explanatory Memorandum to the proposals states that operators importing foodstuffs from third countries must specify the GMOs they contain so that this information can be notified to operators receiving the product at all subsequent stages of production. If this information is not available from the exporter, the importer should determine, via sampling and testing, the identity of any GMOs present.

However, the testing of third country imports to confirm their GM status would be pointless for any ingredients, such as refined oils, which would not contain GM material regardless of whether or not they had been produced from GM products. Therefore, the authorities cannot enforce the requirements and importers cannot guarantee the GM status of the product.

3. SCOPE

3.1 We welcome the fact that the traceability and labelling requirements would not extend to products which are produced "with a GMO" rather than "from a GMO" such as cheese produced using a genetically modified enzyme, and meat products obtained from animals fed GM animal feed. GM declarations on these products are unnecessary and could be detrimental to sales.

Diana Axby
Manager, Regulatory Affairs

31 January 2002

Memorandum by The Reverend Professor Michael Reiss, Professor of Science Education, University of London Institute of Education; formerly ethicist member of the UK Government's Advisory Committee on Novel Foods and Processes and Chair of EuropaBio's Advisory Group on Ethics

LABELLING GM FOODS: THE ETHICAL WAY FORWARD

Those who make decisions and implement policy in the European Commission (EC) are almost all well intentioned. However, since July last year a series of proposals have been rumbling that threaten to waste a great deal of money, to alarm people unnecessarily and to delay the introduction of new biotechnological products.

I refer to the proposals from the EC on traceability and labelling of GMOs and food and feed products derived from them[1]. As is widely realised, the food-labelling proposals go beyond current standards by requiring labels for all foods produced by GMOs regardless of whether detectable DNA or proteins are in those products[2]. A number of objections have been raised against these proposals on the grounds of practically (the availability of the necessary analytical detection methods), fairness (the proposals can be regarded as discriminating unfairly against certain producers and certain countries) and cost[3].

However, here I want to go to the heart of what are usually assumed to be the two arguments in favour of this labelling. First that such labelling is ethical; secondly that people want it. The second issue is more easily dealt with. Of course, if you ask people "Do you want labelling?" they say "Yes" but it is facile and misleading from this to conclude that labelling is really what is wanted. People need to know the consequences of policies, including compulsory labelling, and they need to know if there are other arguments for and against them. The various surveys (eg the Eurobarometer in Europe) that are done do not provide such necessary preliminary education ie accompanying relevant information. You might as well ask people "Do you want lower taxes?" Most people will say "Yes". The real question is something like "Do you want lower taxes and an accompanying reduction in such public services as education, health, transport, law enforcement and defence?"

The ethical issue is more subtle than the one to do with what the public wants. At one point I assumed—and argued in a book I wrote with Roger Straughan—that labelling was the way forward for GM foods on the grounds that labelling provides information, that information allows choice and that choice is a good thing[4]. However, I have come to believe that I was mistaken implicitly to presume that choice requires mandatory labelling. I now feel that in many circumstances it is better not to require such labelling but to permit retailers and restaurants that provide foods to decide, in a free market environment, whether or not to label. In that way the principle of choice holds both at the level of retailers and restaurants and then at the level of individual consumers. If consumers really want to know whether the food they are buying or eating is from GMOs or not from GMOs they will seek out those retailers and restaurants who label. If, as I suspect is actually the case for most consumers, they haven't a deep interest in whether or not genetic modification has played a role, they won't seek out such labels. Exactly the same point holds with regard to the labelling of animal feed and the consequent choices by farmers and others.

The issue can be examined more generally by asking the question "Why do we need regulations (eg in regard to the labelling of food) rather than simply allowing people harmed by actions to take those responsible for the harm to court?" One answer is that people often want regulation to prevent such harms from happening. (I may be able to sue you for harming me because you have failed to show a duty of care, for example by driving too fast, but I may prefer that the harm had never happened, for example by my government having passed laws about speeding limits.) Another answer is that legal recourse is a very imperfect way of attempting

---

[1] Proposal for a Regulation of the European Parliament and of the Council concerning traceability and labelling of genetically modified organisms and traceability of food and feed products produced from genetically modified organisms, IP/01/1095, 25 July 2001, Brussels.

[2] Dorey, E *Nat Biotechnol.* 19, 795 (2001).

[3] Fox, J L *Nat Biotechnol.* 19, 897 (2001).

[4] Reiss, M J and Straughan R (1996). *Improving nature? The science and ethics of genetic engineering.* (Cambridge University Press, Cambridge; 1976).

to redress harms. In particular, those with little money, power or persistence stand only a small chance of successfully taking anyone, certainly a large company, to court.

These considerations suggest that the particular duties of a regulatory system are (i) to prevent certain harms; (ii) to provide especial protection for those unable to take legal actions against those responsible for harms[5]. In the case of GM crops, I would therefore expect regulators to pay particular attention (a) to those especially likely to be harmed; (b) to those who lack agency. Some actors, for example farm animals and young children, potentially fall into both categories. Other actors, for example adults with certain food allergies, fall into just one. Indeed, it is precisely when it can be argued that significant harm would (or might frequently enough) be prevented by labelling that there is a powerful argument for mandatory labelling. For this reason I approve of mandatory labelling of foods that contain important allergens. (Importance here combines aspects both of the severity of the allergy and of the number of people with it.) Given the enormous amount of effort made in the USA, Europe and a number of other regions to ensure that those GM foods that can be bought are at least as safe as conventional foods I do not believe that it can validly be argued that mandatory labelling of GM foods is required.

12 February 2002

Memorandum by The Royal Society

I am responding to your request of 22 January 2002 for a response to the call for evidence by the House of Lords European Union Committee Sub Committee D investigating the European Commission's proposals for assessment, authorisation, traceability and labelling of GM food and animal feed.

I enclose a copy of *Genetically modified plants for food use* which the Royal Society published in 1998 (*not printed*). The issues of labelling and traceability of GM foods are addressed in section five and annex VI of this report. In summary our report concluded:

— We strongly support the labelling of foods containing GM material, where the new foodstuff is substantially changed (according to specified criteria) from that of its conventional counterpart, to allow customer choice.

— We recognise that segregation of commodity crops and derivatives through long supply chains on a global scale will cause difficulties of traceability for those manufacturers and retailers who wish to source products which do not contain GMOs or their derivatives. Problems may also relate to the complexity of international trade, detection limits, complexity of product formulations or processing techniques.

— For enforcement purposes, it will be essential to recognise a minimum level for adventitious presence of GM material, below which a product can be considered to be free of GM derivatives. Scientifically validated testing methods would have to be developed and agreed in order for such enforcement to be carried out in a reliable, readily repeatable and practical basis.

In addition we recommended that the regulatory authorities, the European Commission and relevant bodies work together to resolve this issue.

You will be aware that we have recently published *Genetically modified plants for food use and human health—an update,* also enclosed (*not printed*). Labelling and tracing of genetically modified organisms are discussed briefly in Appendix 4 of this document.

We are pleased that the House of Lords European Union Committee are considering the issue and look forward to the outcome of this inquiry.

Professor P P G Bateson FRS
Biological Secretary and Vice-President

13 February 2002

Memorandum by The Royal Society of Edinburgh

1. The Royal Society of Edinburgh (RSE) is pleased to respond to the request by the House of Lords European Union Committee for evidence on the European Commission's proposals for labelling and tracing of genetically modified (GM) food and animal feed (COM(01)182 and COM(01)425). The RSE is Scotland's premier Learned Society, comprising Fellows elected on the basis of their distinction, from the full range of academic disciplines, and from industry, commerce and the professions. This response has been compiled by the General Secretary with the assistance of a number of Fellows with substantial experience in this area.

2. In principle, arrangements for labelling and tracing GM food and feed and genetically modified organisms (GMOs) are to be welcomed as a means of reassuring the public. However, the Regulations need to be workable, not excessively onerous to administer and understandable by the public and those who have

---

[5] Reiss, M J *J Agricultural and Environmental Ethics,* 14, 179-190 (2001).

to administer them. At present, the proposals have a number of shortcomings in terms of meeting the needs of consumers who wish to exert their choice to avoid foods produced with the application of GM technology, and in terms of monitoring and enforcement.

3. The specific issues identified in the consultation paper are addressed below:

Do these proposals adequately address the requirements of European consumers for regulation, traceability and labelling of GM food and feed and of food and feed products derived from GMOs?

4. The attempts to provide increased transparency and consumer input are to be applauded. However, the proposals will not fully meet consumer demands for clear labelling and in some cases they could add confusion and mislead the public, adding little value.

5. The proposals argue, justifiably, that some consumers wish to exercise their choice to buy "non-GM" products. As a result the proposals have extended the labelling and traceability proposals not only to products containing GM DNA and protein but also to purified and manufactured products (where GM DNA and protein would not be detectable). However, the proposals then fail to recognise that consumer objections are to the application of GM technology. The fine distinctions that the proposals make between products made from GMO as distinct from products made with GMO will not meet consumers' labelling needs, and in some cases they are likely to mislead rather than inform.

6. As consumers begin to understand the detailed nature of the proposals they are likely to voice concerns across a range of areas where the regulations will produce misleading inconsistencies in labelling policy, or labelling policies that do not meet consumer requirements. Notable amongst these will be the legislation's failure to address the question of labelling animal products, since consumer surveys indicate that this is the single greatest point of consumer demand for clear labelling.

7. To better meet consumer demands for labelling, one approach would be to draw a distinction between those food and feed products that are produced without the application of GM technology and those that involve the application of GM technology (including products made from and products made with GM technology). Some countries, for example Germany, Austria and the Netherlands, already have legal provision for a labelling classification of products "Produced without genetic engineering". This classification could be extended across the Community together with the introduction of a second labelling classification "Produced with the use of genetic engineering". This would then provide a simple and easily understood labelling system, which would fully meet the needs for consumer choice and avoid complex and potentially misleading labelling of products. This would also simplify the systems of traceability so that they could be more easily and cost-effectively monitored. As it stands, there is confusion and inconsistency between the use of GM and GMO in the current Regulations. In particular GMO is often used where "products from GMOs" is meant. The labelling of foods with ". . . containing a genetically modified organism" is also highly misleading in that there is an implication that the labelled product is viable (and liable to escape!).

8. Alternatively, informed choice could be improved by providing information on the derived value (or otherwise) of the product to the consumer, or the genetic modification involved, or the involvement of GM technology. For example, the removal of allergenicity, the presence of herbicide resistance genes or the use of genetically engineered enzymes in the making of cheese. The labelling could then be made through the use of the specific code number/letters on the label with the full identification outlined in an official codex in much the same way as E-numbers are presently defined.

How effective are the proposals likely to be in ensuring full traceability of GM material at all stages of the chain from producer to consumer?

9. Traceability is desirable where the withdrawal of a product may be required. However, as noted above, the labelling of foods with "this product contains genetically modified organisms" is highly misleading in that there is an implication that the labelled product is viable. The use of the term "Produced with the use of genetic engineering" should be adequate where appropriate and terminology standardised with the proposed Regulation on genetically modified food and feed.

10. Responsibility for accurate labelling would lie with the importer, who would in turn require the exporter to supply an adequate description. In many cases this would be straightforward, since it would relate to documentation supplied by the primary producer (eg Monsanto, Aventis or Zeneca). In practice, importers may state that imports may contain the full range of GM varieties that might be present as a result of mingling during harvesting and transport.

11. Enforcement is likely to be undertaken by a similar mechanism to the traceability scheme for beef products, laid down under Regulation (EC) 1760/2000. Responsibility for the traceability systems would be placed on the businesses operating in the feed/food chain, and enforcement authorities would need to operate an audit system at the stages of import, storage, manufacturing/processing, distribution and sales. Analytical testing would likely to be required at specific stages along this sequence.

Are the proposals likely to be enforceable in practice, particularly where no novel genetic material is contained in the food or feed?

12. Testing the status of a GM foodstock requires detailed knowledge of the transgene that it carries (or carried). This information is usually readily available and in principle such testing is straightforward. However, there will need to be an obligation on the exporter to provide appropriate documentation. Considerable resources will also need to be deployed for detection methods to be made sufficiently sensitive to apply to a wide variety of products. For highly processed foods, with a complex matrix and in which significant denaturing and losses of DNA occur, protocols which provide definitive answers may be difficult to obtain. In addition, as national laboratories will carry out the safety assessments on behalf of the European Food Authority (EFA), on a rota basis, their methods will need to be standardised and verified with consequent resource implications.

13. Testing for GM contamination is more problematical, because it requires knowledge of all the many transgenes that might be carried by the contaminating GMO, or which might have entered the crop itself by accident. Thus, it is possible to devise tests for the presence of known GMOs of the same and other species, but tests cannot be devised to detect unknown GMOs in most cases. From this it follows that detection of contamination will be simpler and more secure in countries that maintain a database of GMOs approved for both trials and release. The presence of contaminants modified in a manner which is not in the public domain is unlikely to be detectable.

14. In addition, the identification of oils from GMOs will be difficult. The methods of detection normally rely on the detection of DNA or protein. These methods will be difficult/impossible to apply to products with little or no DNA or protein present. If the oil (or other product) is or contains a variant produced as a result of genetic modification, then testing will be simple. Otherwise, if it is free of DNA and protein and is effectively identical to the equivalent product prepared from non-GM organisms, then no test is currently possible.

A threshold level of 1 per cent or lower for the accidental presence of GM material in food and feed has been proposed, below which there would be an exemption. Is a threshold of this level, common to both food and feed, appropriate?

15. If a GM product has not been approved by the relevant European Union (EU) Committee, the 0 per cent tolerance is the only approach that will satisfy requirements and the demands of those who have concerns about GM technology. However, it is the adventitious, non-intentional and unavoidable presence of GM seed in conventional seed lots, which is to be regulated. Given the EU annually imports some 37 million tonnes of maize, soya and rapeseed or derived feed products, predominantly sourced from a world market that contains a substantial and increasing proportion of GM material, and given the supply chain through elevators and silos, and barges, ships, lorries and holding bins, the likelihood of adventitious presence is sufficiently high that a 0 per cent threshold will not be practicable. If the EU has approval systems for GM products that broadly keep pace with those in exporting countries the issue of non-approved material being imported will not be a major consideration. However, it will become an increasing concern if the approval systems of the EU fall behind those in other countries, as is presently the case.

16. In terms of approved GM material, in the harvesting and transport of bulk commodity crops there is some inevitable mingling of varieties. The Commission is considering legislation which modifies current separation distances between GM and non-GM crops in the field and which would restrict the presence of GM seed in seed lots to between 0.3 per cent and 0.7 per cent (depending on the crop species in question). However, even with systems designed for identity preservation, it is unlikely that the present threshold of 1 per cent adventitious contamination that is required for non-GM crops can be achieved consistently on a routine basis. It will also be very difficult to monitor, with the likelihood of picking up contaminants depending upon the methods used to sample, with practical difficulties in particular for crops such as soya, maize and rape.

Are the proposals compatible with obligations towards non-Member States seeking to export food and feed to the EU?

17. There seems little doubt that the impact of these proposals on trade outside the EU and on small businesses and catering establishments will be significant. The requirements will increase the complexity and cost of small business operation, with operators in all groups and businesses involved in the production, purchasing and utilisation chain (including catering companies) having to maintain all necessary records relating to traceability and product identity. This is likely to be met by increased food costs to the consumer.

What other aspects of the proposals require further consideration before the UK Government can sign up to them?

18. With regard to proposals for applications to be renewed every 10 years, under present law any exotic, newly discovered, food plant or any novel plant produced through non-GM breeding could be introduced to the market without restriction of time of approval. The Commission also already has in place Article 16 which allows Member States to bring new information on risk to the Commission at any time. Therefore, as long

as Member States have regular access to information from post-release monitoring, the 10-year limit would not seem necessary and would add additional cost and bureaucracy. However, a 10-year review would allow regulators to keep pace with changes in product production techniques and improved analytical techniques.

19. The long-term reliability and practicality of the process also need to be considered. Storage, transport and shipping of grain from the US involves millions of tonnes and the scale of production may prove problematic for the records of all grain batches to be accurately maintained for a number of years once doors are more fully open to GM imports and when production accelerates in Europe.

20. Another practical constraint will be the success of the determination of the traceability of GMOs and their products from third countries. Detection methods, in particular for certain products such as oils derived from GMOs, are likely to be difficult or impossible to set up and the implementation of the proposals will require comprehensive monitoring and enforcement at all levels. Where it is possible, it will require efficient and effective administration.

21. The cost implications could only be established through an appropriate business analysis but, as indicated by the general cost of identity preservation and audit systems, estimated increases in food production costs might be in the order of 10-15 per cent. In addition, as there will be no requirement for the traceability systems to be adopted by those who are producing food outside the EU, the additional costs involved could make EU food production less competitive against imports than at present. In effect this could result in the EU importing more food of more doubtful provenance.

Additional Information

22. In responding to this inquiry the Society would like to draw attention to the following Royal Society of Edinburgh responses which are of relevance to this subject: *Review of the Framework for Overseeing Developments in Biotechnology* (February 1999); *The Scientific Advisory System-Genetically Modified Foods Inquiry* (March 1999); *The OECD Edinburgh Conference on the Scientific and Health Aspects of Genetically Modified Foods* (February 2000); *Inquiry on European Community Food Safety Policy* (March 2000); *The Assessment of Risk to Biodiversity from GM Crop Management* (December 2000); *The Adventitious Presence of GM Seeds in Seed of Conventional Varieties* (April 2001); *Possible Scenarios for the Uptake of GM in Agriculture* (August 2001) and *Commission Proposals on Adventitious GM Presence in Non-GM Seeds* (August 2001). Copies of the above publications are available from the Research Officer, Dr Marc Rands (email: evidenceadvice@royalsoced.org.uk).

Professor Andrew Miller CBE FRSE
General Secretary

4 February 2002

Memorandum by The Scotch Whisky Association

INTRODUCTION

1.1 We refer to your invitation for comment on the European Commission's proposals in relation to genetic modification.

1.2 We should like to make it clear that to the best of our knowledge no member of The Scotch Whisky Association (SWA) is using or has used any GM cereal in the production of Scotch Whisky. Notwithstanding this, the regulations as currently drafted carry a number of ambiguities and give cause for concern for their application and practicalities for the industry in the future. We thus welcome the opportunity to respond to your invitation.

A QUESTION OF SAFETY

2.1 The industry supports the proposals for a clearer, EU-wide, robust and effective authorisation process. This should be key to ensuring that consumer safety, animal welfare and the environment are protected and give consumer confidence in the products developed using GM techniques.

2.2 It is disappointing that the proposals do not strictly adhere to the question of consumer safety. The proposed regulation on GM food and feed states "food law should be based on risk analysis". Yet the proposals do not apply this principle to highly processed foods such as highly refined oils, and other products that contain no residual DNA or protein from the raw material, making these products identical to "original" versions. By requiring the labelling of such products, the proposals set a dangerous precedent, which could lead to an increased labelling of products for reasons other than consumer safety and health. This could lead to label information overload, and the loss of prominence for health information that might be vital to those consumers with allergies etc.

2.3 Section five of the Explanatory Memorandum of the food and feed proposal states that the proposals are based on a view that "consumers are demanding clear labelling". By introducing labelling that is not based on sound safety and health grounds the proposals are a significant step towards crowded labels that are anything but "clear". The proposals do not necessarily help inform properly those consumers with concerns about GM and may in fact mislead. A product "produced from GMOs but not containing GMOs" will have to be labelled as a GM or GM derived product, while a product that does contain GM DNA or protein need not be labelled if that GM material arises through adventitious circumstances.

TRACEABILITY AND LABELLING

3.1 The proposals on traceability and labelling have a potential to cause further confusion among consumers. These proposals appear to have confused ethical labelling with food safety, so that traceability systems would no longer be primarily linked to consumer safety. This appears to be a departure from the existing international approach on food safety.

3.2 Although the traceability proposals do provide a possible route to reduce the levels of testing, there is still a requirement for enforcement and possible "due diligence" checks. The proposals do not appear to take recognition of the situation outwith the EU, leaving distillers importing grain likely to have to carry out frequent checks. Although only a limited number of GM crop varieties have been approved by the EU, the OECD website lists *inter alia* 18 maize varieties which have been approved elsewhere. Even, if the testing methodology were in place to test for each of these 18 varieties, this requirement would impose significant practical problems for importers and would be likely to lead to substantially increased costs.

3.3 To be effective, laws must be enforceable. However, there are no methods for testing materials such as highly processed foods, which do not contain DNA or protein from the GM version of the crop from which they were derived, nor is it possible to test for the adventitious presence of GM derived material not containing DNA or protein. This means that the 1 per cent threshold is not enforceable.

3.4 As a result, ignoring concerns about the lack of analytical testing as an issue to be addressed in the food and feed proposals means that the traceability and labelling proposals are likely to force the food and drink industries into IP (Identity Preservation) schemes that are mandatory in all but name. Such schemes are only workable in a limited number of applications and a small fraction of the overall world market for particular crops. The widening of the labelling requirements to include derivatives may make such schemes unworkable. The sustainability of such schemes will be seriously challenged as the cultivation of GM crops spreads, particularly if widespread cultivation starts in the EU. The likely result is that IP systems will only have sustainability in narrow applications and more and more foods will include materials with GM origins such that labelling will become meaningless.

IMPLEMENTATION—LABELLING OF EXISTING STOCK

4.1 While a number of the comments in this paper could equally apply to other industries, the comments in this section relate to the unique position of matured spirits such as Scotch Whisky and are fundamental to the industry.

4.2 Spirit drinks which require lengthy maturation are in an unusual situation. Scotch Whisky companies have always carried out quality checks on the cereals used in production and maintained records of suppliers for traceability purposes. However, the onerous traceability requirements within the current proposal cannot be met, and there is no method of testing to confirm the absence of GM raw materials being used in the production of the spirit, notwithstanding that no GM cereals were available at the time of distillation. For many years to come the Scotch sold to consumers will have been made before GM cereal options were ever available, but as a result no IP or traceability audit trail is available. Scotch Whisky distillers who use maize have sought to follow IP systems since the current labelling regulations were introduced.

4.3 The proposal to keep records for up to five years takes no account of products with a longer production cycle such as many matured spirit drinks. For example, some major deluxe Scotch Whisky brands are matured for more than 12 years; and malt whisky is frequently sold at 10, 20 or 25 years old, and occasionally at 50 or 60 years old. Any proposal that requires distillers/bottlers to produce traceability records for aged stock would be considerably onerous, and be of particular burden to smaller firms.

4.4 Thus it is essential that should the regulations come into force, they should apply only to spirits distilled after the date of implementation.

A BARRIER TO TRADE

5.1 The proposed regulations could be construed as barriers to trade by non-EU countries and may precipitate appeals to the World Trade Organisation and the possibility of retaliatory action on products exported by the EU. We have deep concerns that spirit drinks, such as Scotch Whisky, may be targeted in vital major export markets outwith the EU. Scotch Whisky is one of the EU's most valuable manufactured export earners. Exports to non-EU markets were worth £1.3 billion (€2 billion) in 2000.

TIMING

6.1 The proposals stress the need for a one-stop approach yet these Regulations are being introduced before the European Food Authority is properly set up and running.

CONCLUSION

7.1 The Scotch Whisky Association noted with interest the answer given in the House of Commons by the Under-Secretary of State for Public Health when she said: *"The United Kingdom will seek to ensure that any new rules are practical, proportionate and enforceable"* (Hansard—222W, 4 July 2001).

7.2 The present traceability and labelling proposals fail this test and should therefore be reconsidered. This has been recognised in the UK by National Economic Research Associates (NERA), which reported to the Food Standards Agency on the *"Economic Appraisal of Options for Extension of Legislation on GM Labelling"*. NERA concluded that the best option was to maintain the *status quo* on labelling and to introduce an accredited "GM-free" scheme, to provide consumer choice. As with the current approach to "organic", products wishing to make a GM-free claim would have to meet certain criteria. If there is clear consumer demand for GM free products, retailers and manufacturers can choose to meet that demand within the competitive marketplace.

7.3 It is the belief of The Scotch Whisky Association that further consideration should be given to these proposed Regulations.

Campbell Evans
Director of Government and Consumer Affairs

February 2002

Memorandum and Supplementary Memorandum by Supply Chain Initiative on Modified Agricultural Crops (SCIMAC)

INTRODUCTION

0.1 Established in June 1998, SCIMAC is a grouping of industry organisations along the UK farm supply chain. Members are:

— National Farmers Union

— British Society of Plant Breeders

— Crop Protection Association

— UK Agricultural Supply Trade Association

— British Sugar Beet Seed Producers Association

0.2 As detailed in the attached explanatory memorandum, SCIMAC was established to support the open and responsible introduction of GM crop technology in the UK. Member organisations share a commitment to ensuring UK adoption of the technology is carefully managed, and delivers a meaningful choice for farmers, the food industry and consumers.

0.3 SCIMAC represents a broad base of membership, including organisations, companies and individuals not directly involved in the development of GM crop technology. Since these organisations are presenting separate evidence to the Committee's inquiry, this submission focuses on the specific role of the SCIMAC stewardship programme in meeting the objectives of traceability and consumer choice as set out in the Commission's proposals.

0.4 Traceability is central to the SCIMAC initiative. The SCIMAC guidelines include specific provision for the identity preservation of GM crops from initial seed stock through to delivery of the harvested crop ex-farm, and establishes a framework for continued identity preservation and traceability beyond that point. The measures specified build on existing, proven systems within UK agriculture, and combine provisions for record-keeping and transfer of information with specific requirements for on-farm management practice, for example in relation to:

— Seed storage and planting guidelines

— Machinery operation

— Crop-specific separation distances

— Harvesting and post harvest management

0.5 The purpose of identity preservation within the SCIMAC Code of Practice and guidelines is to provide a meaningful choice, for those who wish to make a positive decision in favour of GM crops and products as well as those who may prefer to avoid them. It is important to emphasise that the primary role of labelling is to promote choice, not to provide a route for denial of access and choice.

1. *Do these proposals adequately address the requirements of European consumers for regulation, traceability and labelling of GM food and feed and of food and feed products derived from GMOs?*

1.1 The primary objective of regulations in this area must be to deliver safety and promote choice. Issues of public or consumer acceptance are the preserve of commercial and market forces, not the responsibility of regulators. The "requirements of European consumers" in relation to GM products are neither uniform nor constant. Since customer demands and priorities are continually changing, controls must be sufficiently flexible to enable those demands to be met.

1.2 Once safety has been established, the key objective of the proposed legislation should be to provide a workable framework in which consumers can exercise an informed choice.

1.3 Two issues give particular cause for concern. Firstly, the practicality and enforceability of requiring traceability and labelling for highly refined ingredients and additives whose provenance or composition cannot be detected or verified in the end-product. Secondly, the need to ensure consistency in approach between EU proposals relating to traceability and labelling in food and feed and those addressing the presence of GM material in seed.

2. *Do they make sensible distinctions between the requirements of animal feed and those of food for human consumption?*

2.1 The primary supply chain urgently needs a framework of legal certainty in which to operate. SCIMAC therefore welcomes the proposed establishment of GM labelling thresholds for both food and feed, and the proposal that marketing consents should only be granted to GM products approved as safe for use in both food and feed products.

2.2 Clearly the provenance, volume and trading practice for bulk commodity crops destined for animal feed production differs from those used in food manufacturing. Such differences should be reflected in the final legislation to ensure traceability is workable and enforceable in practice, serves to inform rather than confuse consumers, and does not present unnecessary barriers to international trade.

3. *How effective are the proposals likely to be in ensuring full traceability of GM material at all stages of the chain from producer to consumer?*

3.1 SCIMAC notes that details of the traceability regime are left flexible within the Commission's proposals and will to some extent depend on how individual Member States implement them. Implementation should not seek to re-invent the wheel, but to build upon proven and established systems of traceability and identity preservation.

3.2 Within the farming and food production sectors, such systems have operated effectively for many years at UK and international level, for example in producing seed crops to guaranteed levels of purity and varietal identity, or in segregating harvested crops destined for different end uses.

3.3 In addition, the SCIMAC Code of Practice and On-Farm Guidelines were specifically developed to deliver identity preservation for GM crops grown in the UK, based on the proven experience of existing traceability systems. As such this initiative offers a framework for safeguarding the integrity of both GM crops and neighbouring non-GM crops within a practical farming situation, up to and including the ex-farm delivery of harvested produce.

3.4 Within the Government's programme of GM crop Farm-Scale Evaluations, the SCIMAC guidelines have been applied within a normal farming situation at more than 180 field-scale sites across the UK. This experience has demonstrated that the protocols are workable in practice, robust in safeguarding the integrity of GM and neighbouring non-GM crops (including certified seed and organic crops) and capable of being audited.

3.5 It is important to note, however, that the effectiveness of current traceability and identity preservation systems can be verified through sampling and testing regimes at appropriate points in the chain. As detailed in our response to question 4, there is currently no reliable detection method to verify the full traceability and therefore the accuracy of labelling claims made in relation to certain highly processed ingredients, additives and derivatives.

4. *Are the proposals likely to be enforceable in practice, particularly where no novel genetic material is contained in the food or feed?*

4.1 SCIMAC considers that regulations in this area can only deliver a meaningful and enforceable framework of consumer information by focusing on the product rather than the production process.

4.2 Meaningful because a clear distinction can be drawn between products containing detectable GM material and the almost limitless range of products which could at some stage involve the use of modern biotechnology.

4.3 Examples of such products range from those currently within the scope of the Commission's proposals, such as highly refined ingredients or additives, to those outside, such as foods produced using GM processing aids or livestock products reared with the use of GM medicines.

4.4 Enforceable because the presence of detectable GM protein or DNA can be verified through testing. The practical implications of developing a traceability system around claims which cannot be substantiated through end-product testing—in terms of compliance and enforcement, as well as the considerable scope for fraud—are more likely to confuse than inform consumers, and weaken rather than strengthen public confidence.

4.5 The safe and legitimate application of GM technology should not be subjected to measures which simply add cost and bureaucracy while achieving little (if anything) in terms of informed consumer choice. Labelling exists to promote choice, not to provide a route for denial of access and choice.

4.6 Once GM products have been assessed as safe in terms of human health and the environment, regulations governing their use should not be determined by arbitrary (and potentially transitory) commercial conditions specified by those seeking to make claims about freedom from GM for marketing purposes. The primary responsibility for meeting any additional conditions must lie with those seeking to exploit a marketing or commercial advantage from such claims, and should remain the preserve of market forces rather than regulation.

5. *A threshold level of 1 per cent or lower for the accidental presence of GM material in food and feed has been proposed, below which there would be an exemption. Is a threshold of this level, common to both food and feed, appropriate?*

5.1 SCIMAC supports a benchmark labelling threshold of 1 per cent for presence of GM material, in terms of its practicality, enforceability and clarity to consumers.

5.2 The Commission's proposals also establish a legal basis for the technically unavoidable presence of GM material which has been subject to a risk assessment in the EU, but which has not been fully cleared for marketing. Such a provision is necessary to reflect the practical realities of agriculture and food production, and to protect continued EU research and development activity in this area. However, it must also be supported by similar recognition of equivalent safety assessments conducted outside the EU

5.3 Furthermore, the proposals for accidental presence of GM material in food and feed appear to be at odds with the Commission's current proposals to address GM thresholds in seed (see response to question 10). This inconsistency must be addressed.

6. *Is the role proposed for (a) the European Food Authority and its scientific committees and (b) Member States in the authorisation process for GM food and feed appropriate?*

6.1 SCIMAC supports measures which will improve the transparency and accountability of the risk assessment and authorisation process. The proposed role of the European Food Authority (EFA) as a "one-stop shop" represents a welcome step in this direction. A major weakness in the current approvals process has been the ability of individual Member States to delay authorisation on political rather than scientific or safety grounds. This uncertainty must be addressed to ensure that regulation fulfils its intended role to enable, rather than disable, technological progress and innovation.

7. *Are the proposals likely to be compatible with the requirements of the Cartagena Protocol on Biosafety and with other international commitments, including OECD programmes?*

7.1 With major crops traded globally, there is an urgent need to establish harmonised international regulation in this area, or to introduce the concept of reciprocal recognition for third country GM approvals within the EU regulatory process. Failure to establish such arrangements at an international level represents an unnecessary and unacceptable barrier to the technology, and may have the effect of denying access and choice rather than promoting it.

8. *Are the proposals compatible with obligations towards non-Member States seeking to export food and feed to the EU?*

8.1 In the absence of harmonised international regulation, or reciprocal recognition of third country authorisation procedures (for example under OECD or FAO guidelines), the EU authorisation process and proposed traceability requirements look set to impose additional obligations on importers of food and feed materials to the EU. This will not only penalise importers through increased segregation, sampling and testing requirements, it will also affect cost and availability to customers within the EU, including livestock farmers who rely on imported feed material such as soya.

9. *Should the present EU-wide moratorium on approving GM food and crop product applications be maintained until the issues concerning traceability and labelling of GMOs have been resolved?*

9.1 The *de facto* EU-wide moratorium on new GMO authorisations has no basis in safety or science. Continuing to block new approvals risks serious damage to future European research in both industrial and academic sectors.

9.2 The moratorium has no effect on those GM products already approved for marketing within the EU. For these products, the supply chain is already addressing traceability requirements in response to the demands of customers.

9.3 The market is seeking clarity, consistency and direction. The current moratorium offers none of these, but threatens instead to drive investment and innovation out of the EU, and deny choice and access to the technology's potential benefits for consumers, farmers and the environment.

10. *What other aspects of the proposals require further consideration before the UK Government can sign up to them?*

10.1 The Commission's current proposals to establish legally enforceable thresholds for GM presence in seed via amendments to EU seed marketing legislation are at odds with the proposed traceability and labelling regulation, and could seriously disrupt conventional plant breeding and seed production within the EU. They may also prove a disincentive to EU-based research and development into GM crops. This would disadvantage future progress and competitiveness within European agriculture while other regions of the world forge ahead with the technology (2001 saw a 19 per cent increase in global GM plantings to 52.6 million ha).

10.2 Central to the industry's concerns with the Commission's current proposals in this area is an inherent conflict between the different legislative approaches. While the revised Deliberate Release Directive provides a framework for experimental (Part B) GM crop trials to take place safely, the Commission's seed proposals set a zero threshold for the presence of Part B material in seed. Not only is a zero threshold biologically impossible to achieve (or verify), such a requirement would inevitably impose an "either/or" decision between GM crop trials and seed production. In contrast, the Commission's traceability and labelling proposals explicitly recognise the need to establish thresholds for unavoidable presence of GM material which has been subject to a risk assessment within the EU system.

10.3 This potential conflict must be removed by establishing workable thresholds for the presence in seed of GM material cleared as safe for deliberate release into the environment. A system of international equivalence to recognise and establish tolerance levels for GMOs approved by non-EU authorities must also be agreed as a matter of urgency.

February 2002

Supplementary Memorandum

1. INTRODUCTION TO SCIMAC

The Supply Chain Initiative on Modified Agricultural Crops (SCIMAC) is a grouping of industry organisations along the UK farm supply chain. Members are:

— British Society of Plant Breeders (BSPB)

— Crop Protection Association (CPA)

— National Farmers Union (NFU)

— UK Agricultural Supply Trade Association (UKASTA)

— British Sugar Beet Seed Producers Association (BSBSPA)

SCIMAC represents an extremely broad base of membership, including organisations and individuals not directly involved in the development of GM crop technology.

SCIMAC's activities are managed by a Board of Management comprising one representative from each member organisation.

2. SCIMAC OBJECTIVES

SCIMAC was established in June 1998 to support the open and responsible development of GM crops in the UK. All five member organisations believe GM crops offer benefits to consumers, the food chain and the environment, and share a commitment to ensuring UK adoption of the technology is carefully managed, identifies closely with public opinion, and delivers a meaningful choice for consumers.

This proactive initiative by the whole farm supply chain has been developed well in advance of the first GM crops being grown commercially in this country. Under European and UK law, no GM crops can be approved unless they have been rigorously assessed for food, feed and environmental safety. SCIMAC fully supports effective, science-based regulation of the technology.

Consensus within SCIMAC is based on a shared conviction that access to new technology has been, and will remain, fundamental to the future well-being of UK agriculture—both in terms of our economic competitiveness and our ability to protect and enhance the British countryside and environment.

Consensus within SCIMAC is also built on a common belief that decisions about the future role of GM crops in the UK must be based on sound scientific information.

3. REGULATORY ASSESSMENT OF GM CROPS

Before any GM crop can be released into the environment (ie grown in the open), it must first undergo a rigorous safety evaluation as prescribed under European law. In the UK, an independent committee of experts—the Advisory Committee on Releases to the Environment (ACRE)—advises Ministers on all applications to release GM crops.

ACRE must be satisfied that a GM crop is safe in terms of its impact on human health, animal health and the environment before it can be approved for release.

GM crops must also undergo separate evaluation for food and animal feed safety before they can be approved for marketing. The Advisory Committee on Novel Foods and Processes (ACNFP) and the Advisory Committee on Animal Feedingstuffs (ACAF) conduct these assessments and provide advice to UK Ministers.

Relevant GM crops, including the GM herbicide tolerant crops involved in the current programme of farm-scale evaluations, must also seek separate approval from the Pesticides Safety Directorate (PSD) in relation to the quality, safety and efficacy of the companion herbicide.

In addition, all GM crop varieties are subject to the same seeds regulations as non-GM crops. These require at least two years' testing to establish the genetic distinctness, uniformity and stability (DUS) of each new variety, as well as its value for cultivation and use (VCU) compared to other market leading varieties.

Only after all these regulatory hurdles have been cleared can a GM crop be finally approved for commercial release.

4. SCIMAC ACTIVITIES

SCIMAC's role is essentially two-fold:

(i)   Industry Stewardship—SCIMAC has developed a programme of on-farm management guidelines for GM herbicide tolerant crops. These guidelines have been formally endorsed by Government, and aim to ensure best practice in the way the crops are grown, and to provide choice for consumers via identity preservation of GM crops and neighbouring non-GM crops.

(ii) Farm-Scale Evaluations—SCIMAC is the industry partner in the Government's programme of farm-scale evaluations, and is responsible for identifying a pool of potential sites for further assessment and final selection by the independent Scientific Steering Committee overseeing the research programme.

5. INDUSTRY STEWARDSHIP

Following widespread consultation, SCIMAC has developed plans for the carefully managed and monitored introduction of GM crops, identifying closely with public attitudes towards the technology.

The core aims of the SCIMAC Code of Practice are to provide identity preservation for GM crops, so allowing consumer choice, and to ensure effective adoption of GM crops within UK agriculture through best practice guidelines.

This initiative builds on existing principles of good agricultural practice, and closely mirrors the proven system operated for more than 30 years to control the production of certified seed crops.

Like the official seed certification system, the SCIMAC Code of Practice will be applied through a framework of legally binding contracts, subject to routine inspection, independent audit and penalties for non-compliance.

Government backing for the SCIMAC initiative was announced on 21 May 1999. The stewardship programme is also attracting interest in Europe and beyond as a model for the measured and responsible adoption of technological progress in modern agriculture.

6. SCIMAC IN OPERATION

The SCIMAC Code of Practice on the Introduction of Genetically Modified Crops sets out basic requirements along the farm supply chain for provision of information, record-keeping and good management practice.

To safeguard customer choice, this will ensure a consistent, industry-wide approach to the supply of information relating to GM crops from seed to harvested crop.

The SCIMAC on-farm guidelines address the specific management implications of herbicide tolerance, the first GM application nearing commercialisation in the UK.

The guidelines are designed to promote responsible environmental practice, to maintain the integrity of GM and non-GM crops (including organic and certified seed crops), and to optimise the effectiveness of the new technology within a farm-scale rotation.

All aspects of on-farm operations are covered, including:

— Operator training and competence

— Seed storage and planting guidelines

— Machinery operation

— Crop separation distances

— Crop management and herbicide use

— Harvesting and post-harvest management guidelines

— On-farm monitoring and record-keeping

7. FARM-SCALE EVALUATIONS

The farm-scale evaluations have been established in addition to the regulatory processes described above, and in response to specific concerns raised by groups such as English Nature and RSPB about the biodiversity effects of growing GM herbicide tolerant crops.

The objective of this Government-funded programme is to assess the wider effects on farmland wildlife of growing GM herbicide tolerant crops in direct comparison with current farming practice. It is one of the largest ecological studies of its kind in the world.

The programme is overseen by a Scientific Steering Committee, which includes representatives from English Nature, RSPB, and the Game Conservancy Council.

Ecological monitoring is conducted by a consortium of independent research organisations led by the Centre for Ecology and Hydrology, and including the Institute of Arable Crop Research and the Scottish Crop Research Institute.

Under the terms of a formal agreement reached between Government and SCIMAC in November 1999, there will be no move to widespread commercial cultivation of GM crops in the UK until completion of the farm-scale evaluations following harvest of crops planted in 2002. Through this process, industry has voluntarily put its technology out to independent scientific scrutiny—over and above any regulatory requirements. No other agricultural technology has ever undergone such a comprehensive programme of testing and evaluation.

Within the farm-scale evaluations, the Scientific Steering Committee has specified that data will be required from 60 to 75 sites per crop over the three years of the programme. Four GM herbicide tolerant crops are involved—spring oilseed rape, forage maize, beet and winter oilseed rape.

Each field is planted with a GM crop in one half, an equivalent non-GM crop in the other half. Fields are selected to provide a representative spread for each crop in terms of geographical spread and farm type. Field sizes typically range between two and ten hectares.

None of the crops involved in this programme have yet received all the necessary consents and authorisations for food and feed use. As a result, no GM crops harvested in 2001 will enter the human food or animal feed chains.

8. GM CROPS IN THE UK

The first GM crops trials in the UK took place in 1987. Over the past 14 years well over 600 individual trials of these crops have taken place in a range of different crop species, at different locations throughout the UK.

9. GM CROPS IN OTHER PARTS OF THE WORLD

Since the mid-1980s, there have been more than 50,000 field trials of GM crops in 45 countries around the world. More than 60 different crop species have been modified.

In commercial terms, the rate of uptake for GM crops has far outstripped the introduction of any other new technology in agriculture. Following extensive safety evaluations over many years, more than 300 million acres have been grown commercially across North America, South America, Asia, Australasia and Europe.

An estimated 300 million tonnes of GM crops have already been consumed by humans and animals around the world.

To date there is no evidence of harmful effects from the commercial use of GM crop technology—in terms of food safety, feed safety or the environment. After 15 years of research in 81 separate studies, the European Commission recently confirmed that GM crops pose no new risks to human health or the environment. Indeed the Commission stated that GM crops, because they are developed using more precise technology and are subjected to greater regulatory scrutiny, are "probably even safer than conventional plants and foods."

10. SCIMAC SEPARATION DISTANCES

The crops involved in the farm-scale evaluations have already undergone a comprehensive safety assessment by the Advisory Committee on Releases to the Environment (ACRE). In ACRE's view, these crops can be grown safely without any separation distances.

However, the SCIMAC stewardship programme aims to safeguard the integrity of GM and neighbouring non-GM crops. That means reducing the potential for any cross-pollination to an absolute minimum within a practical farming situation. Zero does not exist in nature, so no separation distance, however large, could offer a guarantee of zero cross-pollination.

The distances specified by SCIMAC are based on well-established scientific knowledge of the characteristics of each crop species in terms of pollen distribution and cross-pollination. These are reinforced by practical experience over many years of growing certified seed crops to specified levels of genetic purity and identity.

According to a review of existing scientific literature commissioned by MAFF in 2000, the SCIMAC separation distances will ensure that any potential cross-pollination is reduced to below 1 per cent under worst case conditions. In practice, the actual level of cross-pollination likely to occur within a normal farming situation will be significantly lower.

The current SCIMAC separation distances are viewed as extremely precautionary and remain subject to continuous review. They will apply on a provisional basis in the context of the current trials, and pending the outcome of gene flow studies being conducted as part of the Farm-Scale Evaluations (FSE) process.

11. GM CROPS AND NEIGHBOURING FARMERS

British agriculture is a diverse industry, producing a vast array of products, in different environments, by a range of different methods. But every farmer's objective is the cost-effective production of safe, wholesome food in sympathy with the environment. In the past, access to new technology has enabled farmers to achieve those objectives—GM crop technology may help farmers achieve them in future.

The SCIMAC stewardship programme was established to support the effective integration of GM crop technology alongside existing forms of agriculture. Like the existing system for growing certified seed crops, it requires the GM crop grower to follow specific management regimes, to consult with neighbouring farmers, and at all times to safeguard the identity and integrity of the GM crop.

Through this stewardship process, farmers as well as consumers can exercise a choice, and keep an open mind on the potential development of GM crop technology in this country.

February 2002

Memorandum by Syngenta

EXECUTIVE SUMMARY

Syngenta is aware of consumer concerns and sensitivities related to food products. We strongly support consumer choice and are keen to achieve a rigorous, transparent and workable regulatory system for food and feed products enhanced through biotechnology throughout Europe.

Consumer confidence in food products could be greatly improved via a robust labelling system and a meaningful, enforceable traceability process. It is essential that labelling should not be considered as a route to deny access to this, or any other technology and should be used positively to promote access and choice.

Syngenta believes it is inappropriate for labelling legislation to be linked to safety issues both in the regulatory framework and also in consumer perception. Labelling of GM products is not an issue of food safety but of consumer choice and it is important that adequate communication is actioned to ensure that consumers are aware of this fundamental principle.

It is important that any legislation on GM food and feed products takes account of the vast range of production, market and delivery systems involved throughout the food/feed chain. Also, as with all regulation, it must be practically applicable on a global/European basis and result in the delivery of information that leads to consumer confidence.

Industry is supportive and committed to the development and implementation of effective regulation however such regulation must be enabling rather than disabling if it is to deliver its objectives.

INTRODUCTION

Syngenta welcomes this opportunity to respond to the House of Lords inquiry on labelling and tracing of genetically modified food and feed.

Syngenta is a leading global agribusiness, we rank first in crop protection and third in the high value commercial seeds market. Formed in November 2000 by the merger of Novartis Agribusiness and Zeneca Agrochemicals, Syngenta is listed on the Swiss, London, New York and Stockholm Stock Exchanges.

As a company that develops both plant protection and genetically modified (GM) seed products, Syngenta is aware of consumer concerns and sensitivities related to food safety.

We strongly support consumer choice and are keen to achieve a rigorous, transparent and workable regulatory system for GMOs throughout Europe.

1. *Do these proposals adequately address the requirements of European consumers for regulation, traceability and labelling of GM food and feed and of food and feed products derived from GMOs?*

1.1 Traceability is an essential part of food production and Syngenta recognises that traceability in the food supply chain allows the source of a particular food or food ingredient to be identified, as in many cases the analysis of food alone cannot provide information about its source. We also believe it is desirable that a suitable and workable traceability process is introduced, as it is the enforcement of this system that will encourage consumer confidence.

1.2 We recognise that labelling regulations vary from country to country according to local legislation and consumer requirements. With major crops being traded globally, the ability of food processors and manufacturers to provide reliable labelling information can also vary. We believe that these standards have to be agreed upon by all parties involved including seed producers, growers, commodity suppliers, processors, food manufacturers, retailers and national regulatory bodies.

1.3 We are concerned that the legislation proposed does not appear to address potential changes in consumer attitudes towards genetically modified organisms. More flexibility is required in the legislation to allow for such changes.

1.4 An important element in developing proposals that meet consumer requirements and attitudes is to ensure that accurate and valid information is available on such attitudes and requirements. Syngenta believes that it is imperative that this information is based on sound direct consumer research. It is also worth noting that consumer attitudes can potentially change dramatically in a very short period of time and therefore it is vital that sufficient flexibility is in-built into the proposals to address this issue.

2. *Do they make sensible distinctions between the requirements of animal feed and those of food for human consumption?*

2.1 The various industry chains are highly complex and can vary widely in volumes, and number of processes and processors. It is important that the proposals address the specific requirements of the various industry production, market and delivery systems through which the "ingredients" pass, if consumer confidence is to be achieved.

2.2 It is imperative for differences in industry chains (eg production, market and delivery systems) to be acknowledged and addressed in order for the final proposals to result in an ability to actually deliver in practice.

2.3 Due to the complexity of industry chain processes, Syngenta believes that it is essential for expert consultation be sought in each of the specific chains to ensure that the proposals lead to the development of enabling, rather than disabling regulation, and to regulation that can be practically applied which will lead to consumer confidence.

3. How effective are the proposals likely to be in ensuring full traceability of GM material at all stages of the chain from producer to consumer?

3.1 We believe it is necessary to highlight the multi-faceted nature of crops as the processes involved in their production, storage, processing and delivery may vary greatly and each may have many different practical constraints that will need to be considered for this legislation.

3.2 The extensive scope of this legislation attempts to cover all areas of the food/feed chain, from seeds and crops, to feed and livestock, and finally food products for human consumption. It is hard to envisage how a single set of legislation can be successfully applied to all elements of this diverse range.

4. Are the proposals likely to be enforceable in practice, particularly where no novel genetic material is contained in the food or feed?

4.1 Syngenta is working with the food supply chain and local regulators to access ways to provide meaningful information to consumers, it is important for the proposed legislation to have clear meaning if it is to build consumer confidence. For example, many crops enhanced through biotechnology, such as refined oils or starches, contain no plant genetic material and are often indistinguishable from food produced by other methods. However, the proposed legislation states that oils would be included within the labelling. We believe that further clarification of this legislation is necessary to avoid confusion—both from industry and consumer perspectives.

5. A threshold level of 1 per cent or lower for the accidental presence of GM material in food and feed has been proposed, below which there would be an exemption. Is a threshold of this level, common to both food and feed, appropriate?

5.1 For any such regulatory system to be workable, threshold levels have to be agreed. It is important that these levels are meaningful and that suitable scientifically validated detection methods are available in order for the public to have confidence in the results produced. Currently, 1 per cent appears to be the agreed threshold level for food products. However, we believe this will require future revision because of changes in cost and consumer expectations.

5.2 Zero tolerance for non-approved events is practically unachievable and so Syngenta would not support any moves to legislate for this. This threshold level would effectively prevent biotechnology research in Europe and would do incalculable harm to European research and agriculture in both industry and academic sectors. In order for this legislation to be workable, realistic threshold levels are needed.

6. Is the role proposed for (a) the European Food Authority and its scientific committees and (b) Member States in the authorisation process for GM food and feed appropriate?

6.1 We are concerned about the proposal to rotate the assessment of GM Food and Feed dossiers to different Member State competent authorities, as we believe there could be different interpretations of the risk assessment process depending on the Member State involved.

6.2 Syngenta believes that the purpose of the European Food Authority (EFA) should be to harmonise the risk assessment process and scientific scrutiny of information supplied for purposes of the risk assessment between Member States. We are concerned that the mechanism to achieve this risk assessment process could become unclear if the risk assessment process is rotated between competent authorities in Member States. It is essential for a sound process to be devised in order to apply risk assessment in a consistent manner.

7. Are the proposals likely to be compatible with the requirements of the Cartagena Protocol on Biosafety and with other international commitments, including OECD programmes?

7.1 Article 7.3 d and e of the proposed legislation and corresponding Articles in the feed section detail the safety and environmental risk assessment process and state that the Authority may ask any Member State or a competent authority to carry out the risk assessments. We feel that this process is only acceptable if the EFA ensure that it is carried out in a consistent manner.

7.2 Syngenta believes it is unacceptable for the proposal to legislate that the presence of genetically modified material due to adventitious or technically unavoidable presence is only acceptable if the GM material has been subject to a risk assessment by the relevant Scientific Committee or the European Food Authority. Syngenta believes that a risk assessment performed by OECD countries should be taken into account in these circumstances. We therefore believe that the legislative systems of other countries, and conclusions from risk assessment carried out in these countries, must be recognised by Europe under these circumstances.

7.3 Syngenta recognises that labelling regulations vary from country to country according to local legislation and consumer requirements. With major crops being traded globally, the ability of food processors and manufacturers to provide reliable labelling information can also vary. We believe that these standards have to be agreed upon by all parties involved including seed producers, growers, commodity suppliers, processors, food manufacturers, retailers and national regulatory bodies.

8. *Are the proposals compatible with the obligations towards non-Member States seeking to export food and feed to the EU?*

8.1 The compatibility of the proposals with non-Member States will depend on the thresholds set for GM crops approved in these countries.

8.2 The inclusion of a *de jure* or *de facto* legislation detailing zero tolerance on non-EU approved events is practically unachievable and would effectively impose a ban on agricultural research and development institutions in non-member states, and in particular in developing countries. This would be contrary to the obligations taken by the EU in the Biosafety Protocol and the Biodiversity Convention, to promote technology transfer in biotechnology. It also poses ethical questions, as most prominently exposed by the Nuffield Council on Bioethics in its report: "*Genetically Modified Crops: the ethical and social issues*" (http://www.nuffieldbioethics.org/publications/pp__0000000009.asp) which clearly states a moral obligation to allow developing countries to acquire the tools (technical, institutional, legal) with which to make their own informed choices on the use (or not) of GM crops as part of their development policy. Imposing a *de facto* zero tolerance on GM components of imported food/feed from these countries is contrary to this principle of self-determination.

9. *Should the present EU-wide moratorium on approving GM food and crop product applications be maintained until the issues concerning traceability and labelling of GMOs have been resolved?*

9.1 Syngenta is concerned that the present moratorium sends the wrong policy signal to the public, giving the public the impression that existing regulatory oversight processes are not sufficient, when this is clearly not correct.

9.2 The systems set in place under EU Regulations 90/220 and 258/97 have worked well over the past decade, and approved products have been on the market for several years and have an outstanding safety record. Under these circumstances, maintaining a ban on further approvals risks invalidating the core of the future approval system, since it will be based largely on the same principle of excellence in scientific risk assessment as exists in the current system.

10. *What other aspects of the proposals require further consideration before the UK Government can sign up to them?*

10.1 Syngenta believes it is essential that the various elements of existing legislation, and legislation under development that relates to and has impact upon this area from seed to shelf, is truly connected in order for each individual piece of legislation to support and build on the regulatory confidence of the other individual pieces of regulation.

10.2 We are concerned that any apparent conflict between elements of the regulatory framework could lead to public confusion and therefore result in a loss of consumer confidence. Syngenta is aware of consumer concerns and sensitivities related to food products. We strongly support consumer choice and are keen to achieve a fully integrated, rigorous, transparent and workable regulatory system for food and feed products enhanced through biotechnology throughout Europe.

CONCLUSIONS

Syngenta recognises the legitimacy of consumer choice and strives to ensure that this is delivered. We welcome the aims of this proposal and are keen to achieve a rigorous, transparent and workable regulatory system for GMOs throughout Europe.

We believe that consumer confidence in food products could be greatly improved via a clear, meaningful labelling system and traceability process.

We are concerned that the legislation proposed does not appear to address potential changes in consumer attitudes towards GMOs. More flexibility is required in the legislation to allow for such changes.

Syngenta believes it is inappropriate for labelling legislation to be linked to safety issues as labelling of these products is not an issue of food safety, but of consumer choice.

A vast range of production, market and delivery systems exist within the food/feed chain. We are concerned that a single piece of legislation attempting to cover all areas of this chain may not deliver the robustness and transparency needed to build consumer confidence.

Syngenta is pleased to partake in this inquiry and would welcome an opportunity to discuss both general or specific topics from this proposal further in both written and verbal form should the inquiry require it.

12 February 2002

Letter and memorandum from the United Kingdom Agricultural Supply Trade Association (UKASTA)

INQUIRY ON LABELLING AND TRACEABILITY OF GENETICALLY MODIFIED FOOD AND FEED

Please find herewith a submission to the Committee's inquiry on behalf of the United Kingdom Agricultural Supply Trade Association (UKASTA). The Association represents around 300 companies involved in the manufacture and supply of animal feedingstuffs, the trading of combinable crops from farm and the supply of seed, fertiliser, agrochemicals and forage additives to farmers. The combined turnover of member businesses is around £4.8 billion annually.

We hope the Committee finds the evidence of use in helping them to reach conclusions. As mentioned in the submission if it would help the Committee to understand the role that assurance schemes are playing in this area we would be more than happy to assist.

Paul Rooke
Policy Director

13 February 2002

1. *Do these proposals adequately address the requirements of European consumers for regulation, traceability and labelling of GM food and feed and of food and feed products derived from GMOs?*

In answering this question we would wish to draw the Committee's attention to consumer research results from both industry and the Food Standards Agency, which has attempted to provide a more objective assessment of consumer attitudes to biotechnology in relation to food products. We highlight this not to draw attention away from the issue, but to try and ensure that we might consider how the requirements of European, and particularly UK, consumers are measured.

The objective measurement, which requires consumers to consider what they believe are their biggest concerns on food safety and food production (rather than giving an answer to a specific question), suggests that whilst there is concern on the subject, it does not have the scale of concern which is normally attached to it.

We would prefer to consider whether the proposals are in line with the commercial demands already being made in the marketplace, which are addressing, in particular, the traceability of GM food and feed. We would suggest that current market demands reflect more accurately the requirements of consumers.

2. *Do they make sensible distinctions between the requirements of animal feed and those of food for human consumption?*

We would suggest that the distinctions between food and feed do not fully recognise the practical differences between the two industries. This is particularly true in relation to the quantities of imported soya and corn (maize) based products in both processed and unprocessed states. The UK imports annually, around two million tonnes of soyabeans and its meal, together with just under one million tonnes of corn gluten feed. These raw materials are used by both feed manufacturers in compound feedingstuffs, and by farmers as straight feed ingredients.

Products are therefore imported from the Americas and often to mainland Europe (ie Rotterdam) before being broken down into smaller lots and moved to one or more EU countries. This system (which is the most cost effective means of transport) does however mean there is a number of additional elements to the supply chain and a number of opportunities for product of different sources to be co-mingled in order to make up individual consignments. As such it becomes impossible to keep a completely accurate check on what mix of varieties may make up a final consignment, delivered to a feed mill.

Relating this to the proposed legislation means therefore that there is a requirement for a user to "play safe" and include information of all possible modified varieties which could be present in a consignment. We would question whether this offers the consumer information of great value. By not recognising the fundamental differences in both volume and trading practice, the legislation becomes self defeating.

3. How effective are the proposals likely to be in ensuring full traceability of GM material at all stages of the chain from producer to consumer?

We would draw attention to the answer given to the previous question which, we believe, gives a clear indication that whilst the proposals might give full traceability, it will achieve this only in so far as it gives traceability back to a range of consignments from which a product may have been produced. In reality this could give traceability back to a wide range of varieties from an even wider range of sources.

Information which is as vague as this, we would suggest, will prove to be of little value to the consumer and result in every stage in the chain being required to manage an increasing volume of relatively worthless paper. We would prefer to find a solution which helps to inform consumers rather than raising the potential to mislead them—resulting in the fear of even greater mistrust.

4. Are the proposals likely to be enforceable in practice, particularly where no novel genetic material is contained in the food or feed?

There is great concern, from an animal feed manufacturing standpoint, that this area will be the source of great cost and delay for no perceivable benefit to anyone further along the food chain. The problem reaches its peak with highly processed products such as vegetable oils, although any degree of processing reduces the effectiveness of any analytical methods.

The regulations rely on an accurate information programme that would accompany the consignment through the various stages in the chain from producer to end-user. Our concern is that early elements of this chain will be concerns outside the EU and therefore outside the direct scope of EU legislation. There may be instances where they are unable or unwilling to provide the necessary information which would allow determination of which events are present. This leaves the importer in an impossible situation, needing to provide onward information but having no basis for that information and no analytical means of confirming what events may be involved.

Given this situation we would question the enforceability of the measures. We are concerned that attempts to force legislation down this road will do nothing more than push up the cost of UK livestock production in comparison to imported products. This will achieve little if anything in terms of the demands for consumer information and choice which is claimed to be the rationale behind the legislation. What it will produce however is a discrepancy between food production inside and outside the EU, irrespective of where it is consumed.

5. A threshold level of 1 per cent or lower for the accidental presence of GM material in food and feed has been proposed, below which there would be an exemption. Is a threshold of this level, common to both food and feed, appropriate?

We believe that, at this moment in time, the proposal for a level of 1 per cent is appropriate for the feed industry. We would however wish to draw the Committee's attention to previous conclusions reached by the EU Scientific Committee on Plants, which has taken the view that the projected upward movement in the production of GM crops will render the 1 per cent threshold unattainable within a few years.

We believe legislation needs to remain flexible to accommodate such changes. Furthermore the Commission must recognise the global changes in the use of the technology and not put in place barriers which affect the ability of EU based business to compete. Imports of livestock products into the Community are high on the agenda at present but we must ensure that there is equivalence, wherever possible, between the production conditions for livestock products, both inside and outside the Community.

6. Is the role proposed for (a) the European Food Authority and its scientific committees and (b) Member States in the authorisation process for GM food and feed appropriate?

We would welcome the adoption of a "one door-one key" approach. We would voice some concern however at the proposal to operate a single risk management process under a regulatory committee procedure. Although UKASTA is not directly representative of those companies submitting applications, we believe that the current approvals system under 90/220/EEC has major weaknesses in its process which can lead to the stalling of applications by a single Member State, often for political reasons rather than scientific or safety grounds. We would therefore wish to see a more open and democratic structure adopted in the evaluation of risk management.

7. Are the proposals likely to be compatible with the requirements of the Cartagena Protocol on Biosafety and with other international commitments, including OECD programmes?

We feel this is an area on which others will be better qualified to comment. We would however wish to re-iterate earlier comments that the Community must recognise both its wider commitments and the basis on which livestock production is managed outside the EU. The prospects of second generation developments in biotechnology, bringing in quality traits, threatens to increase still further the gap in EU production costs with those of third countries. The Commission, and other EU bodies, must weigh carefully these wider issues when developing legislation to govern specific areas of technology.

8. *Are the proposals compatible with obligations towards non-Member States seeking to export food and feed to the EU?*

Our concerns in this area have been voiced in answer to previous questions.

9. *Should the present EU-wide moratorium on approving GM food and crop product applications be maintained until the issues concerning traceability and labelling GMOs have been resolved?*

We would suggest that such an approach would be wrong for one very simple reason. Analysis of the market will determine that companies are already addressing issues such as traceability in response to the demands of their customers. UKASTA operates an assurance scheme in relation to feed raw materials which now offers a non-GM module. This module has received the support of a number of UK retailers as their preferred method of delivering to their specifications for issues such as traceability.

What the market is looking for is certainty and direction. The current moratorium offers neither of these, representing instead a stagnation which threatens to drive food production out of the Community and away from direct control.

10. *What other aspects of the proposals require further consideration before the UK Government can sign up to them?*

We would wish to expand slightly on the issue of assurance, raised in response to the previous question. UKASTA operates two schemes in the animal feed sector—the UKASTA Feed Assurance Scheme (UFAS) and the Feed Materials Assurance Scheme (FEMAS). UFAS is, and FEMAS will shortly be, accredited to EN45011 status. FEMAS is key to the non-GM sourcing and traceability for feed materials at this point in time and, as mentioned earlier, is being specified by retailers as a preferred means of achieving the market demands. We would very much welcome the opportunity to provide greater detail of these schemes and highlight our concern that potentially clumsy legislation may have on their development and expansion.

A second issue we would wish to pick up is in relation to the current conflict between these proposals and GM legislation in other areas of community competency. In particular our involvement in the seed industry means we are very concerned at the existing Commission proposals on adventitious presence of GM material in non-GM seed and the Commission stance on Part B approvals under the deliberate release provisions. At present the Commission view Part B clearances as being unapproved and therefore carrying a zero tolerance—which we believe is simply not going to be achievable. The inability of the Commission to produce a verifiable test for presence of GM which is both repeatable and accurate, despite its confidence that such a test would be in place by mid-2001, only serves to reinforce our concern.

Once again we see the current proposals as being a cost and bureaucratic burden whilst offering no conceivable benefit to the end consumer in either information or choice.

Memorandum by the University of the West of England, Faculty of Applied Sciences

In response to the Committee's request for comments, the Faculty of Applied Sciences at the University of the West of England, Bristol offers the following (numbers relate to the questions posed):

1 NO

Regulations do not deal effectively with the addition of one or more products derived or containing GMOs. Traceability would only be effective if "local" enforcement agencies were empowered to visit and inspect producers and processors on a frequent basis. Although the producers and processors would have a duty to record and monitor GMOs, without close independent supervision, confidence in the industry would be compromised.

2 NO

It is difficult to maintain separate GM streams without effective monitoring and management at national and local level throughout the EU. A significant proportion of UK food is sourced from other EU countries and to maintain customer confidence it is imperative that the European Food Authority (EFA) has the mandate to monitor and inspect national agencies to ensure regulatory requirements are being maintained. The EFA must have the ability and authority to inspect producers and processors within Member States with minimal notice to the Member State and no notice to the producer or processor. It is difficult to appreciate the distinction between animal and human feeds given the food chain to man.

3

Although the regulations will serve to improve customer confidence in the short term, the obvious difficulties of determining GM in food and feed will in time lead to "sensationalised" press articles demonstrating how easy it is for GM food or feed to be combined or introduced into non-GM food and feed.

4 NO

Not without readily detectable levels of GMO. Enforcement depends on paper records and is not related to the actual occurrence of GMO in either food or feed.

5

1 per cent cannot be detected any better than 10 per cent. Surely the level should be risk-based in the first instance and then related to methods and levels of detection rather than a spurious 1 per cent.

6

The roles are appropriate, as is the role of the Member States. It is suggested that the practicalities of checking and determining accuracy in this process expose the Community and UK to the introduction of GMOs by stealth.

7

The protocols are compliant with international commitments. However the absence of scientific evidence of risk rather than the absence of risk drive these protocols itself. Traditionally the EU has taken a high moral position by preventing the introduction of a process or product unless it can be demonstrated as safe as opposed to not being demonstrated as unsafe.

8

If as suggested above it is difficult to have confidence in Member States who have a poor track record of checking (take BSE for example) what confidence can the UK have in non-EU states under economical stress where the economical pressure to use lower cost GMO sources will be compelling.

9 YES

The case for maintaining the moratorium still exists.

10

Testing and local enforcement/verification must be an integral part of the removal of the GM safety barriers. Although a limited number of published works have failed to demonstrate antibiotic resistance transfer to the normal flora of animals fed with GM food, more rigorous and extensive studies need to be completed.

Professor Wendy Purcell
Dean

February 2002

Printed in the United Kingdom by The Stationery Office Limited
5/2002 713892 19585